Fore! Gone.

MINNESOTA'S LOST GOLF COURSES

1897–1999

JOE BISSEN

Photographs by Peter Wong

FIVE STAR PUBLISHING
South St. Paul, Minnesota

Fore! Gone. Minnesota's Lost Golf Courses, 1897–1999

© 2014, 2019 Joe Bissen

Published by:
Five Star Publishing
Sout St. Paul, MN

www.ForeGoneGolf.com

All rights reserved. No part of this book may be reproduced or transmitted in any form or by any means, electronic or mechanical, including photocopying, recording, or by any information storage and retrieval system, without permission in writing from the publisher, except for the inclusion of brief quotations in a review.

COVER: A shelter that was part of Whitewater Valley Golf Course remains on the Whitewater State Park grounds, north of St. Charles, Minn. The course closed in 1975. *Peter Wong photo*

Color prints of photos taken by Peter Wong and Joe Bissen for this book can be ordered at ForeGoneGolf.com.

Cover and interior design, Tamara Dever, TLC Book Design, www.TLCBookDesign.com

Stock images:

Minnesota Interstate map: © Stacey Lynn Payne | Dreamstime.com; Flags on Interstate map: © Natis76 | Dreamstime.com; Golfer in circle: © Daveh900 | Dreamstime.com; Nail heads: © Nuttapong | Dreamstime.com; Nugget icon: © Daveh900 | Dreamstime.com; Old photo frames: © Jakub Krechowicz | Dreamstime.com; Old quarters: © Gavril Bernad | Dreamstime.com; Two old photo frames together: © Andreka | Dreamstime.com; Ch. 44 opening icon: © Daveh900 | Dreamstime.com; Old photo frame with corners: © Ron Sumners | Dreamstime.com; Minnesota flag: © Christian Mueringer | Dreamstime.com; Minnesota counties map: © Deskcube | Dreamstime.com; Diagonal plaid: © Witchera | Dreamstime.com; Bucket of balls: ©iStockphoto.com/simonox; Golfer in the mist: ©iStockphoto.com/cmcderm1

ISBN: 978-0-9911748-0-5

To Warren Bissen, who would have loved
every one of these lost courses and would have
one-putted so many of their greens
it'd make your head spin.

"*If you don't know history,
then you don't know anything.
You are a leaf that doesn't know
it is part of a tree.*"

— MICHAEL CRICHTON

PETER WONG PHOTO

ACKNOWLEDGEMENTS

WITHOUT FAIL — WELL, ALMOST WITHOUT FAIL — everyone I contacted was wonderfully helpful in passing along information and memories on lost golf courses. There was the one guy who hung up on me when I started a phone conversation with, "I hear there was a golf course in your back yard." But beyond that, thanks to all, and special thanks to:

Peter Wong, whose pictures are worth ten thousand words, and Tami Dever, whose skill in combining pictures and words is worth a hundred thousand words (to say nothing of her unflinching patience).

Gary Derong, my astute editor and headline/chapter-title writer nonpareil.

Rick Shefchik, author of the remarkable *From Fields to Fairways: Classic Golf Clubs of Minnesota*, for answering a slew of questions on the state's golf history.

Phil Kostolnik, for allowing me access to a vein from his gold mine of golf history.

The McNulty family of St. Louis Park, for photos, news clippings and much more on Westwood Hills and Matoska.

A handful of people with historical societies contributed mightily: Paul Anderson, North St. Paul; Sue Doocy, Mower County; Charles Gramling, Chisago City Heritage Association; Michael Kirchmeier, Jackson County; Pam Myers, Westonka; and Darryl Sannes, Brooklyn.

Maryanne Norton and Tony Dierckins of Duluth, who helped me cover that city from end to end.

Peggy Roske, archivist at College of St. Benedict/St. John's University.

Joe Oberle and Warren Ryan of *Minnesota Golfer* magazine and the Minnesota Golf Association.

Ian Stade, Hennepin County Special Collections librarian.

Bill Peterson of Coon Rapids, for material on Jake's in Coon Rapids.

Joe Stansberry — props for the props.

Mike Rak, who started as an interview and ended as a friend.

Everyone who contributed to my Kickstarter fundraising campaign, making it possible for this book to get into print. I would be remiss in not making special mention of Tom Barnard and Brad Neuville. Thanks also to Kickstarter for being such an adept fundraising vehicle.

And to Susie, Andy, Nick and Katie — my family.

TABLE OF CONTENTS

1
INTRODUCTION

3
CHAPTER 1
PLANE AND SIMPLE
Rich Acres Golf Course, Richfield

9
CHAPTER 2
GRANDDADDY — AND HIS BROTHER
Winona Golf Club, Meadow-Brook Golf Club

17
CHAPTER 3
CAUSE OF DEATH

21
CHAPTER 4
BANG IT OFF THE TOWER
Hilltop Public Golf Links, Columbia Heights

29
CHAPTER 5
EIGHT IS ENOUGH
Sommerdorf Golf Course, Brownton

31
CHAPTER 6
UNEARTHING A GEM
Westwood Hills Golf Course, St. Louis Park AND BUD'S TALE

43
CHAPTER 7
A MAN, A MYTH, A MONKEY
Joyner's (Brooklyn Park Golf Course)

47
CHAPTER 8
COMMON THREADS

53
CHAPTER 9
PIONEERS OF SPORT
The Minnetonka Club, Deephaven

61
CHAPTER 10
SCOTCH THREESOME
Caledonia Golf Club

65
CHAPTER 11
NORWEGIAN PRIDE
Spring Grove

67
CHAPTER 12
A STORMY PAST
Whitewater Valley Golf Course, St. Charles/Altura

73
CHAPTER 13
DULUTH, WEST AND EAST
Riverside Golf Club and Lakewood Golf Club, Duluth

83
CHAPTER 14
NUTS TO YOU
Bayport Golf Club

87
CHAPTER 15
SHEARED BY SHEEP
Sleepy Eye

89
CHAPTER 16
CAPITAL LOSSES
Roadside Golf Club and Merriam Park Golf Club, St. Paul

93
CHAPTER 17
NINE FOR LUNCH
Quality Park, St. Paul

95
CHAPTER 18
THOR AND TOM'S PLACE
Matoska Country Club, Gem Lake
AND CLUBHOUSE CONUNDRUM

105
CHAPTER 19
VALLEYS FORGED
Southview/Ironwood Country Club, Mankato

109
CHAPTER 20
NOT SO MUCH THE GOLF COURSE …
Mudcura Golf Club, Chanhassen

115
CHAPTER 21
BUNKER HILLS, THE ELDER
Bunker Hills Country Club, Mendota Heights

119
CHAPTER 22
PARK PLACE,
AND WHAT A PARK
Antlers Park Golf Links, Lakeville

125
CHAPTER 23
THE SMELL TEST
Austin Municipal; Hillcrest Golf Course, Austin

131
CHAPTER 24
YA GOTTA WONDER, PART II
Memorial Golf Course, Mankato

133
CHAPTER 25
FEARSOME FOURSOME
Maple Grove Golf Acres, Hermantown

135
CHAPTER 26
THE OLD COLLEGE TRY
St. John's Golf Course, Collegeville

139
CHAPTER 27
UPHILL CLIMB
Hillside Golf Course, St. Cloud

143
CHAPTER 28
ROAD TRIP
Nopeming Private Golf Course, Chippewa National Forest

151
CHAPTER 29
MINNEAPOLIS MYSTERY
Bryn Mawr Golf Club, Minneapolis

Table of Contents

159
CHAPTER 30
HOT, TOASTY REMNANTS
Green Lake Country Club, Spicer

163
CHAPTER 31
UNFULFILLED PROMISE
Royalhaven Golf Club, Hugo

167
CHAPTER 32
URBAN HOTBED
Felder's Golf Center, Plymouth

169
CHAPTER 33
BURIED TREASURE
Wabasha Golf Club

173
CHAPTER 34
JEWISH FORERUNNER
*Northwood Country Club,
North St. Paul*

179
CHAPTER 35
STRIKING VIEW
*Jake's/Mississippi Golf Course,
Coon Rapids*

183
CHAPTER 36
MEMORY SERVES
Mound Golf Course

187
CHAPTER 37
PLAYING WITH CONVICTION
Stillwater Prison

189
CHAPTER 38
SCOTSMAN'S CRAFT
Chisago Golf Club, Chisago City

193
CHAPTER 39
SHORT HITTER
Chisago Lakes Par 3, Lindstrom

195
CHAPTER 40
THE IRON GAME
Chisholm Public Golf Course

199
CHAPTER 41
TAKE IT FROM DAD
Bemidji Municipal

201
CHAPTER 42
SILOS AND FLAGSTICKS
*Southwestern Minnesota
Windom, Jackson, Lakefield,
Heron Lake, Fulda, Chandler,
Pipestone, Tracy*

207
CHAPTER 43
REBIRTHED
*Tatepaha/Faribault; Shattuck, Faribault;
Cannon Glen,
Cannon Falls; Northfield Golf Club;
Ortonville Golf Club; Oakcrest, Roseau*

213
CHAPTER 44
LET'S NOT FORGET ...
Other Courses

221
FORE! GONE. GALLERY

The Lost Courses

Numbers on flags correspond to chapter numbers in the book.

To view an interactive lost-course map, pinpointing locations of many of these lost courses to within a few hundred yards, please visit ForeGoneGolf.com.

A TAD TRIVIAL

First Lost Course
Winona Golf Club, Chapter 2

Last Lost Course (pre-2000)
Rich Acres, Chapter 1

Longest Course
Northwood Country Club, Chapter 34

Shortest Course
Nopeming/Joyce Estate, Chapter 28

Most Holes
Westwood Hills, Chapter 6

Fewest Holes
Mudcura, Chapter 20

*"They paved paradise
and put up a parking lot."*

JONI MITCHELL
"Big Yellow Taxi"

Introduction

WHAT A WORLD OF GOLF COURSES WE HAVE, ALL IN A SINGLE STATE. WE HAVE IN MINNESOTA WINDSWEPT, PRAIRIE-STYLE COURSES IN THE SOUTHWEST. COURSES COZIED UP AGAINST BLUFFSIDES IN THE SOUTHEAST. PERCHED ABOVE A GREAT LAKE IN THE NORTHEAST. CONCEALED INSIDE FORESTS OF THE NORTHWEST. DISPERSED THROUGHOUT THE METRO, FROM 7,000-YARD MONSTERS TO PAR-27 PETUNIAS.

Some of our courses are known worldwide and host million-dollar majors. Others are known "poodneer" (translation: pretty near) into the next county and host quarter skins games.

We have it all here.

We have lost it all, too.

Since the day in 1893 when George McCree, a Scottish-Canadian locomotive machinist, whacked driver-fairway wood-midiron to stake out the first hole on the state's first golf course, Town & Country Club of St. Paul, more than 400 Minnesota golf courses, by conservative estimate, have been created. Most exist today in their original form or something close to it, but there have been casualties, too:

Lost courses.

More than 80 golf courses have disappeared from the Minnesota landscape since 1897, when a fledgling club in a Mississippi River city abandoned a virtually unplayable hillside parcel in favor of a more palatable (i.e. flatter) place to play.

The names of the lost courses likely are unfamiliar to most Minnesotans who play the game today: Antlers Park. Bunker Hills (no, not that Bunker Hills). Bryn Mawr. Green Lake. Hillside. Hilltop. Lakewood. Matoska. Mudcura. Nopeming. Northwood. Quality Park. Riverside. Roadside. Southview (no, not that Southview). Westwood Hills.

Minnesota's lost courses featured the bizarre as well as the boss: one built next to a sewage disposal plant and with, predictably, the shelf life of a carton of milk. One designed by a Minnesota Golf hall of famer and played by a World Golf hall of famer. Courses frequented by sheep, cows, escaped hogs, a friendly dog and a monkey. Sites that turned into not only pastures, subdivisions and megastores but also into a nature center, an antique store and a colossal airport runway.

This is your captain speaking. I'll try not to land in that pot bunker down there.

I wish I could say writing about lost golf courses was my idea. It wasn't. It was conceived by Don Rohrer of Woodbury, who advanced the notion to *Minnesota Golfer Magazine* in 2010 after driving past a course in California that lay dormant. The magazine editors asked me to write about lost Twin Cities courses, which I did for their summer 2010 issue. Best assignment ever. I was hooked.

After writing the story, I poked around the topic for two more years, then plunged into a book-writing project in July 2012.

Upon completion, I feel as though I should ask the printer to drop a gigantic asterisk on the facing page. Because, I must admit, there are issues:

- *Fore! Gone.* is not intended to be Minnesota's be-all, end-all lost-golf-course history. Consider it more of a representative sample. I'm as sure as Tiger on a two-footer that there are dozens more abandoned courses I don't know about. I came up with 87 that have at least some degree of verifiability of having existed, but tracking down extensive histories is like playing a quick nine on a sticky Sunday evening, with gnats swarming around: You take a swat, you get one or two, you get the feeling there are a hundred more that you missed.

- I haven't written about every known lost course in Minnesota. I included only those that disappeared in 1999 or before, which omits dozens of 21st-century perishings caused, for the most part, by golf's demand-and-supply curves whooshing past each other in opposite directions in about 2000. Someone else can write that sequel.

- As much as I would like to say every detail in this book is irrefutably, incontrovertibly true, I can't. I've tried to verify all I could, but often I was left with the necessity of a) choosing between contradictions, b) leaving out the implausible, or c) passing along, sometimes on blind faith, people's recollections. Because so many of these courses disappeared in the 1930s and '40s, those who remembered them were at advanced ages — into their late 80s and 90s. And though I have developed a great appreciation for our octo/nonogenarian set, some of their lost-course memories could be fuzzy. (No sweat, 90-year-olds. Happens to those of us decades younger, too.)

One last note: All printed ages of people mentioned in this book were their ages as of the time they were interviewed — in the latter half of 2012 or early 2013.

Joe Bissen

CHAPTER 1

Plane and Simple

RICH ACRES GOLF COURSE
CITY: RICHFIELD
COUNTY: HENNEPIN
YEARS: 1980-99

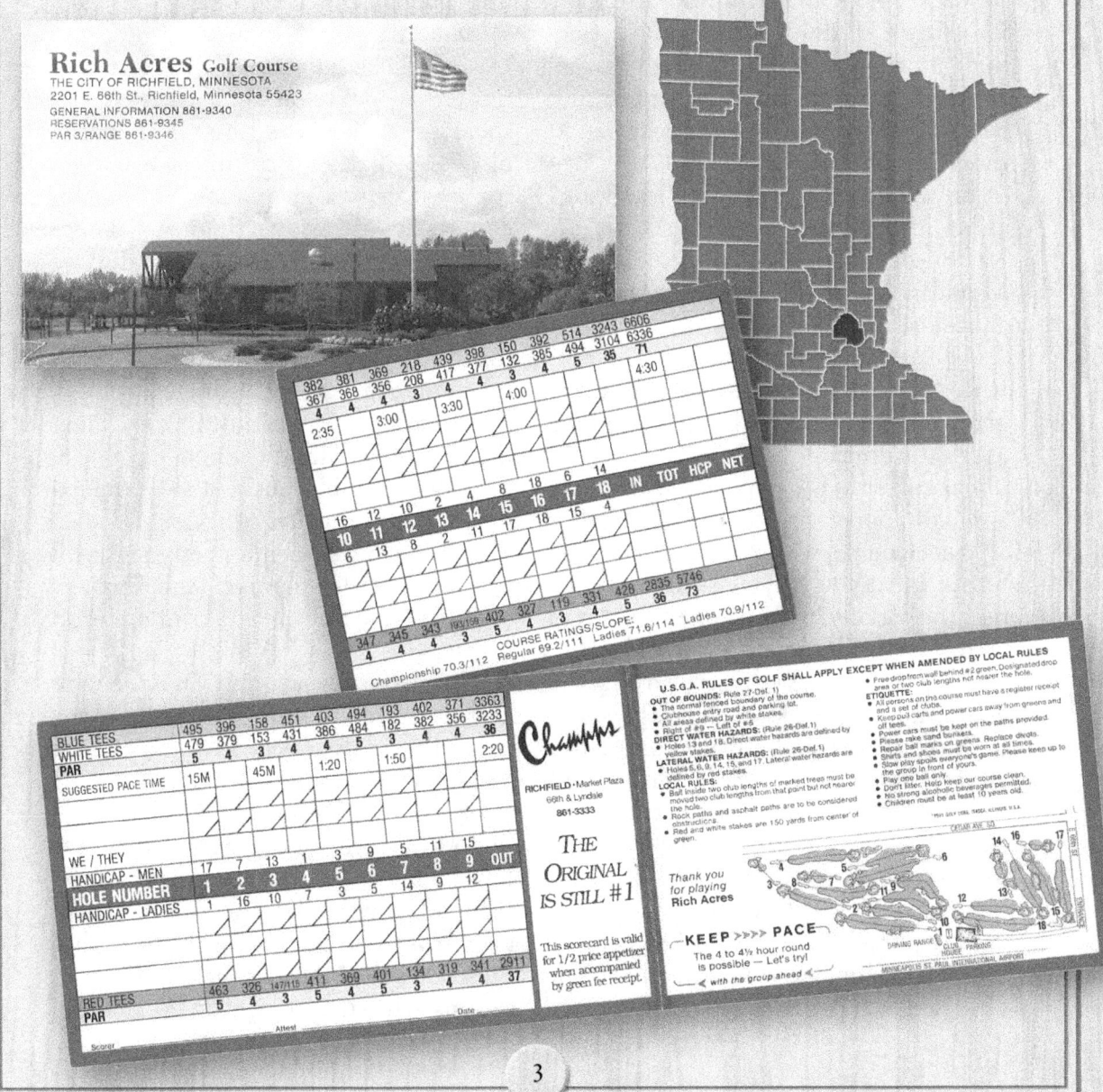

Fore! Gone.

They paved paradise in Richfield, Minnesota. Man, did they ever. Emphasis on "paved," not so much "paradise."

Rich Acres Golf Course never was a threat to win any course-design awards, unless there is some kind of distinction for Top Fifty Fairly Flat Courses You Can Play. But the course was sporty, it was easily accessible at Cedar Avenue between I-494 and Minnesota 62 (the Crosstown Highway), it was immensely popular, and before the cement mixers steamed in and turned it into a gigantic airport runway, it had a certain charm to those who frequented it.

"It was a nice course. Nice and walkable. Through the years it got better; it was improved," said Eileen Nelson of Minneapolis, who played Rich Acres for almost a decade.

Well, ahem, this is not to imply that Rich Acres' certain charm was unmitigated charm. For one thing, the course abutted Minneapolis-St. Paul International Airport, a juxtaposition that had a way of imposing upon the senses.

"Nice course, with the smell of diesel fumes when you played 14 through 16 near the parking lot," said one Rich Acres golfer who shall remain anonymous.

Then there were — insert earplugs, if you would — the planes. Though some Rich Acres golfers said the noise from jets ascending and descending overhead wasn't as disturbing as advertised, the course still was Richfield's 100-decibel playground.

If you were a Rich Acres golfer, learning the phrase "You're away" in American Sign Language wouldn't have been a bad idea.

"They were loud. They were really loud," Dave Podas, who grew up in south Minneapolis and played Rich Acres often, said of the planes.

"They did some experiments. I remember once it was like a bomb going off," Nelson conceded.

"It actually was kind of cool," said Dave Buzicky, a longtime Richfield firefighter who frequented Rich Acres, speaking not of the noise but of the planes-to-players proximity. "You'd get some cool-looking planes coming in, and you could watch them. ... There was this Russian transport plane the one day. It was loaded to the gills, and you never thought it was going to get up in the air. I mean, the thing just lumbered down the runway. It was huge."

The plane, *da*, did ultimately meet the friendly skies, which is good, because a flaming hunk of steel, fueled by a thousand quarts of Russian vodka, would not have been a pretty sight on the Rich Acres fairways. And Buzicky couldn't have put out the conflagration by himself.

The airport wasn't only an issue with golfers. Rich Acres' grounds crew couldn't use two-way FM radios, the course's Glen F. Lentner noted in a 1985 entry in the Minnesota Golf Course Superintendents' Association newsletter. "The reason is the Air Traffic Control Tower," Lentner wrote. "The course is so close to the airport that these electrical devices pick up conversations with the air traffic controllers

Headed toward landing on Runway 17/35 at Minneapolis-St. Paul International Airport, the former site of Rich Acres Golf Course.

JOE BISSEN PHOTO

and the pilots. If the crew gets bored with listening to punk rock or country music during lunch, they can tune in KJJO 104 F.M. and listen to the Controller/Pilot talk show."

Nonetheless, Twin Cities golfers overlooked Rich Acres' foibles and played the place in droves. Buzicky, who played there from its birth in 1980 until its passing in 1999, said that in the late 1980s and early '90s, Rich Acres was the most-played golf course in the state. A 1998 *St. Paul Pioneer Press* story noted that the demise of Rich Acres' 18-hole course, par-3 course and driving range "will dump 87,000 rounds of golf and more than 3 million practice balls on the already crowded public golf courses of the area."

How did Rich Acres wind up with more traffic than the Crosstown during Monday morning rush hour? Two main reasons, the first borrowing from an old real-estate adage and summed up in four words by Buzicky: "The location was wonderful."

Also, there was the notion that most golfers don't consider it necessary to play the second coming of Augusta National every time out. This was addressed in a 1999 column by Tom Powers of the *Pioneer Press*:

"Soon-to-be-closed Rich Acres, which no doubt plays host to some excellent golfers, is a haven for the less talented.

" 'That's where our niche is,' head pro Mike Lanigan said. 'It's spread out, easy to walk, not a lot of rough or bunkers. … You don't have to lose a dozen golf balls.' "

Lanigan was at Rich Acres for 14 years, until the course's closing in 1999. He said in 2013 that annual play at the 18-hole course topped out at 62,000 rounds and that the par-3 course once hosted 32,000 rounds. A reasonable greens fee, a little over $20 in the late 1990s, also contributed to the course's popularity.

"You start when the sun comes up and go 'til the sun goes down," Lanigan said of the business day at Rich Acres. "I don't think we could have done much more."

The busy season at Rich Acres didn't stop at summer's end.

"I remember that Rich Acres was always ultra crowded on November 11 every year if the weather was even slightly reasonable," one former Rich Acres player who did not want to be identified wrote via email. "We always assumed it was the presence of a lot of veterans. Richfield had a solid veteran population in those days, and a big American Legion Club was nearby."

As for the course itself, designed and built by Brauer and Associates on a plot of land largely devoid of character, it wasn't overly memorable. In fact, only one person interviewed mentioned a hole he thought was particularly strong.

"One of the more interesting holes would be the fifth hole," said Rod Lidenberg, Rich Acres' first club pro and manager. "It was a dogleg, uphill par 4 with a grove of trees on the right."

The hole was memorable for another reason — its Alpine slope of a green.

"I had a putt there that was a 20-footer uphill," Lanigan said. "When I hit it, it came up short and rolled back, and I had a 22-footer."

Didja make that one, Mike?

"I did. That's why I remember it."

The fifth green eventually was rebuilt, as was the sixth.

By the way, airplanes weren't the only transportation-related issue at Rich Acres. Windshields were another.

"I forget what hole it was," Podas said, "but it ran parallel to Cedar Avenue, and if you weren't careful, you could whip it right out into Cedar Avenue if you hooked it off about the fourth or fifth hole."

Rich Acres' first nine holes opened on July 1, 1980, Lidenberg said. The city of Richfield procured use of the land in 1979 by taking out a 30-year lease for $1 a year from the Metropolitan Airports Commission, with the stipulation that the MAC could reclaim the land on 18 months' notice. Because of the favorable lease terms, the golf course began turning a profit for the city by 1987, Lanigan said.

The land-lease arrangement worked "very, very well. It made money for both of us (the city and MAC)," said Loren Law, 97, of Edina, who helped get Rich Acres get off the ground while he served as mayor of Richfield. "It was better than having that land sit vacant."

Rich Acres' landscape resembled that of Saudi Arabia in the early years, but trees were added, the course greened up, and it became a more respectable golf grounds. Good enough, even, to host qualifying events for state tournaments and spirited competition beyond that.

Podas was one such competitor. His home course was Hiawatha in Minneapolis, two miles north of Rich Acres. Once Rich Acres opened, a few of the more talented south Minneapolis public-course players exited Hiawatha and began playing for Rich Acres.

"When we were in our 20s," Podas said, "there were enough good players to where we'd go over to Rich Acres and there was pretty good action. ... They got some of 'our' players, if you will, so there was a little bit of a rivalry there, for lack of a better word, between the Hiawatha guys and the Rich Acres guys."

Loren Law, who as mayor of Richfield was instrumental in getting Rich Acres Golf Course off the ground, strikes a shot during an opening ceremony for the course.

COURTESY OF JIM TOPITZHOFER

One of Podas' Rich Acres' "rivals" was Dave Nordeen. The two are no worse for the wear of having played each other, or Rich Acres. Nordeen won two Minnesota State Amateur championships and one Tapemark Charity Pro-Am title and now is head professional at the reputable Somerby Golf Club in Byron, Minn. Podas is director of golf and head professional at the ultra-exclusive Bel-Air Country Club in Los Angeles. He has played in PGA Tour events and, in 2007, according to the *Los Angeles Times*, shot a course-record 63 at Bel-Air while playing in a foursome that included sports broadcaster Al Michaels. *Do you believe in birdies? Yes!!!* (Podas declined to drop names in a 2013 interview, but Bel-Air's membership rolls reportedly have included Jack Nicholson, Pete Sampras, Dennis Quaid, Jerry West, Vin Scully and Tom Cruise.)

Rich Acres retained its popularity well into the 1990s, but the airport lease hung over the course with every takeoff and tee time. By 1997, word got out that Minneapolis-St. Paul International Airport was looking to expand and soon would take over the golf course grounds.

Though many Rich Acres golfers recognized the course's demise as a fait accompli — "You knew it was going to come someday," Buzicky said — the news was met with disappointment.

"There probably was one mature tree on the whole golf course" when it started, Lidenberg said. "All the trees that were planted from that point forward, we had to purchase. We'd plant those trees (through a program with golfers). It was a shame to see all those trees come down, because we'd spent so much time on them."

The bulldozers began lining up off Cedar Avenue, and houses were either

Fore! Gone.

This shelter is one of two at Augsburg Park in Richfield, the only remaining standing structures from Rich Acres Golf Course. One of the shelters stood between the fourth green and fifth tee box; the other was between Nos. 14 and 16 greens. They were moved by City of Richfield crews to Augsburg Park.

COURTESY OF JIM TOPITZHOFER

razed or boarded up in the Rich Acres and New Ford Town neighborhoods.

"It was a very nice golf course, and a lot of us hated to see it go," said Jerry Vick of Bloomington, who founded a singles league at Rich Acres, "but that's progress."

"Progress" took a highly, well, concrete form. Rich Acres survived on life support through the 1999 golf season. "The last day Rich Acres was open was December 13, 1999," wrote the emailer and former Rich Acres golfer. "I showed up to play, but the crowds were huge. I ended up playing the par-3 course as a twosome."

In the spring of 2000, the bulldozers hit Rich Acres full force, and the golf course made way for Runway 17/35 of Minneapolis-St. Paul International Airport — $681 million worth of pavement that when opened in October 2005 would measure 8,000 feet long, 150 feet wide and up to 15 feet deep.

They paved paradise, or maybe something ever so slightly resembling it.

"We always heard that it was built on land leased by the airport and that it could (close)," Podas said of Rich Acres, "but it was one of those things where you never believed they actually would do it.

"Once that golf course was up and running and open, which was really a flat area that was nothing, all of a sudden you had trees, you had ponds, you had this beautiful golf course, you'd be playing there and say, 'Yeah, the airport's going to take this back,' and you'd go, 'No way a guy's going to come out here and plow this up.' And it ended up happening. ... We were wrong."

Portions of this chapter appeared in the Summer 2010 edition of *Minnesota Golfer* magazine and are reprinted with permission of the Minnesota Golf Association.

A FEW RICH ACRES RELICS — WELL, BESIDES SOME OF ITS older golfers — remain. Two picnic shelters from the golf course stand in Richfield's Augsburg Park, at West 70th Street and Nicollet Avenue, and a golf course plaque rests in a Richfield Fire Department station.

CHAPTER 2
Granddaddy—and His Brother

WINONA GOLF CLUB, MEADOW-BROOK GOLF CLUB
CITY: WINONA
COUNTY: WINONA
YEARS: 1897–1918

Sugar Loaf, a Winona landmark

Club House of Meadow Brook Golf Club

Meadow-Brook Golf Club clubhouse, from the book Views of Winona.
COURTESY OF WINONA COUNTY HISTORICAL SOCIETY

Fore! Gone.

Minnesota's oldest known lost golf course rests in peace 1½ miles from downtown in the Mississippi River city of Winona.

So does its next of kin.

As the 19th century was closing, Winona lumberman Addison B. Youmans became smitten with a new game being played on the American continent. He had seen golf played in an informal and primitive manner in his river town, and he had traveled to Europe and witnessed a more advanced version of the game. On July 30, 1897, Youmans helped form the Winona Golf Club. He was made president of the 13-member club, and he laid out a course on vacant property in a valley across Lake Winona near Woodlawn Cemetery.

One printed source says the course was south of Woodlawn. Another says it was east. One source says the course consisted of six holes; another -- the *Winona Daily Republican*, in a July 30, 1898, story heralding the first anniversary of organized golf in Winona — reported that the course was a 12-holer.

On a late-summer day in 1897, one of the 13 founding members brought his A-game to the Winona Golf Club.

"A tournament was held there on Sept. 6," the *Daily Republican* reported, "and was won by Mr. W.M. Bolcom with a score of 54."

Though Bolcom would be heard from again, that tournament closed the recorded history of play at Winona Golf Club. Within months, the club, and Addison Youmans' course, were history — and Winona Golf Club had become Minnesota's first lost golf course.

"As the players became more thoroughly acquainted with the game, they began to appreciate that the grounds were entirely unsuited to the purpose," the *Daily Republican* reported. "They were rough, rocky, and were filled with trees. They then began to cast about for a new place which was more adapted to the game, and where links could be laid out on which the players would not be constantly handicapped."

The Winonans' "casting about" led them to a tract 1¼ miles to the northwest. By the 1898 golf season, or possibly even in late 1897, Meadow-Brook Golf Club (also referred to as Meadowbrook and Meadow Brook) had opened, on a leased tract more acceptable to the club members. The *Daily Republican* reported the parcel as being "gently rolling."

A 2004 *Winona Post* story on Meadow-Brook, written in thorough detail by James A. Miller, pinpointed both the course's location and its mien:

"Located in the western part of the city, now mostly recognized as Cotter High School's St. Michael's Athletic Field bordering Fifth Street and Gilmore Avenue, Meadowbrook boasted a difficult and picturesque nine-hole links.

"... The clubhouse at Meadowbrook was an elaborate one-story wood frame building located at Fifth and Lee streets, now the sites of St. Mary's Catholic Church and St. Anne Extended Healthcare. Open-air porches, a dining hall and a large dance floor made the clubhouse the perfect location for social gatherings as well as golf."

The *Daily Republican* reported that "the wives and daughters of the members are also entitled to the privileges of the club." The 1898 membership roster included six women.

Meadow-Brook covered 2,097 yards at the time of its opening and played to a "bogey" (the equivalent of par, in today's terms) score of 39. If the newspaper reports are to be believed, Meadow-Brook was held in high regard by all who played it. Players had to navigate deep sand bunkers, tall grasses and a creek. In modern-day design terms, the layout appears to have been decidedly penal.

The Meadow-Brook layout was tinkered with from the get-go, and throughout its 21-year history. An April 8, 1898, *Daily Republican* story mentioned improvements planned, including two sand bunkers, one fence bunker, two new bridges and several greens. A 1901 *Minneapolis Journal* story portending the most important event in club history mentioned the addition of two "deep sand pits" near the first and second greens.

The *Winona Post* and the anniversary *Daily Republican* stories described the holes in detail. Highlights:

- No. 1, called Home Tee or The Pond, crossed the creek and measured 217 yards.

- No. 2, The Straightaway, 232 yards with no hazards.

- No. 3, Roadside, parallel to Gilmore Avenue, 229 yards with a 4-foot-high sand hill.

The Creek Running Through the Golf Links

Meadow-Brook Golf Club, with a "view" of the creek running through the course, from the book Views of Winona.

COURTESY OF WINONA COUNTY HISTORICAL SOCIETY

- No. 4, Bullrushes, 210 yards across the creek.

- No. 5, Midway, 201 yards, recrossing the creek. Meadow-Brook members often played into the adjacent sixth fairway to avoid trouble.

- No. 6, Lone Tree, 203 yards, again across the creek.

- No. 7, The Fence, 240 yards, played toward Hilbert Street, with a tall board fence as a hazard.

- No. 8, named Long Hole by perhaps the first Mr. Obvious in Minnesota golf history, measured 335 yards and was, knock me over with a feather, the longest on the course. (The *Winona Post* story referred to No. 6 as Long Hole, No. 7 as Lone Tree and No. 8 as Out-of-Sight Hole, suggesting those three holes were re-routed at some point.)

- No. 9, Home Hole, 225 yards with a sand bunker.

The *Daily Republican* anniversary story — remember, these were the very early days of golf in America — offered a short primer on the game:

"At the beginning of each hole or link is a teeing ground. This is a square of hardened ground, slightly raised above the level. A box called the tee clay box is nearby and is always filled with moist clay. At the end of the link is a hole several inches in diameter and about three inches deep. In the center of this hole is a flag, by which the hole can be easily located. The idea in the play is to drive the ball from the teeing ground into the hole in the fewest number of strokes.

"At the start the ball is teed up, or slightly raised from the ground, by placing it on a small portion of the clay. The club, called the driver, which is used for a long swing stroke, is used and the ball is sent as far as possible. ...

"When the ball finally reaches the putting green, which is a level place about thirty yards in diameter surrounding the hole, the putter, a straight iron club, is used to drive the ball, much as in croquet, into the hole."

Croquet. Now, there was a game the 19th-century Winonans could relate to. Golf? Not so much.

"It is true that the game has been subject to much ridicule, not only here but throughout the country," the *Daily Republican* reported, "but this is due to the fact that people do not understand it. ..."

Meadow-Brook (or Winona Golf Club, technically speaking) is believed to have been the first golf club in outstate Minnesota, rivaled in that regard only by Northland in Duluth (1899) and Tatepaha Golf Club of Faribault (1900). Perhaps with that distinction as a calling card, Meadow-Brook secured its place in Minnesota golf history on Aug. 20, 1901, when approximately 15 men convened a meeting at the Winona club and formed the Minnesota Golf Association. Seven clubs were founding members: Bryn Mawr (Minneapolis), Meadow-Brook, Merriam Park (St. Paul), Minikahda (Minneapolis), Rochester GC, Tatepeha and Town & Country (St. Paul). John M. Barfield of Meadow-Brook was chosen the MGA's first president.

Nine days later, Meadow-Brook crested. The club hosted Minnesota's first "state tournament," an event that would come to be known as the Min-

St. Mike's field creek in Winona, which once cut through the grounds of Meadow-Brook Golf Club.
JOE BISSEN PHOTO

nesota Golf Association State Amateur. There were 43 entrants, all from MGA founding clubs. Entry fee was $2.

"The links are in splendid condition for this tournament, never having been better in this or any previous season," the *Winona Daily Republican-Herald* reported on Aug. 28, 1901.

The *Minneapolis Journal* of Aug. 12, 1901, had reported similarly: "The Meadowbrook golf course at Winona is being fitted up in fine shape, at an outlay of a large sum, in readiness for the coming state golf tournament. ... When the tournament arrives the links will be in the best shape that they have ever seen." The newspaper reported that a new caddie house had been erected and improvements had been made to the clubhouse.

Two weeks later, the newspaper reported that Meadow-Brook had spent $260 on prizes for the tournament. Included in the outlay was a large, three-handled loving cup, made of sterling silver and gold-lined and including an enameled golf scene, for the champion. Samuel R. Van Sant, a Winonan inaugurated as Minnesota's 15th governor earlier in the year, returned to the city during tournament week, in part to follow the competition.

The tournament covered three days: one day of stroke-play qualifying and two days of match play. Michael Doran Jr. lovingly eyed the cup after leading qualifiers with rounds of 40 and 42 for an 82, 4 over bogey. But Bolcom ended Doran's hopes the next day, defeating him 1-up in the first round of match play.

St. Michael's Athletic Field in Winona, the home of Winona Cotter High School athletics and formerly part of the grounds of Meadow-Brook Golf Club. Photo, looking southward, was taken from the fifth floor of St. Anne of Winona, an assisted living facility on West Broadway Street which also was likely on the former Meadow-Brook grounds. In view to the left are the former buildings of the defunct College of St. Teresa.

KATIE BISSEN PHOTO

Bolcom must have been an imposing foe. He won a driving contest during the tournament with a blast of 227½ yards, "a distance mark that the (Meadow-Brook) membership yearly practiced for and aimed to surpass," the *Winona Post* reported.

But Bolcom fell to a higher power. On Aug. 31, 1901, he lost the 36-hole championship match 2 and 1 to the Rev. Theodore Payne Thurston, a charter Meadow-Brook member and minister at St. Paul's Episcopal Church in Winona. The ninth hole of the first round featured a critical error by Bolcom, as described by the *Minneapolis Journal*: "Bolcom drove into a bunker and in an attempt to extricate his ball fouled the sphere, and thus forfeited the hole to Thurston."

Thurston clinched the title match by sinking a long putt for a birdie 3 on No. 8, "Long Hole."

Meadow-Brook continued to host competitions, including the Marfield Cup and the Bolcom Loving Cup, but it never again approached its late-1901 status. The *Winona Post* story reported that the course consistently had flooding problems and that club management eventually abandoned the nine-hole course for a six-hole layout on higher ground.

By 1910, many of the club's top players had left Winona. That year's State Amateur tournament, played at Town & Country Club in St. Paul, included no golfers from Winona. Play continued at the six-hole Meadow-Brook Golf Club through 1918, but on a far-from-grand scale.

In early 1919, the 2004 *Winona Post* story reported, the club was presented an opportunity to purchase approximately 140 acres of farmland in Pleasant Valley, 3½ miles southeast of downtown Winona. The purchase was made, and Winona Country Club was established, with a voting membership of 150 men. It opened in 1920 as a nine-hole course, designed by Scotsmen Tom Bendelow and Ben Knight.

Winona Country Club acquired more land in the 1960s and, with a redesign plotted by Robert Trent Jones, expanded to 18 holes. The course is now called Bridges and is semi-private.

Back on the old Meadow-Brook site, there is not the slightest hint that a golf course ever existed there. As mentioned in the *Winona Post* story, the grounds are mostly occupied by a large senior care center and Winona Cotter High School's athletic fields. Gilmore Creek, which ran through the course, now runs mostly underground through the Cotter fields. The entire grounds, once described as "gently rolling," is now as flat as a slice of pita bread.

THE MEADOW-BROOK GROUNDS, JUDGING BY AN OLD MAP, extended as far north as the southern edge of Fifth Street. That particular area is now residential. But two blocks west, on the north side of Fifth Street, lies Westfield Golf Course, a nine-hole, public course that opened in 1923.

CHAPTER 3

Cause of Death

MINNESOTA'S LOST GOLF COURSES LIE IN PERMANENT REPOSE NEAR EVERY BORDER OF THE STATE, FROM BAYPORT TO AUSTIN TO ORTONVILLE TO TWIN VALLEY TO WARROAD, AND IN SCORES OF PLACES WITHIN. BUT WHEN WERE THEY BORN? AND WHY DID THEY DIE?

There are a hundred answers to those questions. The earliest lost course was born in 1897. The latest, not including post-2000, died in December 1999. Some looked like well-groomed, verdant expanses. Others looked like, well, Farmer Farmall's back 40, which they sometimes were. They died because of hard times. They died because higher powers — city or state authorities, anyway — wanted the land. And they died because selling the real estate to a developer made a lot more dollars and sense than continuing to run a golf course.

Still, with all that said, there is one distinct, unmistakable pattern among Minnesota's lost golf courses. It's so uncannily common that it's almost a template:

Born during good times of the 1920s. Expired during gloomier days of the '30s and '40s.

A step back in time is required here. Remember the WABAC Machine from *The Rocky and Bullwinkle Show?* Crank it up, Peabody and Sherman.

The year is 1920. The United States has weathered the latter half of a decade in which a world war claimed 8.5 million lives worldwide and a Spanish influenza pandemic claimed almost 30 million more. After a brief economic depression in 1920 and 1921, America picks up steam like a runaway locomotive. The byword for the new decade is "prosperity."

Radios, refrigerators and ranges appear in Americans' homes. More and more of Ford's Model-T's appear on their driveways, giving Americans never-before-imagined access to places near and far. As the decade advances, most people have more money. In 1920, the average income for a Minnesota wage earner is $2,940. By 1927, that figure will rise to $4,812.

The good times are rolling, and they are rolling right into the growing game of golf. Newspapers and magazines trumpet the achievements of the game's great players, including the consummate gentleman Bob Jones and the consummate swashbuckler Walter Hagen. The American public is enamored of the game, and to sate the thirst, golf courses are built. Everywhere.

"By the 1920s," Minnesota author Rick Shefchik wrote in *From Fields to Fairways*, his remarkable compendium of Minnesota's classic golf clubs, "golf had become so popular and fashionable that no self-respecting community of any size wanted to be without a course of its own ..."

No kidding. Only seven Minnesota courses were listed in the 1916 *American Annual Golf Guide*. By 1926, the same guide listed 75 Minnesota courses. The year before, the book *Tee Party on the Green* had reported 82 Minnesota courses, ranking 14th in the nation.

But a five-day span in late October 1929 changed everything.

The morning of Oct. 24, 1929 — "Black Thursday" — opened a mass sell-off on Wall Street and precipitated a cataclysmic stock market crash. By the time sunset arrived five days later, on Black Tuesday, Wall Street had been reduced to a figurative pile of rubble. According to one estimate, the value of U.S. stocks dropped by $16 billion over the final months of 1929.

Soon, the nation was plunged into an economic depression — the Great Depression, it would come to be called. By 1933, the U.S. unemployment rate had reached 25 percent. In 1934, the Minnesota unemployment rate was 22 percent. Thousands of Americans took to government bread lines just to eat. Personal income dropped by 50 percent. Crop prices dropped by 60 percent.

Farms failed. Banks failed. So did golf courses.

Golf courses, to be blunt, dropped like flies in the 1930s and 1940s. More than 50 courses are known to have expired in those two decades, and it's more likely that at least 70 or 80 actually did.

Down they went, like tomato cans versus Joe Louis. First, construction all but stopped. Through the 1920s, the Minnesota golf magazine *The 10,000 Lakes Golfer* included nearly ceaseless reports or updates on new-course construction in Minnesota. By 1932, similar reports in the magazine's successor, *The Amateur Golfer & Outdoor Magazine*, had vanished. By 1936, only 36 courses remained on the Minnesota Golf Association's roster of member courses.

How tough were those times? The website of Jackson Golf Club, in southwestern Minnesota, reports that the club's cash on hand at the end of 1931 was $1.73.

Private courses, because they tended to have backers with deep financial pockets, bobbed and weaved and generally survived the Great Depression. Northwood Country Club in North St. Paul was one such example. Almost all of the other lost courses of that era were municipally owned, daily-fee or semi-private.

The summer of 1936 produced another blow — a scalding one. The Great Heat Wave of 1936 was both extraordinary and deadly. The temperature peaked at 106 in Duluth, 108 in Minneapolis and 114 in Moorhead, an all-time high in the state. Grasshoppers were fried alive in farmers' fields. There was a human toll as well: Over a 15-day period in July, nearly 800 Minnesotans were reported to have died from the heat. In a nine-day period early in the month, the heat wave killed 240 people in St. Paul, according to a 1936 *White Bear Press* story.

Though there is no direct evidence the 1936 heat wave contributed to the demise of any golf courses, it couldn't have helped any of them.

"Everything was burned," Hilltop golfer Mike Rak remembered.

Amid unprecedented hard times for golf courses, a shot in the arm finally came on Dec. 17, 1936, with the announcement that $10.5 million in relief funds would be spent on new and existing golf courses through President Franklin D. Roosevelt's Works Progress Administration. WPA projects put unemployed Americans back on the job — many of them on the golf course.

Sports Illustrated noted in a 2009 story that the WPA and Civil Works Administration built or renovated nearly 600 municipal golf courses in the United States. Among the WPA projects in Minnesota: a clubhouse and pro shop at Keller in Maplewood, five new greens at Columbia in Minneapolis, and at least a dozen new-course projects statewide. WPA contributed to at least one course going "lost," as well: Ortonville Golf Club moved its club from north of town to a superior location overlooking Big Stone Lake.

But not every ailing golf course received WPA elixir, and more Minnesota courses passed into oblivion in the late 1930s.

Then, one more sledgehammer's blow for American golf: U.S. entry into World War II in December 1941. The war put 16.1 million Americans in military uniforms. More than 15½ million of those were men, and when it's considered that golf still was largely a man's game in the early 1940s, that translates to a huge loss in numbers of people available to pony up a daily greens fee.

Al Schultz, late mayor of Bayport, estimated in 2012 that 50 percent of that city's males enlisted in World War II. Peanuts Bell, who caddied and played at the old Bayport golf course, was one of them, having served in the 15th Air Force in Italy. In fact, the vast majority of men who were interviewed for this book and who remembered lost courses of the 1930s and '40s were World War II veterans. Rak served in the Army's 91st Infantry in Africa. Don Dostert (Bunker Hills) served with the 1st Marines in the Pacific. Bud Chapman (Westwood Hills) flew B-29s. John Burton (The Minnetonka Club) served with the Navy in the Mediterranean. Thor Nordwall (Matoska) served with the Army Signal Corps in Europe.

While the men were away, the women did not play — golf, nor much of anything else. American citizens were singularly focused on the war effort. Government policies underlined those efforts. On Dec. 17, 1941, the Office of Price Administration ordered an 80 percent reduction in the production of new golf balls. On April 9, 1942, the War Production Board ordered a full stop to the manufacturing of golf equipment as of May 31, 1942. That edict was eased

Fore! Gone.

The old sand greens at Chisago Golf Club are long gone, as is all other physical evidence of a golf course having existed on the site. All that remains is a tribute: This photo was taken near Fairway Lane and Eagle Drive in Chisago City.

JOE BISSEN PHOTO

the next month, when the WPB permitted clubs to be manufactured with material already on hand.

Those who oversaw golf responded in kind. On Jan. 11, 1942, the United States Golf Association canceled all of its championships for the duration of the war. The 1943 PGA Tour season consisted of only three events. Augusta National closed in 1943 for the duration of the war, and the club allowed 50 cows to graze its property.

In the words of Frank Fiorito, a longtime St. Paul-area golf professional: "During the war, you couldn't get no golf balls, couldn't get no clubs. They were making bullets."

The war's momentum turned by 1944, and in 1945, it concluded in victory for the Allies. America suffered more than 400,000 casualties (dead or missing), and thousands more came home seriously injured. Comparatively, the war's cost on the game of golf was, of course, a pittance. Still, it was real. More Minnesota courses folded during the war years or shortly after — Hilltop in Columbia Heights and Bunker Hills in Mendota Heights, to name just two.

Postwar, America recovered. So did its golf courses, as the game enjoyed a period of expansion — thank you, Sam, Patty, Ben, Arnie, Jack, Lee, Gary, Tom, Nancy, Shark, Freddie and Tiger — that lasted nearly 50 years.

But for the lost golf courses of the 1930s and 1940s, almost nothing remained, except for faded memories.

CHAPTER 4

Bang It Off the Tower

HILLTOP PUBLIC GOLF LINKS
CITY: COLUMBIA HEIGHTS
COUNTY: ANOKA
YEARS: CIRCA 1927–46

Please Replace Turf

HILLTOP PUBLIC
Golf Links

2201 45th Ave. N. E. — Dinsmore 3114
Minneapolis, Minn.
Western Golf Association Rules Govern All Play

SCORE CARD

These cards are furnished by

JAPS-OLSON CO.
PRINTING - STATIONERY
Loose Leaf Devices - Binders
LITHOGRAPHING
417 So. 7th St.
Minneapolis, Minn.

SCORECARD COURTESY OF PHIL KOSTOLNIK

Fore! Gone.

It's a radiant Sunday morning in July 2012, and 91-year-old Mike Rak is in a familiar place. He's on the golf course.

Sort of.

Underfoot, there is asphalt, not bentgrass. Alongside, split-levels, not flagsticks. There isn't a tee box or two-tiered green in sight — and there hasn't been for 65 years.

Rak (pronounced "Rock") is riding shotgun in an SUV turning onto Fairway Drive in the northern Minneapolis suburb of Columbia Heights. As the vehicle completes its turn, Rak's memory is jogged. He goes back in time.

"See that? There's a tower by the 12th green," he says.

To his left, behind a row of houses, beyond a chain-link fence, across a service road that borders the property of the Minneapolis Water Works and up a three-foot rise, is a round, brick tower with a cone-shaped, metal roof, about 25 feet tall and 15 feet in diameter.

"The 12th hole was 160 yards," Rak says. "Where the tower was, balls would hit off that tower and go on the green.

Doink! Nice par! Golfers at Hilltop Public Golf Links in Columbia Heights occasionally bounced tee shots off this gatehouse, now part of the Columbia Heights Ultrafiltration Plant, and onto the green of the par-3 12th hole.

PETER WONG PHOTO

... The green was right back of this house there."

In his mind's eye, Rak is back on his old stomping grounds: Hilltop Public Golf Links, born in the 1920s, deceased 1946, occupying 150 acres or so in the northwest corner of Columbia Heights. Rak caddied at Hilltop in the 1930s and played there in the 1940s.

The house to which Rak refers, and its back yard, now own squatter's rights to the old 12th green at Hilltop. From the street, neither Rak nor the SUV driver can see the slightest evidence that anyone ever hopped on the bogey train and finished 4-4-5-5-6-5-5 anywhere near here.

In this part of Columbia Heights, there is an almost standard response when residents are asked if they know about the neighborhood's history:

There was a golf course here?

Yep, there was. Most likely, nobody alive remembers it as well as Rak.

So, Mike, true confessions: Did you ever bounce one off the tower and onto the green?

Rak smiles.

"Yeah. *Everyone* did."

The brick towers near Hilltop's old 12th green are technically referred to as gatehouses. A handful of them dot the grounds of the Columbia Heights Ultrafiltration Plant, which processes up to 70 million gallons of Mississippi River water daily, makes it potable, and sends it downhill to nearby Minneapolis.

The Hilltop golf course wrapped around the grounds of the current Ultrafiltration Plant and an adjacent, previously existing, plant in an upside-down "L" shape. This, incidentally, was news to a supervisor at the Minneapolis Water

Mike Rak of Columbia Heights, a former top-flight golfer at Hilltop, Gross and Columbia golf courses in Minneapolis and its northern suburbs.

PETER WONG PHOTO

Department, which operates the plant. The supervisor, answering an inquiry about the gatehouses, asserts in a voicemail message that "there may have been an employee who went up there and swung a club up there once in the past, but it's really not a golf course; I don't believe it ever was."

Yeah, right. And Mike Rak never hit a 7-iron pin-high, either.

The SUV turns right, eastbound now on 49th Avenue Northeast.

"You see a straight line here; this is 49th," Rak says. "In other words, this was the 15th fairway. ... The 15th green was right here. Fifteen was a drivable par 4."

Fore! Gone.

Mike Rak studies the map of Hilltop that he sketched out in detail on a manila folder.
PETER WONG PHOTO

The SUV is at the southern edge of Albert A. Kordiak Park. A parking lot occupies part of what was the 15th fairway. A small restroom stands within probably 50 feet of where the 15th green was. Where once a Hilltop golfer's putting stunk, now ... well, never mind.

Just beyond the restroom is the corner of a marsh, its shoreline thick with trees and brush. It is the southern edge of Highland Lake, which Rak knows as Peck's Lake. Rak and his pals used to hunt ducks and pheasant nearby. Rak also used to tee off on Hilltop's 16th hole here.

Couldn't happen now. Today, a good drive, if it managed to sneak through the thicket and clear the lake, might land in somebody's backyard begonia bed.

Tough lie. Try to pick it clean without clipping too many petals.

Rak, undaunted by the sight of the old Hilltop golf course paved here and overgrown there, describes the 16th.

"After 15, you walked to the left, and you hit across the lake, straight, 600 yards," Rak says. "That was the longest hole in town then. This one went all the way up to Stinson Boulevard. You had to carry the ball over a hundred yards (off the tee). It was 615 or 620 yards long." (An old scorecard lists its length as 510 yards, though an estimate based on a modern-day map indicates it might have been in the 550-yard range.)

The 16th green was at the northeast corner of Hilltop golf course and close to the very northeast corner of Columbia

Heights. A 1947 aerial photo indicates that the green was within a few yards of what is now the intersection of Stinson and 5th Street Northwest.

The SUV heads south. The air is rare up here, relatively speaking. This is one of the highest points in the Twin Cities area — 1,065 feet above sea level at the base of the Columbia Heights water tower, which stands between the former 17th green and 18th tee at Hilltop GC. The roadway names in this neighborhood attest to the elevation: Matterhorn Drive, Khyber Lane, Rainier Pass, Innsbruck Parkway.

Downhill from here: No. 18 at Hilltop, a 370-yard par 4, descended back to the clubhouse. The 18th tee "had a nice view of Minneapolis," former Hilltop caddie Chet Latawiec recalled in Irene Parsons' book *Columbia Heights: Bootstrap Town*.

Today, Minneapolis is not visible from the water tower. Houses and treetops are.

Latawiec, incidentally, was among a group of gifted golfers who played Hilltop. The late founder and namesake of Chet's Shoes in Columbia Heights, he won a state junior boys championship and two state public links championships and qualified for the U.S. public links championship 17 times. He is a member of the Minnesota Golf Association Hall of Fame. Rak, a welder, played in the national public links four times and won a Minnesota senior public links championship (1977), a state senior four-ball and a state senior masters. He has eight holes in one. Rak's brother John was a long hitter who once played No. 1 man for the University of Minnesota, and his other brother Joe played in three U.S. Public Links Championships.

Then there were John and Bill Lakotas, fine shotmakers whose family owned a hog farm near the 17th hole at Hilltop. John was a three-time state public links champion. The Lakotases perhaps were better at golf than animal control. Rak sketched out and passed along a remarkably detailed, in-scale map of Hilltop on a manila folder that included this notation near the 17th, referencing the Lakotas farm:

"Watch out for wild hogs."

As adept as the Hilltop crew was, the best player to navigate the course was an outsider. Wally Ulrich, an Austin, Minn., native, served briefly as the Hilltop pro in the mid-1940s before playing the PGA Tour in the late 1940s and 1950s. Steve Walters, a longtime manager at nearby Gross and Columbia golf clubs in nearby northeastern Minneapolis, recalled that the Hilltop regulars, gifted as they were, never could get over the way Ulrich commanded the ball on Hilltop's elevated greens.

Rak agreed.

"He'd hit a wedge," Rak said, "and that son of a buck would back 'em up, and we'd hit the same shot and go over the green."

The Hilltop clubhouse no longer stands, but the course manager's residence does. It is a tall, squarish house at the northeast corner of Chatham Road and 45th Avenue Northeast. In the Hilltop days, a stone archway extended over what is now Chatham and led to the clubhouse.

"There were no homes no place here," Rak says, looking over an area that now is nothing but homes, yards and streets. "The driving range was right next to where that second house is, and

Fore! Gone.

Hilltop Public Golf Links, 1940 aerial photo
THE CRAIG DISHER COLLECTION

Hilltop now: Near the southeastern corner of Albert Kordiak Park in Columbia Heights, the view includes Highland Lake, formerly known as Peck's Lake. Golfers had to clear the corner of the lake with their tee shots on the par-5 16th hole at Hilltop Public Golf Links.

JOE BISSEN PHOTO

it went to Stinson." Between the manager's residence and the driving range was an open-air reservoir with wooden banks at a 45-degree angle that held water used to irrigate the golf course.

Hilltop's front nine traversed the interior of the course grounds, where, Rak says, you couldn't hit a ball out of bounds. The back nine bordered the exterior, with water often in play and out of bounds always in play. The course's western border was the 14th hole, now occupied by Highland Elementary School.

Hilltop was one of the first Twin Cities public courses with grass greens. The greens were fast, Rak said, and there were trees and heavy rough off the fairways. The routing was peculiar, to say the least: The first three holes were par 5s, as was the seventh, though Rak said that routing changed in the course's latter years. The course measured 6,210 yards. Greens fees in the 1930s were 35 cents for nine holes.

Walters, recalling area golfers' appraisal of Hilltop, said: "Players thought the golf course ... was the cat's meow compared to Gross."

Rak said Hilltop's boxes and greens were watered every night and that the "greens were always perfect and tees were perfect."

Rak, the son of a Polish immigrant woman who brought her young family to the United States and raised four children by herself in Columbia Heights, was born in 1921, the same year M.J. Lamberton bought farmland that would become Hilltop Golf Course.

The exact year Hilltop opened is unclear. The June 1927 issue of the magazine *The 10,000 Lakes Golfer* includes an advertisement for J.A. Hunter, Golf Architect, Minneapolis, with "Hill Top" listed as one of the courses Hunter designed or worked on. The ad, however, includes the notation "plans only" after "Hill Top." The same magazine's September 1927 issue reports that Hilltop had hosted a St. Paul Real Estate board tournament. A 1927 Minneapolis telephone directory includes Hilltop Golf Links.

An old scorecard includes admonishments by Lamberton: "Ignorance of the Etiquette of Golf and the principal rules governing the game are inexcusable and reflect discredit on the player. ... It is the desire of the owner to maintain Hilltop Links on a par with the finest courses in the country. Please help us to keep it so. Replace turf. ... Players who in any way make themselves objectionable or fail to observe any of the rules may be denied the privilege of the course."

Parsons wrote about the ownership history of Hilltop in her *Bootstrap Town* book:

"Lamberton died about 1934, and his nephew took over the golf course, leading it to a man named Clovour who operated it until 1939. At that time, about 50 club members bought it for $25 a share and operated it until World War II. During the war years, money to operate golf courses was scarce and, according to Latawiec, 'the course went to seed.'"

It was revived by Ralph Arone, who bought Hilltop for $10,000 from the Central Avenue Merchants after the city of Columbia Heights turned down a proposed purchase, said Bob Fetzek of New Brighton, who grew up in Columbia Heights. Fetzek said Arone bought the course in 1942 or 1943; Fetzek helped him repair pipe and restore the watering system. "That course was a big hayfield" at the time, Fetzek said.

"Arone improved the course and ran it through 1946," Parsons wrote, "but when his efforts to obtain a liquor license were unsuccessful, he sold the property to Wilkinson Realty." Fetzek said the purchase price was $75,000.

"The area was replatted and 20 homes were completed in 1947," Parsons wrote. "By 1955, homes in the Hilltop area were advertised in the newspaper: 'Homes from $13,900 to $16,400 are available. ...'"

There goes the neighborhood. Well, the neighborhood golf course, anyway.

HILLTOP WAS REGARDED WELL ENOUGH TO HAVE HOSTED the 1930 Minnesota Public Golf Association championship and three Minnesota Golf Association Senior Public Links championships, in 1938, '39 and '40.

CHAPTER 5

Eight is Enough

**SOMMERDORF GOLF COURSE
CITY: BROWNTON
COUNTY: MCLEOD
YEARS: 1928-35**

Charles A. Sommerdorf of rural Brownton, sensing in 1928 he didn't have enough room on his property to create a standard nine-hole golf course, thought out of the box and came up with the next-best thing: eight-ninths of a nine-hole course.

"It was an eight-hole course, and they used one hole twice," said Sommerdorf's grandson, Ron Sommerdorf.

Call it Charles Sommerdorf's 89 percent solution.

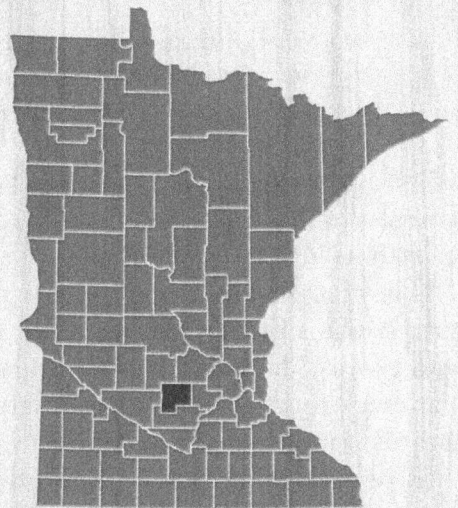

Sommerdorf's creativity might have been maxed out at that point. He did not go fancy-shmancy in naming the place, choosing to call it simply the Sommerdorf golf course, his grandson said. But the course was good enough to have lasted for seven years.

The Sommerdorf course had 35 members when it opened, Ron Sommerdorf said, and served not only golfers in Brownton, current population 762, but also those in Hutchinson, 11 miles north.

Sommerdorf's course was on his farm in Sumter Township, two miles east of the south-central Minnesota city of Brownton. The course was immediately north of U.S. Highway 212, south of railroad tracks that are a half-mile north of the highway, and just west of Lewis Lake, which is now dry. The course was near Buffalo Creek but did not go that far south or west — it was alongside a smaller creek.

Ron Sommerdorf moved to a farm on the golf-course property in 1938 and now owns the property — all eight former holes' worth. His brother Charles lives on the "home" place that was Charles A. Sommerdorf's residence.

"We saw where the remains of the greens were. We used to fish golf balls out of that little creek," Ron Sommerdorf said.

Harry Sommerdorf, son of Charles A. Sommerdorf, tilling land near Brownton, Minn. The sign in the background points to Charles Sommerdorf's golf course.

PHOTO COURTESY OF RON SOMMERDORF

Ron Sommerdorf isn't old enough to have played the course, but he was familiar with its history.

"They just laid it out on the cow pasture. It was all fenced in, and they had sand greens," he said. "You had to cross that creek three or four times. Natural hazards were the cows, of course.

"I remember as kids where those greens were. We used to play there; there were three or four of them at that time, and then there were the tee boxes, just an elevated — it looked like an Indian mound — where they teed off. ... I haven't seen them for years now."

Marlys Fredrick of the McLeod County Historical Museum noted in an email that the course was played even during the winter if weather allowed. She added that the course closed in 1935. The museum has a display of the golf course, including an old map showing its routing and an old golf club.

CHAPTER 6

Unearthing a Gem

WESTWOOD HILLS GOLF COURSE
CITY: ST. LOUIS PARK
COUNTY: HENNEPIN
YEARS: 1929-61

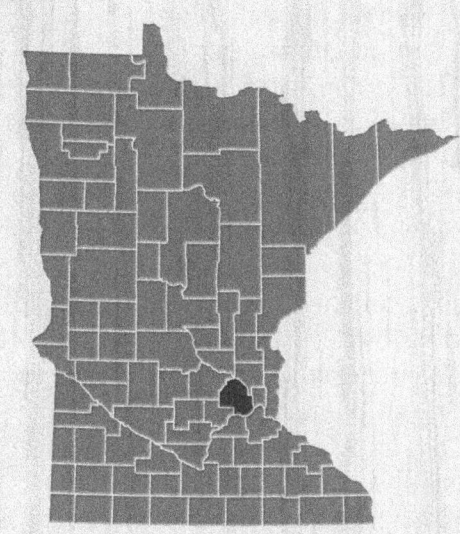

Fore! Gone.

Knock, knock. "Who's there?" "Just me. Any lateral water hazards in your back yard?"

Now, walking into a neighborhood you don't know, randomly rapping on doors and asking a question like that could be bad for your reputation, your health or even your criminal record.

But I am unswayed.

I'm scoping out a neighborhood in the northwest corner of St. Louis Park on a summer's Sunday evening because I know a good portion of it used to be home to Westwood Hills, a once-popular 27-hole public golf course. I've been told remnants of the layout might still be underfoot, a half-century after the course closed, so I'm willing to try to find out the hard way.

By knocking on doors. Well, door, actually.

I never make it to the door on the first house I stop at, on Texas Avenue. I take two steps onto the lawn.

"Where did you come from?" the woman in the front yard asks sternly.

"Right over there. I parked my SUV there and walked here. I'm doing research on old golf courses that aren't around anymore."

Yeah, right, she's thinking. And I'm the scratch-handicap queen of England.

I tell her there used to be a golf course right about here, where my feet are planted. She's sizing me up, and I sense she already has the "9" and the first "1" somehow secretly dialed on her cell phone. She tolerates my inquiry anyway.

Wasn't any golf course here, she says. She is polite, but she also is self-assured.

"We've been here since 1967. I don't know anything about it. No one on this street has been around any longer than that. They won't be able to tell you anything."

We shall see.

I head south down Texas Avenue and take a right. Atop a small hill is the abode at 8112 Westwood Hills Drive.

Knock, knock.

A woman answers.

Bingo.

"This house is where the 10th green used to be," says Laura Callahan, one of the homeowners. "That's one thing they first told us when we bought the house, was that this is where the 10th green was."

In your face, Texas Avenue lady.

The Callahans, Laura and Mitch, have heard of the old golf course but know nothing more about it. They say no signs of it still exist on their property, but they say their oak trees predate the 1958 construction of the house. In other words, those oaks once defended No. 10 at Westwood Hills, spitting shots back at anyone inept enough to have fanned a 6-iron in their direction.

One hole pinpointed, 26 to go.

Across the street, I am told, is the former McNulty home. A few houses up from there, I'm also told, on Westwood Hills Curve, is another McNulty home, the one the family moved to after outgrowing the first one.

The McNultys, I would learn, *are* Westwood Hills Golf Course. Thirty-three years' worth of it. And Westwood Hills, in its totality — history, design, popularity, present-day surroundings — stands as the signature entry in Minnesota's roll of lost golf courses.

James A. McNulty was the patriarch of Westwood Hills — the golf course and the neighborhood. In the early 1900s, McNulty owned a 600-acre parcel of land, mostly in northwestern St. Louis Park, and established the Hyland Homes company. In 1916, Hyland, wishing to establish a golf club on its land, hired noted Scottish architect Willie Park Jr. to lay out a course, and Minneapolis Golf Club opened in 1917, north of Cedar Lake Road and east of what is now Flag Avenue.

MGC was a private club, and McNulty wanted to establish a public alternative, so he hired noted Minnesota-based architect Tom Vardon to design a 27-hole layout immediately east and north of Minneapolis Golf Club. "The fairways will be undulating and the greens large," the November 1928 issue of *The 10,000 Lakes Golfer* reported.

Westwood Hills Country Club, as it was then known, opened as an 18-hole course in June 1929. The course and the neighborhood were named for the Westwood area of Los Angeles, where McNulty had business interests and had played a role in the early formation of Los Angeles Country Club.

Westwood Hills measured 6,400 yards and had bentgrass greens averaging 5,200 square feet, *The 10,000 Lakes Golfer* reported. That was a relatively large green size in that era. Gerald McNulty, secretary of Hyland Homes and son of James McNulty, was club manager. He is listed in some accounts

James McNulty, founder of Westwood Hills Golf Course.

as the course's founder and/or owner, but he was involved with the course only briefly; his father was the driving force behind Westwood Hills.

Vardon was an exemplary hire. The head professional at White Bear Yacht Club in Dellwood, he designed more than 40 golf courses in the Upper Midwest, including Southview in West St. Paul, Eau Claire Golf & Country Club and the University of Minnesota course.

Vardon knew his stuff, "and the course showed it," said John McNulty, 89, of St. Paul, Westwood Hills' longtime manager and grandson of James McNulty. "It was beautifully laid out. A beautiful design."

15th green, Westwood Hills Golf Course.

Westwood Hills' first nine lay south and east of the clubhouse, which was situated atop a hill off Westwood Hills Drive. After an opening par 5, golfers crossed Texas Avenue for the next seven holes, then finished back at the clubhouse. The second nine proceeded south toward Cedar Lake Road, then continued west, paralleling Minneapolis Golf Club. The third nine, which opened in 1933, then closed and reopened again, went north, to the west of what is now Westwood Lake and almost to Wayzata Boulevard, then returned home. That nine included Westwood Hills' best-known hole — No. 22, a par-5, 540-yard double dogleg, the No. 1 handicap hole on all 27.

There was, however, one pesky little issue with the routing.

Westwood Hills and Minneapolis Golf Club "were adjacent," John McNulty said. "Matter of fact, on the 15th hole (at Westwood), many a golfer got confused and ended up on the 11th hole of Minneapolis, and they'd end up at the Minneapolis Golf Club clubhouse and didn't know how they got there.

"And vice versa."

When the old Westwood Hills ads touted private club-style golf on a public-course setting, they weren't exaggerating.

Regardless, the Westwood Hills layout "was terrific," said Ted Stark of Edina, who played there in the late 1940s before joining Edina Country Club. "It was a great course. It's the one we liked the most; it's the only one we went to."

Stark did, however, feel compelled to affix an asterisk onto Westwood Hills' third nine — as did almost everyone who talked about Westwood Hills.

"I'll tell you what I remember about it: Their fairways were all peat," Stark said.

"And they went up and down. So when they mowed them, the mowers wouldn't catch all the low spots, and they'd scald the top spots. So every 10 feet there'd be 8 inches of grass, and then every 10 feet there wouldn't be any grass."

David Chapman of Minnetonka, who grew up nearby, summed up the peat-bog effect more succinctly.

"Four-foot divots," he said.

"You bounced up and down as you walked," noted John Hubbell of Minnetonka.

"Like you were walking on a waterbed," said Chapman.

"You'd have big peat fires," added Jim McNulty, whose father, Robert, operated the course with John McNulty from the 1940s on and who grew up on Westwood Hills Curve. "I remember the St. Louis Park fire department out there for days on end trying to control them."

"The course had a lot of peat," conceded John McNulty, "and keeping the peat under control was really difficult when the moisture stopped, when we were in a drought. The peat would dry out, and fissures would develop. If it stayed moist, it wasn't too bad."

Peat — and re-peat — notwithstanding, the quality of Westwood Hills showed in the popularity of the course and the people who left imprints there. John McNulty said that in the peak days of the course, just before World War II and just after, 550 to 600 golfers a day would play there.

And what a crowd it was.

Les Bolstad was Westwood Hills' professional for most of the 1930s. Bolstad won the 1926 U.S. Public Links championship at age 18, became one of Minnesota's premier teaching professionals

Hall of Fame pro golfer Gene Sarazen at Westwood Hills, standing with young brothers John and Bob McNulty.

and is the namesake of the University of Minnesota's Bolstad golf course.

In the early 1930s, seven-time major champion Gene Sarazen played an exhibition match at Westwood Hills. One of the McNulty family's favorite photographs is of "The Squire," natty in plus-fours, sportcoat and necktie, arms folded around young John and Bob McNulty. The boys' father, John, was the second-generation owner of the course at the time.

Before leaving Westwood Hills to become pro at MGC in 1938, Bolstad frequently gave lessons at Westwood to young Patty Berg of Minneapolis, who would go on to win 15 women's major championships and help found the LPGA Tour, where she won 60 titles.

Bolstad was replaced as Westwood Hills' pro by Gunnard Johnson, who

Westwood Hills clubhouse (main photo).
The view from the clubhouse (inset) featured a sweeping look at the golf course.

came to the course with four state PGA championships in tow and six more in waiting.

On May 5, 1936, famed golf-course architect A.W. Tillinghast visited Westwood Hills while on a two-year, whirlwind tour of U.S. golf courses set up by the PGA of America. Two days earlier, "Tilly" had finished planning Rochester Golf & Country Club, his acclaimed layout in southeastern Minnesota. At Westwood, Tillinghast designed a new 13th green.

Then there was the Brown Bomber, who showed up one day at Westwood Hills. "Joe Louis came out and wanted to play," John McNulty said of the great heavyweight champion boxer. "He couldn't get on another course (because he was black). I said, sure, go ahead and play."

One last brush with greatness. Well, kind of: In 1959, as Westwood Hills was shutting down, nine by nine by nine, the grounds served as a parking lot for the PGA Championship, played next door at Minneapolis Golf Club.

As much as Westwood Hills was a golf course, it was a neighborhood. A neighborhood that Helen McNulty, Jim's mother and Bob's wife, watched out for.

"Westwood Hills Drive was the main road to go to the golf course; up to the clubhouse was a dirt road at the time," Jim McNulty said. "I remember my mother coming out of the house, yelling at all the drivers to slow down because she had all the kids running around. They (drivers) were flying around, trying to get to their tee times."

Jim didn't specify whether "all the kids" meant all five of Helen and Bob McNulty's kids or the scores who occupied the yards and streets in the Westwood Hills Drive and Curve area.

"That neighborhood was wonderful," said Helen McNulty, 90, who now lives in Bloomington. "We had 72 children on that curve." She said neighborhood picnics were common and that residents still get together for reunions.

Many of those children lived in homes built by Bob McNulty, Westwood Hills' co-owner/manager and president of Hyland Homes (John McNulty was vice president). Bob McNulty did not have a construction background, and, Helen McNulty said, got into the business almost by happenstance. He was helping build a home for the family at the same time as a man across the street also was building a home, "and in the middle of it," Helen McNulty said, "he (the man across the street) decided he wanted to go to South America and sell road building materials."

Bob McNulty took over construction of that home and finished his own. "That's when Bob started the building (trade)," Helen McNulty said. "He didn't know anything about golf courses, but he didn't know anything about building, either. But he did very well in both."

Bob McNulty put in most of the roads in the Westwood Hills neighborhood and built many of its homes. Construction became his occupational focus, and his brother John assumed day-to-day management of Westwood Hills Golf Course.

The course still had good years after World War II. John McNulty recalled two "extraordinary … mammoth" fireplaces in the clubhouse that would heat the place for New Year's Eve parties. Elmer Carlson, who had won the 1933 state PGA championship, became the Westwood pro in the course's latter years and had a successful tenure, John McNulty said.

But there were tragedies, too. On Sept. 3, 1942, 15-year-old Patsy John-

The Westwood Hills clubhouse burns to the ground, as reported in the Oct. 1, 1956, Minneapolis Star.

son, daughter of Westwood Hills course manager Pat Johnson, was struck on the head by a golfer's mis-hit shot on the 13th hole. After spending 36 hours in a coma, she died without regaining consciousness.

In the early hours of Oct. 1, 1956, Helen McNulty woke up her 5-year-old son Jim. "I remember my mother at 2 in the morning showing me out the window a big fire up the hill," Jim McNulty said.

The clubhouse was ablaze. "Bob's mother arrived, with dark glasses on; she was crying, she felt so bad," Helen McNulty said. A St. Louis Park Historical Society entry on Westwood Hills reported that the fire was put out but then reignited, burning the building to the ground at a loss estimated at $100,000.

As 1950 approached and passed, Westwood Hills' decline began, for various reasons. Helen McNulty pointed to a decision in 1948 or 1949 to close nine holes in an effort to ameliorate the peat problem. "They had advice from Northrup King," Helen McNulty said,

No. 2 tee, Blue Nine, Westwood Hills Golf Course

referring to her husband and brother-in-law, who were operating the course. "They dug up the golf course; they dug up the first tee, which was the dumbest thing they ever could have done. ... Nobody wanted to tee off with their ball in the dirt, and they kept losing business."

Westwood also lost business to the increasing number of municipal courses popping up. Those courses, John McNulty pointed out, had a significant financial advantage over privately owned public courses because they did not have to pay city taxes.

John McNulty said Westwood Hills always was able to pay its bills, but by 1955, according to the St. Louis Park Historical Society, the course was no longer profitable, and the family began to develop the land for housing. The first nine — easternmost — was abandoned first; it turned partly into residential development and partly the site of the current St. Louis Park Junior High School, just across Texas Avenue.

That action compromised Westwood Hills Golf Course's character. "When we cut off the first nine," John McNulty said, "the course really wasn't the same. It was on its death knell after that."

By 1955, the Murri-Mac Company and Westwood Hills Construction Company had been formed as successors to Hyland Homes. Bob McNulty started the latter business to do home construction in the neighborhood. At the same time, John McNulty had enrolled in law school, no doubt sensing the looming demise of Westwood Hills Golf Course.

Westwood Hills still was an 18-hole course in mid-1956, but the McNultys faced sentiment in favor of continuing to develop the land. They also faced sentiment to do the opposite. After Murri-Mac bought 117 acres in 1957 and proposed to build 400 to 500 homes, a 450-member "Save the Green" committee was formed in St. Louis Park, intent on halting residential development. In 1957, Carl L. Gardner and Associates was retained to investigate the feasibility of the city acquiring Westwood Hills Golf Course and using it for park and recreation facilities.

By 1958, Westwood Hills was listed as a nine-hole course in the *DeWitt* golf course guide. The remaining nine was the "northwestern" nine, near what are now Franklin and Westmoreland avenues. That nine also was near Westwood Lake, which wasn't a lake at the time but became one around 1960 when, according to a St. Louis Park Historical Society entry, a water pipe broke on Franklin Avenue, flooding and filling the lowland.

Westwood Hills Golf Course soon was gone — the historical society's web page indicates that 1961 was its final year of operation — but Westwood Lake remained. It became the centerpiece of Westwood Hills Nature Center, which was phased in in the late 1970s and officially opened in 1981. Today, the center features 160 acres of lake, woods, wetlands and trails. Naturalists tend to flora and fauna and conduct programs for youths at an interpretive center. And they do one

Westwood Hills' greens were larger than many of their counterparts on fellow public courses.

Aerial view, Westwood Hills Golf Course. In the background is residential St. Louis Park; to the left is what would become Westwood Lake and the Westwood Hills Nature Center.

more thing: They tell you that part of Westwood Hills Golf Course remains.

I returned to Westwood Hills in late summer 2012, visited the nature center and happened upon naturalist Mark Zembryki. "There's an old green from the golf course in the woods," Zembryki told me, and he marked its location on a trail map. About one-third of a mile later, after a hike on the Marsh Trail and a sharp left into the woods near a fork in the trail, I found the now-unpolished

Fore! Gone.

It's next to impossible to tell by looking at a photograph, but this is a former green site at Westwood Hills Golf Course, now reposing in the woods at Westwood Hills Nature Center. In the background is Westwood Lake.

JOE BISSEN PHOTO

Tom Vardon gem: a green site, unmistakable even if it was now a mere collection of moss and fallen, blackened stumps and trees. But it takes the shape of a green — larger than many old-style greens, just as that *10,000 Lakes Golfer* magazine article had foretold 84 years earlier — with a rim, maybe a foot high, around the sides and an entryway at the front.

A visitor to the Westwood Hills Nature Center may or may not also see what David Chapman saw on the grounds years ago. Chapman, who grew up in a home adjacent to the 10th tee at Minneapolis Golf Club, on higher ground than the old Westwood Hills third-nine site but within 100 feet of the lost course, apparently was something of a boyhood paleontologist.

"They did have flooding problems," Chapman said, "and at one time there was a farm there, before the golf course, apparently. It flooded out and killed all the livestock. Where Westwood Hills, where the day camp is, the lower areas in there, we used to call it Bones Woods, because we could always go back there and find big cattle skulls, and huge arm and leg bones. To us, it was like dinosaur bones."

Chapman's interests ultimately evolved from bones to brushes; he is a wildlife artist and winner of seven Minnesota outdoor stamp competitions for turkey, duck and pheasant depictions. As for the Westwood Hills Golf Course principals, they also met with success. John McNulty completed law school and spent six years as a municipal judge in St. Louis Park. Bob McNulty's construction firm designed the Met Center sports arena in Bloomington, and he became an

BUD'S TALE

Nobody paints a picture like Bud Chapman. Few tell stories like him, either.

Loyal "Bud" Chapman, a Minneapolis native, is known worldwide for his *18 Infamous Golf Holes*, spectacularly contrived paintings of fictional holes in world-famous locations: Grand Canyon, Wall Street, Machu Picchu, places like that.

I called Chapman in mid-2012 because I knew he once lived near a lost golf course, Westwood Hills. In fact, he lived within yards of the course, in a home adjacent to the 10th green at Minneapolis Golf Club.

Chapman's first story was short and sweet. Asked about his golf game, he said: "I'm pretty good for my age, but otherwise I'm lousy."

Yeah, right. As of that day, Chapman, 89, had shot his age or better 2,382 times. (Yes, he keeps track.) He had shot a 70 at formidable Seminole Golf Club earlier in the year and had been above his age "only two or three times" all year.

As for Westwood Hills, Chapman said he remembered the course but offered no specifics. Well, except for this, retold in inimitable Bud Chapman fashion. Judge its veracity for yourself:

"I do remember one hole at Westwood because it was so unbelievable. I witnessed probably something that has never probably been done in the history of golf.

"The first hole is a par 3, a short par 3 down the hill, and we had our girlfriends over there, and we were going to see if they wanted to play golf, and they said, 'Yeah.' Well, they didn't know anything about golf. I don't know if they'd ever even had a club in their hand. They come out there with their high-heeled shoes like they were going to a party. But we said, well, OK. …

"This one, Mickey McNair (exact spelling unknown), she'd never had a club in her hand in her life, and she took the club back to swing on the first hole there, and she took the swing, and it just ticked the top of the ball, and it just started rolling and was going real slow, but she ticked it enough where it went over the hill and the ball rolled down the hill, picked up speed as it was going, it got back up on the green, and it went in the hole.

"First time anybody ever took a first swing and got a hole in one on the first swing on the first hole of their life. I mean, that's got to be in the *Guineas* (that's how Chapman pronounced it) *Book of World Records*, for sure. It'll never be duplicated."

investor in the Minnesota North Stars hockey team. His sons, Jim and Tim, own and operate McNulty Construction in downtown Minneapolis.

The old golf-course site is now approximately half nature center and half residential and school development. The website historicaerials.com allows a unique view of Westwood Hills, then and now, with a "slide" function that allows one to see 1947 or 1957 Westwood Hills alongside its modern-day counterpart. Voila: Yep, there's the old 10th green in the Callahans' back yard — and in the neighbor's swimming pool. There's a good-sized pond, a former water hazard, bordering the back yards of homes along Utah Street and Utah Avenue. There's a green, right in the middle of the junior high school, and another inches off the school's south wall.

Oh, and one last thing. A parting shot. Memo to the lady who lives on Texas Avenue and thought I had screws loose: I'm 99 percent sure there's a fairway running through your foyer.

Fore!

Note: All historic photos of Westwood Hills are courtesy of Jim McNulty.

CHAPTER 7

A Man, a Myth, a Monkey

**COURSE: JOYNER'S
(BROOKLYN PARK GOLF COURSE)
CITY: BROOKLYN PARK
COUNTY: HENNEPIN
YEARS: 1962-96**

A GOLF COURSE DOESN'T HAVE TO FEATURE THE UNIMPEACHABLE PEDIGREE OF ST. ANDREWS OR THE SEASIDE SPLENDOR OF PEBBLE BEACH TO BE CONSIDERED A SUCCESS.

Al Joyner operated his Brooklyn Park Golf Course for more than three decades, and the words "pedigree" and "splendor" might never have been uttered there, certainly not in the same breath.

Pedigree? The golf course was an offshoot of a bowling alley. Splendor? Topographically speaking, think central Kansas.

All that aside, Al Joyner's family would defy you to not label the place a success.

Brooklyn Park Golf Course, also known as Joyner's Golf Course, was a source of pride for Al Joyner and a source of camaraderie for many who played it.

"It was a place where people maintained friendships," said Joyner's son, Jay, a Minneapolis attorney.

Two fellows named Frank and Bob, for instance, were friends who frequented Joyner's. They worked together at a bar, Jay Joyner said, one as a bartender and the other as a bouncer. As with many who played Joyner's, their handicaps were most likely north of single digits and their divots most likely prodigious.

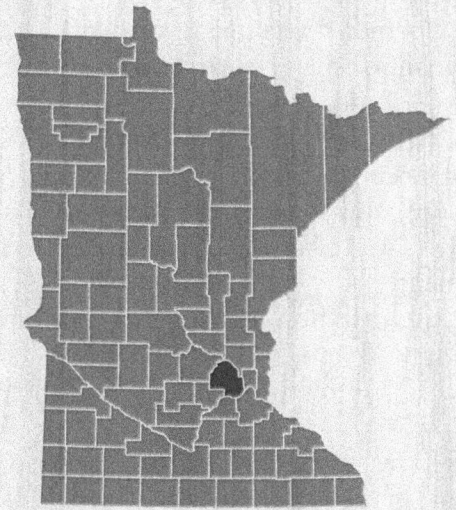

"One time," Jay Joyner said, "one of them came in with a roll of sod under his arm, and he said, 'This is overdue. I'm paying for the damages.'"

Then there was the monkey.

Either Frank or Bob — Joyner didn't remember which — owned a pet monkey that traversed the golf course on its owner's shoulders. One day, Joyner said, the monkey shrieked, ruining the concentration of a golfer on an adjoining hole and causing the player, in a moment of rage, to hurl his club, the offending implement whirling through the air like a helicopter.

So now — and this admittedly is off topic — the next time someone asks what you know about monkeys, you can name three things: long tails, advanced intelligence, deplorable golf-course etiquette.

But back to Joyner's.

Former Crystal resident Larry Hennig, now a realtor and auctioneer in St. Cloud, used to golf at Joyner's because, he says, "it was close to Crystal. It was always in good shape, and it was close, and it was near Mr. Bob's." Mr. Bob's was a bar Mr. Hennig used to frequent.

Oh, by the way — you might know Larry Hennig by his nickname: "The Axe." Or his other nickname: "Pretty Boy."

Larry "The Axe" Hennig, a Robbinsdale native and former University of Minnesota wrestling star, was best known as a professional wrestler in the old American Wrestling Association. He and "Handsome" Harley Race formed a generally reviled 1960s AWA tag team, and Hennig is a member of the International Wrestling Hall of Fame.

Hennig offered no other particular memories of Joyner's, but considering his celebrity status among the working-class stiffs who watched "The Axe" smack noggins into turnbuckles on 1960s Saturday morning TV, Al Joyner no doubt approved of his presence at his golf course.

Joyner opened his course in 1962 at the intersection of Brooklyn Boulevard and Hennepin County Highway 81, adjacent to his 12-lane bowling alley, Joyner Lanes. No high-priced consulting or construction firm was necessary for Al; he forged ahead with the layout himself even though he had no formal golf training or experience.

"He just loved the game," said Pam (Joyner) Dane, Al's daughter.

Al Joyner, in fact, was better known in bowling circles than golf circles. He eventually expanded his bowling operation to 24 lanes, opened another bowling center in Monticello in 1976, was an officer in state and national bowling organizations, once rolled a 298 game, and was inducted into the Minneapolis Bowling Association Hall of Fame in 1982.

As for his golf course, "My dad started this on kind of a shoestring," Jay Joyner said.

A frayed one, at that.

"The first summer we were open, we didn't have a clubhouse," Pam Dane said. "My dad would put me down there every morning with an umbrella-table and a cigar box."

Green fees went into the cigar box. Pam Dane, de facto club manager of Brooklyn Park Golf Course, was 11 years old.

"We didn't have much business that first year," she said.

The Joyners also sold golf balls out of that operation, Jay Joyner remembered: Spaldings and Wilsons, Kro-Flites and K-28s and Dots, the latter with their black and red and green labels color-coded to coincide with their compression.

In its infancy, Joyner's had an underground watering system but not much else.

"The first year, he did not have a maintenance cart," Jay Joyner said of his father, "so he dragged hoses from one place to the next and carried the copper and brass fittings around to water the golf course."

A small metal building was erected later. The building multi-tasked. It served as combination clubhouse, maintenance headquarters and storage shed.

The course's length fit the parameters of what would be considered an "executive" course, though that term seems an oxymoron at such a blue-collar place. Dane called Joyner's a "tweener" course. Par was 32, with five par 4s and four par 3s. Total yardage was 2,355. The par 3s, Jay Joyner said, had enough length to be challenging even for better players — the longest three were 205, 225 and 230 yards.

Still, this was not a course that would fit the skills of someone looking for a training ground from which to advance through PGA Tour Q-School. For instance, a 1977 *Metropolitan Area Golf Course Directory* noted that the course had no bunkers.

"It was geared so that families could come out and get a round in after work," Jay Joyner said. "People that liked to hit a ball far could swing away … and yet it wasn't as laborious for a shorter hitter to go through. A 3,600-yard course would get kind of tiresome" for a player like that.

Al Joyner's wife, Lorraine, ran the course for much of its 35-year life span. The Joyners hired area youth to help during the summers.

"During the '60s and '70s, it worked really well," Pam Dane said. "We had the bowling alley and golf course. He (Al) was pretty proud of the fact that a lot of kids worked with him, and he helped them go to college."

Shingle Creek, first a meandering stream and then dredged and straightened via a public works project in the early 1960s, ran through the course grounds. Pull carts could be rented, but the Joyners never acquired or rented out motorized carts. Greens were bentgrass and good-sized, Jay Joyner said. A driving range was added.

Ed Mattingley grew up in Brooklyn Park, played Joyner's frequently as a youth and remembered it as the first place he ever hit a golf ball. He also remembered the ever-present cigar smoked by Al Joyner, and the Joyners' graciousness.

"They were wonderful people," Mattingley said via email, "and if we were a little short on greens fees, or short on balls or tees, they always made sure we were able to play."

After serving in the military, Mattingley married and returned to Brooklyn Park. He started golfing again at Joyner's, and in the late 1970s, he began playing in "The Muni Open," a tournament named for the Muni, a bar in Robbinsdale that Matttingley hung out in.

"The fun thing," wrote Mattingley, who now lives in Monticello, "was that the guys played and the wives pulled wagons full of coolers of beer and wine … quite the happy hour … always fun."

Operating a golf course generally was a good business prospect into the 1990s, though the tide began to turn late in the decade as golf course supply caught up with, then surpassed, demand to play the game. Combined with an increased demand for suburban development space and higher land prices, course owners could hardly be blamed by the late 1990s for selling their land and exiting the business.

Jay Joyner did not explicitly say whether those were factors in the demise of the golf course. The more significant factors, he said, were the deaths of Al and Lorraine Joyner in 1993 and 1994. There was no one left with adequate time to manage the golf course. Jay Joyner had his law practice, and his sister Pam Dane was running the Monticello bowling alley and a Monticello golf course, Silver Springs (that course closed in 2007).

The Joyners shuttered Brooklyn Park Golf Course in 1996, according to Jay Joyner's best estimate, and sold the land for development. Much of the course grounds, in an area immediately west of Broadway Avenue and not far southwest of North Hennepin Community College, remains vacant. Another portion, north of Shingle Creek, is occupied by a large marsh. Still another portion is business development. The clubhouse is gone, a car dealership occupying that area. The golf course grounds was behind what is now a Menards store. The driving-range area is now the site of a Rainbow Foods store.

A one-hour hike through the knee-high weeds and across the sandy surface covering the old Joyner's Golf Course grounds reveals not a shred of evidence about the course. But there is still evidence of golf, in a manner of speaking: A handful of shin-high flags are stuck in the ground, each bearing the label "Disc Golf." The area is said to have served as a disc golf course after the "real" golf course closed.

BROOKLYN PARK'S CLAIM TO GOLF FAME (IF ONE DOESN'T count Joyner's) is that the city's municipally owned Edinburgh USA course hosted an LPGA Tour event, under three different names, from 1990-96.

CHAPTER 8
Common Threads

Fore! Gone.

Where there are lost golf courses, there are ...
Lost golf course sites.
Lost photographs.
Lost scorecards, lost scrapbooks and lost memories.
And, sadly, lost golfers.

Little tangible evidence remains from most of Minnesota's lost golf courses, especially from those abandoned before 1950. The people who played them are mostly gone, too. The precious few remaining men and women who remember the lost courses of the 1930s and '40s are well into their 80s, and often into their 90s. Someone like Mike Rak, the former Hilltop player and caddie with the sharply focused recall of the golf course that disappeared almost seven decades ago, is just about one in a million.

Reconstruction of these courses, then, is a challenge. Did they all look the same? Did they have common characteristics? If we're trying to compare an old, lost course to a modern, existing one, how do we do that?

The answers to those questions are "no," "yes" and "it ain't easy, but think small."

First, of course the lost courses didn't all look alike. This is Minnesota, after all, not high-plains West Texas. The courses were built on prairie flatland (as at Lakefield, for instance) and on hillsides (Hilltop) and on terrain that rolls and folds like the bedding you just climbed out of (Caledonia). They were built next to bodies of water (Riverside, Duluth; Green Lake, Spicer) and in forests (Joyce Estate, Grand Rapids).

But there are common threads, too. Remember that most of these courses were built in the 1920s, a decade not only of quantity in golf construction but quality as well. The '20s, in fact, are referred to as "The Golden Age" of golf course design.

Nationally, architects such as Donald Ross, A.W. Tillinghast and Seth Raynor were designing world-class layouts in the 1920s. All three plied their craft in Minnesota at one time or another. Regionally, the prolific Tom Vardon, who also served as head professional at White Bear Yacht Club, and the even more prolific Tom Bendelow of the Chicago area, who is credited with close to 800 U.S. designs, were among those who laid out notable courses in Minnesota.

Though it would be laughably presumptuous to think that every man who designed a 1920s Minnesota golf course was a disciple of Ross or Raynor or "Tilly," there were distinctive characteristics among many of the state's 1920s-designed courses. Notwithstanding the farmer or banker who strolled into an empty field, blithely planted nine flagsticks in the ground and declared his golf course open for bad-bounce business, they tended to look like this:

"It was very much a matter of fitting the golf hole to the land," said Chaska golf course architect Kevin Norby, "as opposed to today, where we just go out there and take the land and scrape away and do whatever we want to do."

Tom Fazio, a golf course architect known worldwide, said much the same in his book *Golf Course Designs*:

"Many of the things done by Donald Ross or A.W. Tillinghast or William Flynn were dictated by the limitations of machinery and construction methods," Fazio wrote. "Their design decisions might fairly be described as 'rub of the green,' rather than rub of the designer's pen, because they didn't have the equipment to do otherwise. Nature made the decision for them."

Island greens and amphitheater mounding were a half-century off. Early course architects rarely had more than a couple of teams of horses drawing plows with which to carve the landscape, if they even had any desire to carve the landscape in the first place.

Still, pure minimalism was not a good option on green sites. Any designer worth a five-dollar retainer's fee would recommend at least some moving of the earth for the benefit of the short game.

Norby cites Keller, the estimable public course in Maplewood which opened in 1929 and was laid out by Paul N. Coates, a Ramsey County engineer who received golf course design advice from Ross, as a case study of early-1900s courses.

"You go to a classic golf course," Norby said, "and the greens are elevated, round and small. They were built with a horse and buggy, and they were put on top of hills.

"Keller's a really good example. You look at the backs of greens, and those little bumps are areas where the dirt was pushed off to make the green."

Norby said greens on classic courses tend to be flatter and smaller than present-day greens — approximately 3,000 to 4,500 square feet, compared with some of the behemoths of today, which can reach 11,000 square feet.

Bunkers, similarly, "tend to be small," Norby said, mentioning specifically the work of Raynor, who in 1919 designed Somerset in Mendota Heights and in 1920 designed Midand Hills in Roseville. Norby said classic-style bunkers tend to be 250 to 550 square feet, in contrast to those at most modern courses, with bunkers up to 3,000 square feet, irregularly shaped and "cape and bay" style with flashed edges.

Green construction on classic courses was relatively simple, Norby said. Manure, sand and topsoil were mixed to create putting surfaces.

Often, the formula was even less complex than that. A lot of sand, a little oil, and, voila, there's your green — your sand green. If ever a golf term belonged in the Oxymoron Hall of Fame, "sand greens" would be it.

Many of Minnesota's early golf courses featured sand greens. Half of the state's lost courses, perhaps more, featured them. The "design" concept was simple: Dig out a circular target area, fill it with sand, apply some form of oil — crank-case was said to be the most effective — to keep the sand in place and the texture constant, and provide a special two-sided rake, one side with a toothed edge and the other side with a smooth edge.

Yes, golfers did (and do) actually putt on sand greens. When a group com-

A sand green on the lost Chisago Golf Course. As with most sand greens, not what you'd consider long on architectural inspiration.
COURTESY OF CHISAGO CITY HERITAGE ASSOCIATION.

pletes play on a hole, the "green" surface is to be raked or swept to make it as smooth as possible for the next group. Protocol, as explained on the website pasturegolf.com, is as follows:

"Task of sweeping the greens usually falls to the loser of the hole."

Sand greens could be positively microscopic. An April 26, 1934, *Mower County News* story on the construction of the lost Hillcrest Golf Course in Austin reported that the course was to feature "sand greens that are approximately forty feet in diameter."

Though there are a few sand greens courses in existence in the Midwest — Northwest Angle Country Club, in Minnesota's geographical anomaly, the Northwest Angle, is a hybrid, with seven sand greens and two grass greens — the concept of having to putt on these tiny beasts is, and was, attractive to few golfers.

"They were hard to putt," said Irous Nelson, 94, of New Richmond, Wis., who recalled playing a sand-greens course in the Windom, Minn., area. "In the first place, on the old courses, they weren't taken care of."

An even less-ringing endorsement came from Dave Palmquist of Winona, who played the lost sand-greens course at Whitewater State Park near St. Charles.

"I remember they were horrible to golf on," Palmquist said. "They're not nearly as predictable as the greens today, that's for sure. It's like putting in a sand trap. Nothing rolls very predictably. I never was a good golfer, but I struggled a lot on those sand greens."

From a construction and maintenance standpoint, however, sand greens often were the only reasonable option for a fledgling course with limited funds. They were cheaper to maintain than grass greens. Special mowers were of course unnecessary, as were aeration, herbicides and pest control — well, unless there was concern about the extremely remote possibility of a desert iguana setting up camp on a sand green.

One other thing about lost courses of the early 20th century: They were economy-sized, at least in relation to those of today. Golf in those days was played with hickory-shafted clubs (steel shafts were introduced in 1925) and non-high-tech-gizmoed balls. A smite of 250 yards qualified as mighty in those days. Courses, in turn, had to fit the game as it was played then — no 7,000-yard titans allowed.

A sampling of 15 lost Minnesota layouts — all would have been considered "regulation" courses in their heyday — reveals an average length of 2,509 yards for nine holes. They ranged from minuscule (Mississippi in Coon Rapids, 1,952 yards) to relatively broad-shouldered (Northwood Country Club in North St. Paul, 3,362 yards). By comparison, a random sampling of 14 courses found in the 2012 Minnesota Golf Association media guide reveals an average length, off the "regular" or "men's" tees, of 3,303 yards per nine holes. That's a difference of almost 100 yards per hole on a lost course as opposed to a modern-day course.

CHAPTER 9

Pioneers of Sport

THE MINNETONKA CLUB
CITY: DEEPHAVEN
COUNTY: HENNEPIN
YEARS: CA. 1897-1930

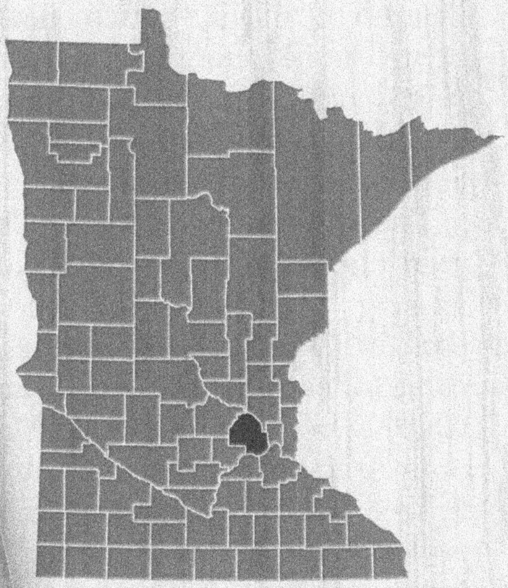

Fore! Gone.

J OHN BURTON, 89, REACHES INTO A FILE IN HIS HOUSE PERCHED ABOVE THE EASTERN SHORE OF LAKE MINNETONKA AND SHOWS ME THE MOST REMARKABLE LOST-GOLF COURSE RELIC I HAVE SEEN.

It is a card, vanilla-colored, six inches tall, made of medium-stock cardboard, with rounded corners. It is a bit rough around the edges, but its ink imprints and hand-written pencil markings are legible. The card is titled "The Minnetonka Club." Beneath the title is a dotted line on which a date can be entered, with the notation "190_" on it, the long dash intended to provide a space to designate an exact year in which the card was used.

The artifact, more than a hundred years old, is a golf scorecard. Nothing is missing. The card includes hole numbers, yardages, "bogey" ratings, even a name for each hole on The Minnetonka Club — from No. 1, named Onagon (a drum used by Chippewa Indians) to No. 9, Tree Tops. On the reverse side, there is more information on the club, including this notation: "The new Chalet for Golf and Tennis players, with shower baths, dressing rooms, etc., is two minutes walk from the Deephaven station."

Two gentlemen had navigated the golf course on this particular day a century ago, with a third party apparently serving as scorekeeper, marking the scores in pencil and totaling them near the bottom of the card:

First player: 344 335 353-33
Second player: 453 344 364-36

As mentioned, a remarkable piece. But, as it turns out, no more remarkable than the story of The Minnetonka Club and the Burtons.

John Cotton Burton, born March 12, 1923, is a third-generation member of an esteemed, accomplished Lake Minnetonka family. To be sure, esteem and accomplishment are not uncommon along the 110 miles of Lake Minnetonka's shoreline, where wealth and status veritably seeps into the bays and inlets at frequent intervals. Still, the Burton family history is exceptional.

Hazen James Burton, born in 1847 in Boston, was the patriarch. Educated at Massachusetts Institute of Technology, he moved to Minnesota and in 1880 established The Plymouth Clothing House at 14 Washington Avenue in downtown Minneapolis. John Burton relates that his grandfather had intended to operate the business as a wholesale and retail outlet but was so successful on the retail end that the business continued in only that capacity. "No establishment west of Chicago carries such a complete line of clothing and furnishings, hats, caps, furs, etc., for men and boys as the 'Plymouth,'" reads an entry in the *Tribune Hand-Book* of Minneapolis, published in 1884.

Hazen Burton was an accomplished baseball player in his youth, but his sporting passion later became sailing, and he helped found the Minnetonka Yacht Club in 1882. He bought a 90-acre plot on the southern tip of Carson's Bay, named it Chimo — John Burton said the name means "welcome" and speculated that it

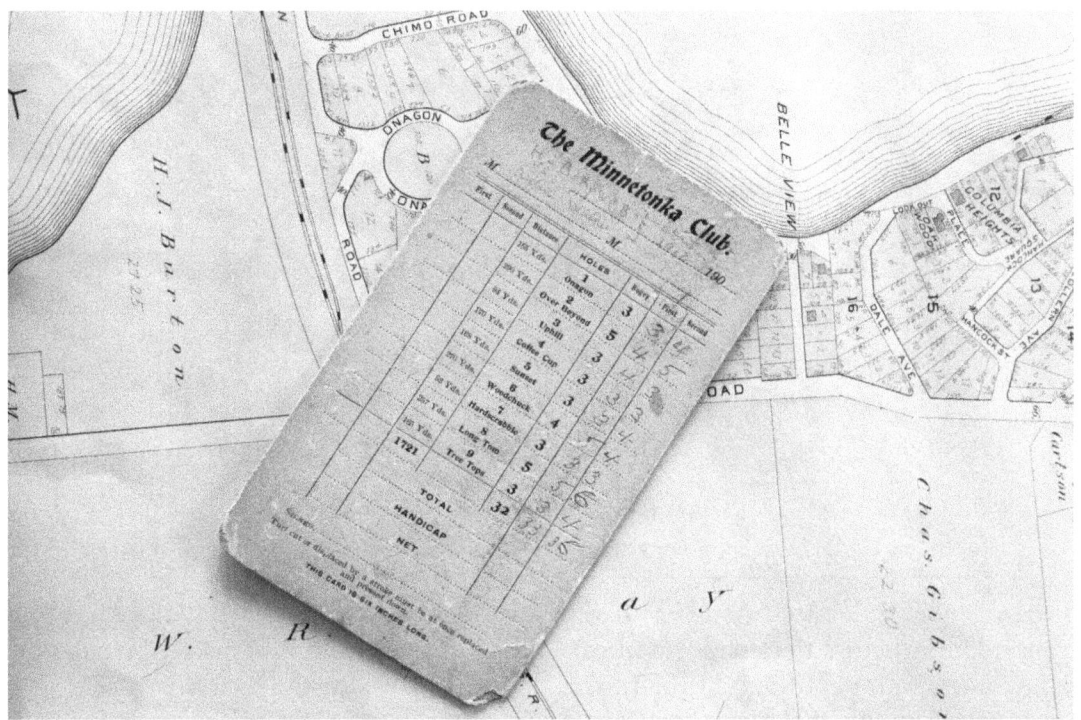

This scorecard from The Minnetonka Club golf course dates to the 1910s. In the background is a plat map showing part of the Chimo estate in Deephaven upon which Ward Cotton Burton built the course.

PETER WONG PHOTO

has American Indian origins — and established a compound of homes and sporting grounds hard by the lake. Center stage belonged to Burton's Chimo mansion, also known as Chimo Forest. The mansion was built in 1890 and still stands today, high on a hill, which a century ago afforded Hazen a vantage point from which to watch yacht races.

Chimo — pronounced "chime-oh" — became a Lake Minnetonka social and sporting hub. City residents had easy access to Chimo via a rail station, built by Hazen Burton himself along the Minneapolis and St. Louis Railroad line. The station was named Deephaven, and Hazen Burton became the first mayor of the new city, established in 1900.

Folks trekked out to Deephaven to watch yacht races and tennis matches. The Burtons built grass courts on the estate and started the prestigious Northwest Lawn Tennis Tournament, which ran from 1886-1941. The first family of Lake Minnetonka sports also staged field hockey games on the Chimo grounds.

Oh, and golf games, too, thanks to Ward Burton.

Ward Cotton Burton, Hazen's son, graduated from Harvard in 1899 and became secretary of the Plymouth Clothing House, but he was best known as a champion sailor. At age 17, he had a revolutionary craft named Onawa built for him by Arthur Dyer of Excelsior.

Fore! Gone.

Photo of Ward Burton on his golf course.
EXCELSIOR-LAKE MINNETONKA HISTORICAL SOCIETY

Onawa, which debuted in 1893, had a canoe-like structure that made it unbeatable on the waters of Lake Minnetonka, and both the craft and young Mr. Burton gained national renown.

Ward Burton, sailor nonpareil and skilled tennis player to boot, fancied another sport as well. In the late 1890s, while in his early 20s, he opened a nine-hole golf course on the south side of the Chimo property. An entry in the Burton Family Photograph Collection, by way of the Excelsior-Lake Minnetonka Historical Society, is dated 1897 and reads, "Ward Burton on his chip and putt golf course."

The reference is understated, perhaps even unfortunate.

Strictly from a golfing perspective, Burton's course was more than "chip and putt." The Burton Private Course, as it also came to be known, measured 1,721 yards, perhaps "chip and putt" on today's golfing barometer but still a moderately substantial length by 1897 hickory-stick standards. The shortest hole, No. 7, named "Hardscrabble," was a paltry 52 yards, but the following hole, "Long Tom," presented 357 yards of challenge. Bogey score for the course was 32.

John Burton, Ward's son, retains only vague memories of the golf course but remembered that "it was on both sides of the (railroad) tracks. In fact, there were two holes where you teed off and had to go across the tracks."

The course is known to have occupied at least part of the grounds of the present-day Deephaven Elementary School, and it likely occupied part of what is now Burton Park, which lies along the southeastern tip of Carson's Bay and was gifted to the city of Deephaven in 1959 by Ward Burton. Based on John Burton's recollection, the golf course likely occupied land on both sides of what is now Minnetonka Boulevard and lay partly on or near what is known as the "Cow Bowl," where the Burtons' tennis courts and field hockey grounds were situated.

The Minnetonka Club has been billed as the first golf course in the Lake Minnetonka area, predating the Lafayette Club, 5½ miles to the northwest in

Minnetonka Beach, which was established in 1899.

The Burtons' competitive spirit manifested itself in tournaments staged on Ward Burton's golf course. An early reference is from the July 21, 1901, *Minneapolis Tribune*. The sailing Burtons and their teammates might have been preoccupied with jibs and spinnakers that day; they dropped a 6-up decision to the Lafayette Club.

The Sept. 2, 1901, *Minneapolis Journal* featured a story headlined "Ladies' Golf Match/Interesting Play at Deephaven Links." The "ladies" tournament was in reality a mixed event, with one woman-man team playing another. The winning team, by two up, was H.J. Burton (Hazen James Burton, presumably) and "Mrs. Belknap."

The Burton club's golfing organization also was known as the Minnetonka Ice Yacht Club, and it joined the Minnesota Golf Association in 1902, a year after the MGA was formed. The Ice Yacht Club and Northland Country Club in Duluth became the eighth and ninth member clubs of the MGA, and the Ice Yacht Club participated in competitions around the Twin Cities and farther outstate.

Play at The Minnetonka Club peaked with the staging of the first home meet in University of Minnesota varsity golf history. In October 1915, Ward Burton offered his course for use by the U of M golf team for the remainder of the season, according to a *Minnesota Daily* newspaper story, and in late autumn 1915, the Gophers hosted an intercollegiate competition there.

The meet was recounted in the Nov. 8, 1915, *Minneapolis Morning Tribune*:

"With the determination of the first golf championship at the University of Minnesota last week, the links game has established itself as one of the sports on the Gopher campus. Harold C. Genter will go down in the annals of the Scotch game as the first winner of a Minnesota university tournament. It will also be a fact that in the history of the sport that the first title was held by a Wisconsin son. Genter's home is Sheboygan, Wis.

"Richard Cullum of Duluth, the native Minnesotan who was depended on to make the event strictly a domestic affair, fell before the Wisconsin boy in the 18-hole final match played on the private course of Ward Burton at Deephaven, Lake Minnetonka." Genter's victory was by a 5-and-4 margin.

The Gophers moved to a new course, north of the agricultural campus in St. Paul, for the 1916 season.

Burton, however, remained connected to the University of Minnesota. In 1916, the *Minnesota Daily* reported, he hosted members of the university's Garrick Club, which staged plays, for golf, dinner and election of officers.

The Burtons' Chimo estate, and The Minnetonka Club, included remarkable social, business and sporting connections. For example, remember the golf scorecard? The participants that day — a pencil marking on the card dates it as "about 1910" — were "HJB," again, Hazen James Burton, and Archie Walker. John Burton said the latter gentleman, who finished bogey-bogey to lose the match to HJB, was the son of Walker Arts Center founder T.B. Walker, a lumber baron who in 1923 was considered one of the 10 wealthiest men in the world. Archie Walker, who would

John Burton, reading at his Deephaven home. In the background are some of the trophies won by Burton during a remarkable sporting life; in the foreground is material from the 1952 Oslo Olympics, in which Burton participated as a Nordic skier.

PETER WONG PHOTO

have been in his 20s at the time of the golf match, was a Minneapolis business and civic leader and a partner in the Walker-Burton Company, which built the Shubert Theatre in downtown Minneapolis in 1910. The Walkers also were instrumental in the founding of Superior Country Club in Golden Valley in 1922; that course is now known as Brookview.

John Burton's social and sporting connections are similarly impressive. He married Janette Johnston, the granddaughter of Clarence H. Johnston Sr., one of the most prominent architects in Minnesota history, designer of 42 homes in the Summit area of St. Paul and the Glensheen Mansion of Duluth. Clarence Johnston's son Harrison was no less than the greatest golfer in Minnesota in the first half of the 20th century. Harrison was better known as Jimmy Johnston.

Jimmy Johnston — John Burton's father-in-law — was labeled "Minnesota's Bobby Jones" by Rick Shefchik in *From Fields to Fairways*. Johnston, who developed his game under the tutelage of White Bear Yacht Club pro Tom Vardon, played on four Walker Cup teams and won seven consecutive Minnesota State Amateur championships, 1921-27. His coup de grace came in 1929, when he beat British star O.F. Willing to win the National Amateur title, then considered one of golf's four major championships. The victory earned Johnston a ticker-tape parade through the streets of St. Paul, where he lived.

John Burton, who had only a passing interest in golf and did not play the game as an adult, said he "didn't really know" who his father-in-law was, in a golfing sense. "He was a very modest, unassuming person," Burton said.

The same could be said of John Burton. An initial interview with Burton at his Deephaven home produced only a mention of his interest in fly fishing on Minnesota waters, with no further talk of sports. You are too modest, sir: Subsequent research, plus a follow-up interview at Burton's home, revealed the man's exceptional background.

Burton played hockey at Harvard, served with the U.S. Navy in the Mediterranean in World War II, then took up cross country skiing while enrolled in law school at the University of Minnesota. He became a member of the U.S. Ski Team and participated in the 1952 Winter Olympics at Oslo, Norway. At 52, he took up distance running and completed his first marathon. At 55, he finished the AAU Masters Marathon in 3 hours, 6 minutes, 7 seconds. He completed 55 marathons in all, including 20 Twin Cities Marathons. He coached hockey at The Blake School in Minneapolis, skied and laid out cross country trails with his wife, and competed in inline skiing marathons and Nordic ski races into his 80s.

It seems likely that John Burton would have plied his waxed-and-wooden planks across his father's fairways at some point, but Burton in 2012 remembered little about the Ward Burton Private Course. "I have a recollection of teeing off up here," he said, referring to a photo that showed the old Chimo field hockey grounds. As well, the golf course's latter years are shrouded in mystery. There is a reference to the course in a 1917 *Minneapolis Tribune* story, but no mentions later than that were uncovered. Still, if John Burton, who was born in 1923, recalls having teed off there, it is likely the course lasted into the early 1930s.

John Burton offered only one quote that hints at the demise of The Minnetonka Club golf course. He remembered that Hazen Burton, who died in 1934, came to believe there was one sport too many being played on the Chimo grounds. "My understanding was that my grandfather figured, we've got tennis balls flying around, and maybe having a bunch of golf balls flying around" wasn't such a great idea.

And so, another lost golf course.

DEEPHAVEN'S BEST-KNOWN GOLF CONNECTION IS THAT it is the residence of Tim "Lumpy" Herron, who has won four tournaments in 10-plus seasons on the PGA Tour. Listed as 5 feet 10 inches and 250 pounds, Herron authors the fairly hysterical "Dear Lumpy" advice column for *Golf Digest*.

CHAPTER 10
Scotch Threesome

CALEDONIA GOLF CLUB
CITY: CALEDONIA
COUNTY: HOUSTON
YEARS: 1929–CIRCA 1940; 1949

PHOTO OF SAMUEL McPHAIL
COURTESY OF HOUSTON COUNTY
HISTORICAL SOCIETY

Fore! Gone.

Excerpt, edited liberally, from a July 2012 telephone conversation: "Hi, Mom. Happy 90th birthday.

"But that's not why I called. Remember how you said there used to be an old golf course in Caledonia? Think anyone in town would know about it?"

Brief pause, mother no doubt taken aback by lack of gratitude. Then:

"Well, there's your Uncle Bob. I think he knows about it. Or …"

Thus begins a long processional, both during that phone call and in subsequent weeks, of names and places and connections that lead to a rather remarkable discovery about my hometown.

In a town like Caledonia — the seat of Minnesota's southeasternmost county, resting on high land surrounded by bluffs and ravines, a close-knit place known for its strong farmers and strong sports teams — almost everybody knows everybody. If you're trying to find out who, to use a fictional example, back in the '60s owned that farm out by the Freeburg ridge, you know, the one with the round barn and the knotty old oak tree, the one whose family sat two pews up from us in church every Sunday and they had 10 kids and a couple of them always had runny noses and when the dad blew *his* nose it sounded like a foghorn, you can usually find that out by talking to somebody who knows somebody who knows somebody.

So, while searching for Caledonia's lost golf course, I talked. To a Schwartzhoff, a Johnson, a Bauer, a Koel, a Ganrude-turned-Fisch, an Ellingson, a couple of Syllings, a Trehus-turned-Wiebke, a St. Mary, a Wieser-turned-McCormick, a Wiebke-turned-Schwartzhoff, a Nicole (sorry, didn't catch the last name) and a dude doing construction work at a farm whose occupants weren't home. I shared memories of a Steffen and a Merzenich and a Simon and fellow Bissens.

It was true — somebody did know somebody who knew somebody who knew somebody.

And what they told me led to this startling conclusion: In a state with 5.3 million residents, a one-stoplight town of 2,800 stands alone, in a lost-golf course sense.

Caledonia has *three* lost courses. That doesn't quite make it the undisputed king of Minnesota's lost courses, but it is the per-capita czar.

This is not a well-known fact in town. Old-timers might be able to tell you about Caledonia's three lost root beer stands, but three lost golf courses? No way.

Even City Hall was unaware.

"I had no idea. … That's news to me," said the city's longtime mayor, Bob Burns.

No thread of golfing logic explains Caledonia's lost-course status — not even the town's Scottish roots.

"Caledonia" is the ancient Latin word for Scotland. Its Minnesota incarnation was established in 1853 by Samuel McPhail, a U.S. Army colonel of Scottish descent. The city annually holds Scottish-themed events honoring its roots. Still, the townspeople's ancestries are mostly German, Irish and Scandinavian, so trying to tie golf in Caledonia, Minn., to golf in the home of the game is a stretch.

It's unlikely McPhail, who was born in Kentucky, ever hunkered down behind a grass bunker during a gale-force storm on the inward nine of the Old Course at St. Andrews, it's unlikely he ever packed a midiron with him on a trip to Caledonia, and it's unlikely he ever smote a featherie in anger within the confines of what is now Houston County.

Honestly, there's no explaining why a place like Caledonia should have three lost golf courses.

The city's golfing roots were first planted about a half-mile north of town, atop a hill, alongside Minnesota Highway 44, on a plot that was known as the Beranek farm. The "course" there consisted of probably only three or four holes, and the best guess is that it operated in the 1920s. A speakeasy is said to have been in operation nearby, though there is no established connection between the golf course and any alleged purveyor of illicit suds.

As golf grew in popularity, the presumption is that the golfers of Caledonia looked for more land on which to establish a "real" course. In 1929, according to a report in the *Caledonia Argus*, Caledonia Golf Club negotiated a ten-year lease of the Bowers farm, near the southwestern corner of the city limits, from Mrs. Anna Bowers.

The course occupied 40 acres, with Highway 44 bordering the north side of the farm. (That would be "old" 44; the highway was since rerouted. Across Old 44 from the former golf course is the Allen Farm, well known to locals as a dairy operation.) Caledonia Golf Club had nine holes with sand greens and measured 2,717 yards, playing to a par of 36. It was designed by Ted Smith, club professional at La Crosse (Wis.) Country Club, and a La Crosse CC associate, Arthur Bakkum.

The land, the *Argus* reported, "is looked upon by the general membership as being quite ideal." A subsequent 1929 *Argus* story reported that the golf club was in "splendid condition financially."

Greens fees were 50 cents a day, as reported in the 1930-31 *American Annual Golf Guide*, and the club had 49 members. The guide listed A.M. Eiken and E.C. Hellickson as presidents.

Melba Krett, who grew up as Melba Metcalf, was raised on a farm adjacent to Caledonia Golf Club and worked there as a teenager.

"I used to sell green fees, and I had a pop stand," said Krett, 88, who moved to La Crosse as an 18-year-old and has lived there since. "And my mom always used to say I drank more pop than I sold."

Krett remembers little else about Caledonia Golf Club, except that it had "a lot of sand traps."

There's nobody left around town who would remember any more than she does.

"I used to play golf a lot. I liked it," Krett said. "I remember one hole, No. 7, that was kind of a rough one. You could lose balls there.

"None of my friends played there," she said of the course. "Just me. Dumb old me."

The date and reason for the demise of Caledonia Golf Club on that site is unknown. It's reasonable to assume that, as with many other lost courses of its generation, either the Great Depression or the onset of World War II, or both, contributed.

In the late 1940s, golf in Caledonia re-emerged on a farm just northwest of town, adjacent to Minnesota Highway 76, about 500 yards from the current Caledonia High School. Peter Koenig (pronounced "King") bought 40 acres and moved to the farm in 1947. At the urging of townspeople, he established a golf course on the land in probably 1948 or 1949, said his daughter, Ann Koel of Caledonia.

Koel's recollection of the course is less than idyllic.

"All these big shots from town came out and tried to talk him into starting a golf course," Koel said of her father. "They were making a great big deal about this and collected all the dues and everything.

"Dad made sand greens, and of course they wanted grass greens and all that big-shot stuff."

The course's life span was measured in months.

"I don't think it lasted even a year," Koel said, "because the guys who collected all the money kept it, and Dad couldn't keep going into debt.

"He worked hard at it, but when there wasn't any money there, you can't go too far with it. He had just bought the farm and planned on farming."

Koenig operated a bar, Pete & Margaret's, for many years on the property, and the golf course grounds went back to cropland — though for a brief period it also hosted car polo matches, with locals bringing their junker Fords and Studebakers around to push a ball five feet in diameter back and forth across the grounds, dents and scratches and smashed quarter-panels be damned.

Golf in Caledonia apparently vanished again, for more than a decade, although the 1953 *DeWitt's Golf Year Book* still listed a Caledonia Golf Club. (No one I talked with, however, mentioned or had any recollection that the town had an operating golf course in the 1950s.)

On Labor Day 1961, Ma Cal Grove Country Club opened, a nine-hole course with grass greens south of town and only a quarter-mile from the old Caledonia Golf Club. The club flourished through the 1970s and '80s, is respected throughout the tri-state area, and has served as the training ground for seven girls state championship teams out of Caledonia High.

CALEDONIA'S CURRENT GOLF COURSE, MA CAL GROVE Country Club, was established as a semi-private club and was named for residents of the towns of its primary shareholders: Mabel, Caledonia and Spring Grove.

CHAPTER 11

Norwegian Pride

COURSE: UNKNOWN NAME
CITY: SPRING GROVE
COUNTY: HOUSTON
YEARS: UNKNOWN

TEN MILES WEST OF CALEDONIA LIES THE EVEN SMALLER TOWN OF SPRING GROVE, WHERE THERE IS NOT A SPECK OF A CHANCE THAT SCOTTISH HERITAGE PLAYED A ROLE IN THE CREATION OF A GOLF COURSE THAT NO LONGER EXISTS.

That's because Spring Grove isn't the slightest bit Scottish. It's Norwegian — as Norwegian as lefse.

Think it's not? The town of 1,330 is the first Norwegian settlement in Minnesota (in 1852) and celebrates Syttende Mai (Norwegian Constitution Day) every May 17. Every September brings another celebration, called UffDa Fest.

You betcha.

Spring Grove couldn't be more Norwegian if King Harald V were to buy a summer cottage on Grove Avenue and organize a lutefisk-eating contest over by the 12-foot Tovar the Terrible Viking statue. Oh — too late. The lutefisk-eating contest was held during Syttende Mai 2012. Eric "Silo" Dahl of Delano, Minn., won first place, somehow managing to stomach 9½ pungent pounds of the stuff. *Svaert god, Eric.* (English translation: You rock, Silo.)

None of which has anything to do with golf or lost courses, but it's just impossible to say much of anything about Spring Grove without paying tribute to its Norwegian roots.

As for Spring Grove's lost golf course, precious little is known about it, but the site was near the western edge of town, just west of the current Spring Grove High School and just north of Main Street, or Minnesota Highway 44. The course was on the old Muller Field grounds.

Today, the area is occupied by streets and houses.

"I could be on hole No. 5, my house," said Dale Buxengaard, a longtime area optometrist who lives on Second Street Northwest and knew a bit about the course, surmising that it closed probably in the late 1930s and became a pasture for a dairy farm before being developed.

Al Sylling remembered the course, too, if only in snippets. Sylling, 98, was in 2012 believed to be the only living charter member of the board of directors at Ma Cal Grove in Caledonia, and his wife, Shirley, 92, is believed to be the only living charter member of the ladies' auxiliary there. But before Al Sylling plied his flat, compact swing on Ma Cal Grove's fairways, he played in Spring Grove.

"It was a short course," Al Sylling said of the Spring Grove course — nine holes, par 34, with sand greens. Sylling believed it might have opened around 1925. He recalled that he once won a match when he hit the green on the par-5 ninth in two shots and sank the eagle putt. And he recalled that fate was less kind to him on another occasion.

"I jumped over a fence and landed on a rusty spike. I got lead poisoning," he said.

That didn't stop him.

"Then I played on crutches."

Al Sylling died in October 2013.

CHAPTER 12
A Stormy Past

WHITEWATER VALLEY GOLF COURSE
CITY: ST. CHARLES / ALTURA
COUNTY: WINONA
YEARS: CIRCA 1930-75

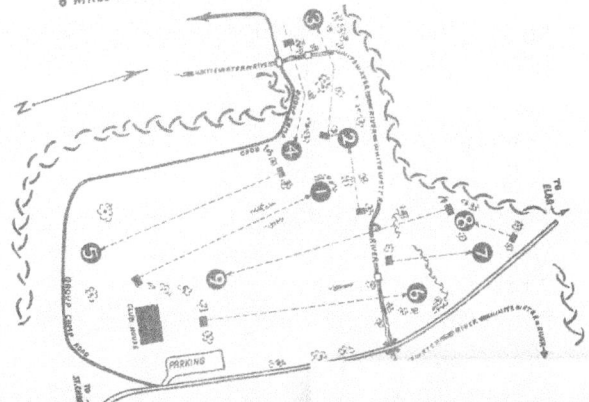
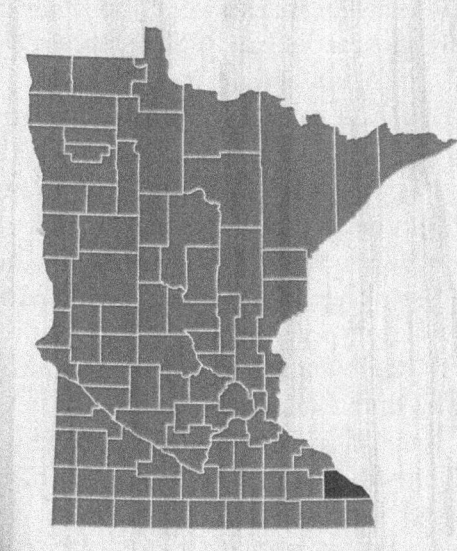

COURTESY OF WHITEWATER STATE PARK

Fore! Gone.

In 1975, the powers that be at the Minnesota Department of Natural Resources decided enough was enough for Whitewater Valley Golf Course. Out came the rubber stamp that would shut down the place.

Though the DNR did not require her assistance, Mother Nature deemed it appropriate to moisten the inkpad for the rubber stamp. Only she didn't just moisten it. She went about her business most indelicately. She slobbered all over it. Again and again and again.

And so, the golf course met its watery grave.

Whitewater Valley Golf Course was opened in 1930 within the confines of Whitewater State Park. The course and park were situated next to Minnesota Highway 74, along the Whitewater River and near the small southeastern Minnesota towns of St. Charles, Altura and Elba. The course was run by authority of the state park and, ultimately, the Minnesota DNR.

Whitewater Valley Golf Course was "Minnesota's Most Scenic." At least that's what an old scorecard boasted. The label is arguable but certainly had at least some merit. Limestone bluffs rising close to 100 feet high placed the course in an amphitheater setting, and four of its holes crossed the Whitewater River.

"It was a beautiful golf course," said Ken Bohks of Mankato, who grew up in the nearby burg of Bethany and remembered playing Whitewater Valley when he was young.

"It was very rustic," said Dan Goodenough of Edina, who grew up in Rochester and played the course a half-dozen times. "With the stone buildings all around, it was kind of like Yellowstone."

Bohks, who as an adult owned Minneopa Golf Course in Mankato, remembered water as a prominent feature at Whitewater Valley.

"Back then they had a golf ball that was called a floater," Bohks said, "and they had water on the course. If the ball went in, it'd float, and they'd go downstream and find it."

Besides the possibility of watching your floater drift down the Whitewater River toward the Mississippi and the Gulf of Mexico, there was one other foreboding concern at Whitewater Valley. A minor one, really.

Rattlesnakes.

Bohks noted that rattlers populated the bluffs surrounding the course. Actually, they still do, although those who live in Minnesota's Bluff Country know their forked tongues are seen infrequently and their fangs rarely are bothersome.

Whitewater Valley Golf Course was a nine-hole layout measuring 2,872 yards. The longest hole, the 475-yard, par-5 ninth, was preceded by the shortest, the 135-yard eighth. The course had sand

The resting place of the former Whitewater Valley Golf Course is in a valley on the grounds of Whitewater State Park near St. Charles.

PETER WONG PHOTO

Fore! Gone.

An old bench and shelter that was part of Whitewater Valley Golf Course still occupies a trailside resting place in Whitewater State Park.

PETER WONG PHOTO

greens, the material taken from the Kellogg-Weaver Dunes area 20 miles to the north.

Dave Palmquist of Winona, a Whitewater State Park naturalist for 38 years before retiring in January 2012, echoed Bohks' appraisal of the place.

"It was a beautiful course," Palmquist said. "I golfed it myself as a youngster when my family camped here back in the '60s, and I lost some golf balls there in the Whitewater River, so I've got some history related to the golf course."

During World War II, the course was closed, and crops were grown on its land. The course reopened after the war.

In May 1974, the rains came.

A "hundred-year flood," often defined as an event resulting from more than 6 inches of rain in a 24-hour period, struck the park, and the golf course was partially flooded out, forcing its closure.

The course reopened the next year, and Mother Nature returned for an encore. A spring in her time clock must have ruptured, because she had miscalculated by a mere 99 years the recommended interval between hundred-year floods. The course was washed out again and closed again — this time for good.

Flooding was the final nail in Whitewater's coffin, but it was not entirely the cause of death.

A couple of years before the 1975 flood, the DNR had crafted something called SCORP — State Comprehensive Outdoor Recreation Plan — which

A patch of light-colored grass grows on the south side of the grounds of the former Whitewater Valley Golf Course. It's possible the grass corresponds with the site of a former sand green on the course, perhaps No. 9, though that could not be confirmed.

PETER WONG PHOTO

posited, in part, that golf courses in state parks were not necessarily good fits for ownership by the state of Minnesota. Whitewater Valley GC became nine round holes in a square peg.

"It wasn't my decision, but I didn't disagree with it," said Palmquist, who became the messenger in telling golfers the course was on its last legs.

"One of the things I was asked to do," he said, "was to share with the public through the media how golf courses maybe don't belong in state parks and that actually there was an excess of golf courses in this area."

By the mid-1970s, the nearby towns of Plainview, Lewiston and Chatfield all had golf courses, and Winona and Rochester, not much farther away, offered multiple options for the game.

"You can't be everything for everybody," Palmquist said. "You have to look at what percentage of the people are using what part of the park, and you know, there's plenty of golf courses out there."

So the course closed, but Mother Nature continued her temperamental ways. Two more significant floods washed through the park in 1978. Then, from Aug. 18-20, 2007, cataclysmic flooding struck southeastern Minnesota, with more than 14 inches of rain falling on Whitewater State Park. The park incurred more than $4 million in damage and was closed for the rest of the year. Had the golf course still been around, it might have been washed halfway to Memphis.

The rains have changed the park's very geography.

"The road that goes by what was the golf course, Highway 74, goes through a valley that was right by the park's nature store," Palmquist said. "And that valley it goes through now is a former Whitewater River channel. So the river doesn't flow there anymore, but it did, and these floods of '74, '75, '78, 2007, when the river gets up high enough, it reclaims its former channel … and that takes it right across some of the golf course."

Palmquist said that had the course somehow survived, it would have suffered from sediment deposits and erosion. He allows that some golfers who pass through the park miss the course, but, really, it's hard to argue with Palmquist's logic on its closure.

Oh — if you want to visit the park, you can see remains of Whitewater Valley Golf Course. In the woods near the start of the Meadow Trail, which traverses much of the old golf course grounds, there is an old bench that was used by golfers. Its roof is grown over with moss and debris from trees. And, Palmquist said, those who venture onto the park's upper trails can see a curious sight when looking down on the meadow.

"Those circles that used to be the greens have nice little circular sand prairies," Palmquist said. "A lot of the prairie plants from the sand greens are growing there."

ON JUNE 19, 1949, ROBERT FLECK, A DENTIST FROM Plainview, Minn., was struck by lightning and killed while on the fifth fairway at Whitewater Valley Golf Course.

CHAPTER 13

Duluth, West and East

RIVERSIDE GOLF CLUB
CITY: DULUTH
COUNTY: ST. LOUIS
YEARS: 1919-44

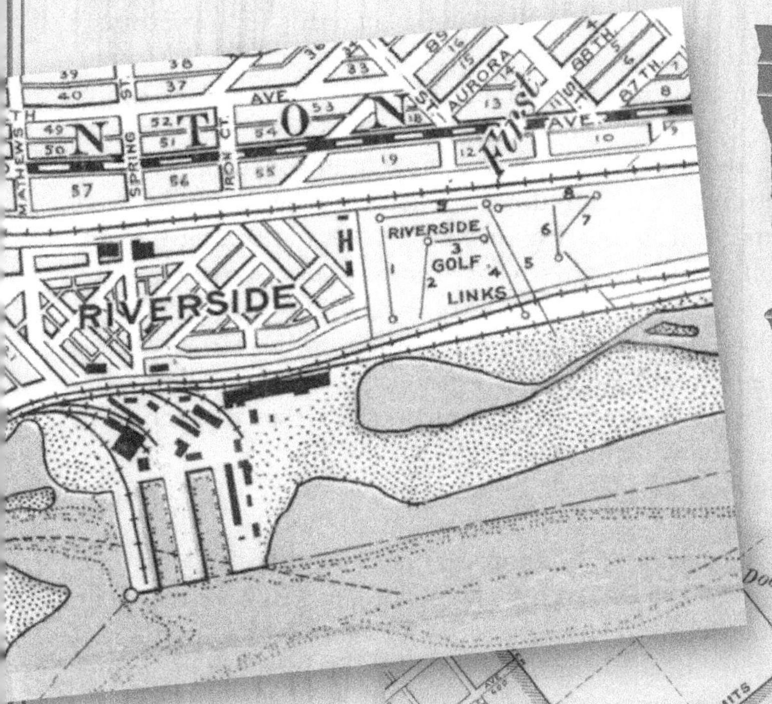

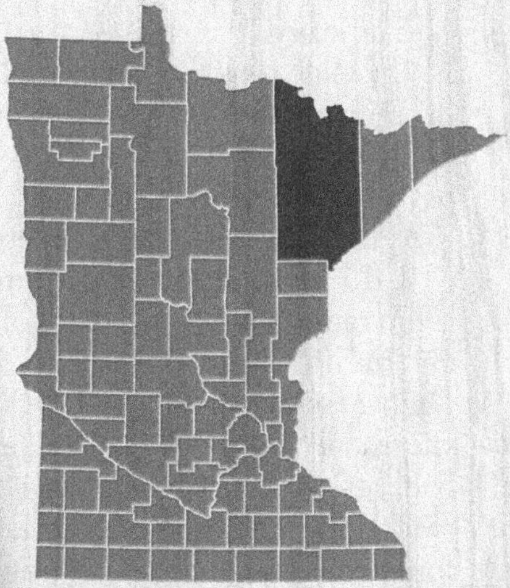

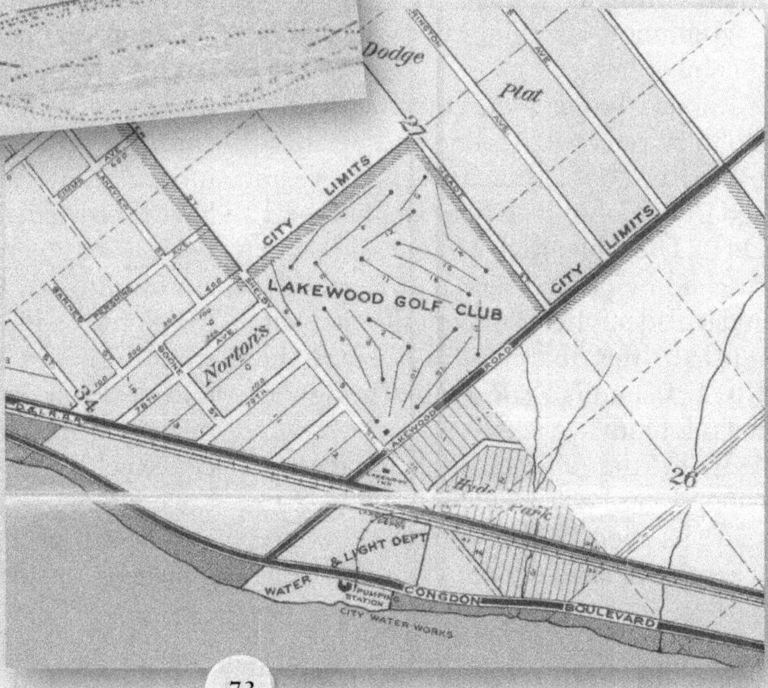

ABOVE: Old plat map shows the location and layout of Riverside Golf Club in Duluth
COURTESY OF DULUTH PUBLIC LIBRARY

RIGHT: Old plat map shows the location and layout of Lakewood Golf Club in Duluth. The map shows an 18-hole layout, but it isn't believed Lakewood ever became an 18-hole course.

Fore! Gone.

A GROVE OF TREES IN THE MIDDLE OF THE OLD RIVERSIDE GOLF CLUB SITE REMAINS. BEYOND THAT, RIVERSIDE HAS BEEN REDUCED TO PERHAPS ONLY ONE STANDING RELIC.

A hundred-sixty miles away.

In a suburban Twin Cities dining room.

It has four legs and a flat top.

Give?

It is a poker table.

True story.

Riverside Golf Club was a solid citizen of Duluth for 2½ decades, yet even Duluthians who know the city's golfing past don't seem to know much about it.

At first, there was only this tidbit:

"I do know that my parents' dining room table came out of that golf course's clubhouse," Mary Kohlbry, a longtime Duluthian now living in Florida, wrote via email. "It was a poker table that dad had refinished. Dad had a round top made for it and it served our family well for the all the holidays. It now belongs to my cousin in Cottage Grove."

Well, then, last things first: the tale of the poker table.

Rhoda Moone is the cousin to whom Kohblry referred. Moone and her husband, Rick, bought the table many years ago from Kohlbry and her late husband, Dick. The table, Rick Moone said when reached by phone, served at Riverside, and it also might have spent time way up north in the Yukon, as well as at the Kitchi Gammi, a social club in downtown Duluth.

Today, the table hosts meals for the Moones and occasionally is allowed to relive its good old days in Duluth, where it accommodated full houses and straight flushes at Riverside. The club's membership, judging by what Kohlbry said she had heard, enjoyed frequent games of I'll see that and raise you twenty.

Your deal, Rick.

"When we play cards or something, we just lift the top off it," Rick Moone said of the old poker table. "It's quite unique."

As is the story of uncovering much of anything about Riverside Golf Club.

I hadn't heard of the place, not even after 15 years as a sportswriter in the Zenith City in the 1980s and '90s. It wasn't until the lost-golf course bug bit me that I grew curious about the abandoned layout in the western reaches of Duluth.

At first, there was little information to be had.

I knew that Jerry Rychlak lived in that part of town, so I called him, but he didn't know much about the Riverside course. Rychlak, who incidentally is the most accurate driver of the golf ball to have ever lived — an imprecise drive for Jerry would be to aim for the left eye of a mosquito at 240 yards and strike it in the right eye instead — mentioned that when he was a kid, his dad would tell him of a golf course that was along the railroad tracks, near the St. Louis River. But Rychlak knew nothing else about the course.

I heard of references to Riverside golfers having played Northland Country

Club golfers in long-ago matches, so I tried a couple of Northland connections.

Warren Askeland didn't know much about the Riverside course. Askeland, who had just turned a sharp-as-a-tack 96 and still golfed at Northland, remembered that he had played Riverside but could offer no details.

The next possibility was Kohlbry, whose Duluth golf connections included many years of employment at Northland Country Club and many years of marriage to the late Dick Kohlbry, one of the city's iconic players. Before passing along the poker table tidbit, Mary Kohlbry said it was too bad I couldn't talk with Ev Stuart, the longtime Northland professional, because Stuart often mentioned Riverside — but Stuart died in 2010.

Kohlbry suggested I call Tom Bell, who grew up in West Duluth and knew old-time golfers from that part of town.

Bell remembered Riverside, albeit in a somewhat foggy manner, like the clouds that would have enveloped the golf course on a Lake Superior-cold meets top-of-the-hill-warm day in Duluth.

Bell said he thought Frank Wade, for whom a baseball stadium in Duluth's West End was named, might have had a hand in establishing Riverside, that Bell's grandfather also might have had a hand in it, and that Bell's grandfather had told him, "You can almost see the remains of such and such a green."

Getting warmer. (Which, in Duluth, is an achievement.)

Next phone call: Paging Will Bibeau ...

"The clubhouse was down below the railroad tracks, directly down from Spirit Mountain ... and I think the clubhouse was facing east," said Bibeau, 80, who grew up in Duluth's Riverside neighborhood, five blocks from the old golf course.

Bibeau, like Rychlak, mentioned the course's proximity to the railroad tracks. But he clarified: In the days of Riverside Golf Club, there was more than one set of tracks near the St. Louis River. The "upper" tracks were the Third District tracks of the Northern Pacific Railroad, just below Grand Avenue, aka Minnesota Highway 23. Those tracks are gone, their path now occupied by the blacktopped Willard Munger State Trail. Two lower sets of tracks, essentially adjacent to each other and within 100 yards of the St. Louis River backwaters, served the old McDougall-Duluth Shipyard in the Riverside neighborhood.

Judging by a 1939 aerial map, the golf course lay below Grand Avenue and completely or mostly between the sets of railroad tracks. Its westernmost green was about 150 yards from the St. Louis River and only 5 or 10 yards from the lower railroad tracks. A green that close to railroad tracks? Wouldn't be surprising if more than one Riverside golfer, standing over a 5-foot birdie putt, was scared shirtless by a locomotive's blare.

"I walk by there about twice a week," Bibeau said of the old layout. "I go right by the golf course, but it's all grown in."

Much appreciated, Mr. Bibeau. Still, no one had relayed any firsthand memories of the golf course from its playing days — until the telephone rang in Jim Walkowiak's West Duluth home.

Walkowiak, 83, remembered having played Riverside.

"When I was a kid I did, yeah," Walkowiak said. "It was a nine-hole golf course, a nice one. A nice, little one. It had nice grass greens."

Near the western edge of the former Riverside Golf Club grounds, the view includes the St. Louis River in the distance.

JOE BISSEN PHOTO

Walkowiak spent 17 years in the Riverside neighborhood. Here is his course tour, in snippets:

"On one side there was a creek running; I know they used to slice the balls down in the woods there by the creek. There was a little creek where you teed off for hole 3, a little creek down below in the gully, and you had to hit it across the gully.

"On the first tee, you'd hit the ball down towards (the railroad tracks). ... And then you'd go over, up and hit No. 2, and No. 2 would go up the hill, way up above.

"The 'shack' (clubhouse) was on the hill by the upper tracks but below Grand Avenue.

"(Behind No. 1 green) the pond was down there, too, it was called the pond, and then the river ran into the pond. And then on the other side, where you teed off for No. 2, there was a creek running on that side, too.

"We made a lot of money on golf balls as kids. I found pails of golf balls when we first moved out there, *pails* of them ... all over in the woods there, they'd slice 'em and they'd go in the woods, and in the creek sometimes. Some of them got only a dime and stuff — that's a long time ago — then we used to turn them in to the caddie shack and we'd get candy bars and pop."

Chatting with Walkowiak closed my pursuit of folks with eyewitness knowledge of Riverside Golf Club. Opening books and web pages revealed other details.

Riverside was indeed a nine-hole course with grass greens. It was established in 1919. A 1919 *Duluth News-Tribune* story on the club's inception listed its address as Eightieth Avenue West. "There are 75 members in the organization and they expect to spend $25,000 in making this club one of the leading clubs in the state," the newspaper reported. John Wright was the first club president, and T.A. Kedward and Albert McDonald were to be its first instructors. Par for the course was reported variously as 29 or 30, and length was 1,800 yards.

In one sense, the club was decades ahead of its time. Trophies? Not on Riverside's watch. "The club," the *News-Tribune* reported, "has adopted the policy of offering useful articles as prizes rather than the regulation cup."

By 1925, membership had been limited to 50, and J. Gordon MacDonald was club president. The book *Tee Party on the Green* listed all of the members' handicaps; H.G. Glenn and Wm. Glenn, both of Zenith Furnace Company, had Riverside's two lowest handicaps — 10 and 11, respectively.

In 1926, greens fees were 75 cents on weekdays and $1 on Sundays and holidays.

Riverside became a Minnesota Golf Association member in 1928, and the July 1928 issue of *The 10,000 Lakes Golfer* reported, "The club is made up of local business and professional men who reside in the western part of the city."

The magazine reported that a $5,000 clubhouse had been recently completed.

Perhaps seeking to capitalize on their proximity to the golf course, a group of six boys created and managed an 18-hole miniature golf course in the neighborhood, the *News-Tribune* reported on Aug. 6, 1930. The miniature course was at the east end of Penton Boulevard, likely within about 200 yards of Riverside Golf Club.

Duluth city directories for 1930 and 1940 listed Riverside's address as 85th Avenue West, though that address appears to be a couple of blocks northeast of the golf course site.

Walkowiak estimated that Riverside closed in about 1940. It probably lasted slightly longer. The course is not listed in the 1942 Duluth telephone directory but is listed in city directories for 1942, '43 and '44 before vanishing from the 1945 directory.

The Riverside terrain remains much as it did 70 years ago, sans the flagsticks. There are two clearings in the woods below Grand Avenue, undeveloped and separated by a stand of trees that rise from a gully. Most of the land is shin-high grass, with elevations and vegetation that suggest old tee boxes and greens. On the other side of Grand, about 350 yards from the golf course grounds, overlooking the spot in the woods where Walkowiak once hunted for balls, is the bottom of Spirit Mountain's major eastern ski run, Four Pipe, which leads to the newly opened Grand Avenue Chalet and Riverside Bar & Grill.

Fore! Gone.

**LAKEWOOD GOLF CLUB
CITY: DULUTH
COUNTY: ST. LOUIS
YEARS: 1931–41**

Fifteen miles northeast of the vacated site of the Riverside Golf Club clubhouse — but in the same city — lies the vacated site of the Lakewood Golf Club clubhouse.

What's there now? John Lofquist can tell you, right down to the asphalt-covered nitty-gritty.

"The clubhouse set in the northbound lane of Highway 61," Lofquist said.

Not averse to stating the obvious, Lofquist added:

"It wouldn't be a good spot for it now."

Indeed. Imagine trying to lace up your FootJoys with an 18-wheeler bearing down at 60 mph.

Lakewood shared so many characteristics with Riverside that you'd have thought it was its eastern Duluth alter ego. Both courses were nine holes, private, near a set of railroad tracks and wedged between an ascending mountain of trees on one side and a sweeping body of water on the other. Both were abandoned in the same era.

Lofquist is 73, too young to remember when Lakewood Golf Club, which occupied a plot just northwest of the intersection of Lakewood Road and the Minnesota Highway 61 expressway, was open. But he most definitely remembers the neighborhood — his neighborhood.

"We lived in the clubhouse for the golf course," said Lofquist, who now lives in the Iron Range town of Nashwauk. "In 1949, we moved in there. The golf course was already shut down and grown over."

What remained was at once quaint and spectacular.

"The fields that used to be the fairways and stuff, I used to go out there picking strawberries," Lofquist said. "On one of the greens, we used to plant a garden back there because of the nice, black soil."

Lofquist's "back there" was partway up the side of a behemoth of a hill known as Moose Mountain. A portion of the hill's southeastern face served as Lakewood Golf Club. A 1939 aerial photo shows the land that had been cleared for the course, including a set of, presumably, two holes that climbed and then descended the hillside. At the course's highest point, the clubhouse was about 500 yards distant, at a drop of about 80 feet. Just below the clubhouse were the Duluth and Iron Range Railroad tracks. And below that, two-thirds of a mile from the mountainside golf holes, was Lake Superior, at a total drop of almost 200 feet.

Lakewood Golf Club clubhouse, after the club had closed. In the state shown, it was the boyhood home of John Lofquist.

COURTESY OF JOHN LOFQUIST

A golfer facing southeast at the course's zenith would have seen Lake Superior panoramically sprawled out for miles — maybe 30, 40 of them.

"You could really see a long ways," Lofquist confirmed.

The view likely would have rivaled the stunning lake views golfers have from the third tee on the Lake Nine at Lester Park, 1½ miles southwest of the Lakewood site, or from the 15th and 16th tees at Northland Country Club, 4½ miles to the southwest. (Yes, the author is aware that, for Northland members past and present, comparing *anything* to that course's vistas is tantamount to sacrilege.)

Construction on Lakewood began in 1930, and the club likely opened in 1931 — the May 1931 issue of *10,000 Lakes Golfer* reported that the club was certain to have nine holes open in June or July of that year. That made it Duluth's fourth private course, joining Northland, Riverside and Ridgeview Country Club, situated "over the hill" on the north side of Duluth. Duluth also had a municipal course, Enger Park, at the time, and Lester Park was dedicated in 1933. Though Duluth's population exceeded 100,000 in 1930, that's a fair amount of competition for the golfing dollar in a city with a relatively short golf season. Whether the relative abundance of golf courses, plus the effects of the Great Depression, ultimately did in Lakewood and/or Riverside is speculative, but it seems a good possibility.

Lakewood is listed as a nine-hole course in guides and newspapers, but a 1935 plat map of the area shows an 18-hole routing. The 1939 aerial photo, too, clearly shows only nine holes. It seems likely that 18 holes were planned but never built.

Lakewood — one person interviewed said the course was known as Lakewood Gardens — was mentioned in publications as late as 1941, listed as a nine-hole course in that year's *WPA Guide to Minnesota Arrowhead Country*, but it almost certainly did not last much longer than that. It was not listed in the 1942 Duluth phone directory. Another former neighborhood resident, Pat Osterloh of Fridley, said her family moved into a house on 79th Avenue East when she was 2 or 3 years old, in about 1940, and that "when we moved in, there wasn't any golf course left … the grass wasn't mowed or anything."

That did not stop the golf course grounds from postmortem utility. Harvey Vanhorn, who lives on Lakewood Road, near the old course, said he believed his late brother, Rusty, operated a riding academy on the grounds. Vanhorn and Bill Elstad of Duluth both said a downhill ski run with a rope tow was set up there, and Elstad suspects the ropes and pulleys still lie along the mountainside, now fully grown over with trees.

Osterloh remembered walking along the hillside as a girl and seeing deer, bears and moose (hence the name Moose Mountain, duh). Her brother, Elstad, used to go hunting just beyond the grounds and recalled that "you could see where the rose bushes came up to the greens." Another former neighborhood resident, Ted Dallos of Two Harbors, said that as a kid in the 1960s, he found many golf balls on the grounds.

Duluth Mysteries,
continued

Well, there is the mystery from 1977 — the one about the mansion along Lake Superior, and the heiress and the night nurse and the adopted daughter, but we won't go there. The Glensheen-Congdon murder mystery isn't exactly in the wheelhouse of someone trying to solve lost-golf course mysteries.

Besides, the remaining lost-course mystery in Duluth is a tough enough nut to crack.

The *Harper's Official Golf Guide* of 1901 included this entry: "A golf club was organized in 1900, having a nine-hole course located west of the Mesaba Railroad, between Superior and West Third Streets."

That would appear to place the course near the current site of Wade Stadium, in West Duluth. That area is said to have served as an airport and staging ground for a circus in the early days of the 20th century. Searches of the *Duluth News-Tribune* from that era turned up no further information except for two utterly confusing reports from 1907.

Exhibit A: "Charles P. Craig & Co. have also sold several lots on Fourth Avenue west, two blocks above Superior Street, and bordering on the golf grounds. These lots are intended as a Christmas present, and terms of sale are private."

Currently, that address is in downtown Duluth. Judging by a 1908 Sanborn map of the city, there were houses and business all around. Even if there had been enough undeveloped land nearby to install a golf course, it would have been on a steep hillside, where the only entities capable of playing it would have been a family of mountain goats.

On the chance that the *News-Tribune* report actually intended to reference Fourth "Street" west, that would fit with the notion that there once was a golf course in the Wade Stadium/Wheeler Fields area of West Duluth.

Exhibit B: "The Lakeside Land Company has sold, through C.P. Craig & Co., two lots on Fortieth avenue west and Puleston street for $600. These lots are within half a block of the golf grounds."

If that location actually had been Fortieth Avenue *East*, it would have been very near Northland Country Club, which at the time had some holes on the south side of Superior Street. Puleston Street was renamed Luverne Street in 1910; Luverne in eastern Duluth is within a 9-iron of the old Northland CC grounds, but there is no Luverne or Puleston Street in western Duluth.

Nut uncracked.

CHAPTER 14

Nuts to You

COURSE: BAYPORT GOLF CLUB
CITY: BAYPORT
COUNTY: WASHINGTON
YEARS: CIRCA 1922-35

Peanuts Bell takes in the scenery at the Croixdale senior care facility in Bayport.
Part of Croixdale is on the grounds of the former Bayport Golf Club. Bell, who lives in Bayport, caddied and played at the golf course in the 1930s.
PETER WONG PHOTO

Fore! Gone.

Eugene Bell stands at the corner of 7th Avenue North and 3rd Street North, right about where players at Bayport Golf Club once tried to decide between a mashie and a niblick to the first green.

Um, wait a minute. Before we go any further ...

Don't call him Eugene. Nobody else does.

Peanuts Bell, 89, turns and looks back across 3rd Street, better known as Minnesota Highway 95 in the St. Croix River town of Bayport.

"You know that old yellow house there?" Bell says. "There was an old French lady, Mrs. Babien, who lived there. She always used to see my mother and me come by. She'd say to my mother, 'If you've got that little peanut with you, can I hold that little peanut?' Then the guys at the grocery store heard it. That's how I got my name. Been that way ever since."

Bayport might be the nickname capital of Minnesota, because so many people in the city of 3,471 have one. "You move to town, you get a nickname," Bell says. "They had some beauties."

There was Peanuts. There was Packey Schultz, the former mayor and police chief, who got his nickname because he was an expert packer and mover. There was Happy McPherson, the banker, who was "Happy" because he often was not.

Peanuts never mentioned whether any Bayporter bore the nickname Bogey, Birdie, Par or Dammittohellithree-putted. Maybe Bayport Golf Club just wasn't around long enough to offer such inspiration.

Bayport GC, in the northeast part of the city, served its patrons for only about a dozen years in the 1920s and '30s. Today, it is a lost course. Almost no one remembers the place.

Except for Peanuts Bell.

"I remember it had sand greens," Bell had said of Bayport Golf Club in a 2012 interview, "and it had a man taking care of it by name of Andy Vickstrom. He had a horse. The horse was trained and never went on the greens. He pulled a sack behind him and leveled out the greens, and he used to do that when everybody got through golfing or was golfing and messed them up. He'd take the horse and straighten out the greens."

Presumably without leaving behind a minefield of horse apples.

Bayport Golf Club's divots, and the horse's business-end expenditures, have been gone for almost 70 years, replaced by excavations that, coincidentally, produced three significant features of modern-day Bayport: Highway 95; Croixdale, an expansive senior care residence; and part of the grounds of Andersen Windows, Bayport's largest and most prominent employer.

Two old maps, property of the Washington County Historical Society in nearby Stillwater, sketch the former Bayport Golf Club tract. Actually, they are not maps so much as rough outlines, not professionally drawn, not particularly to scale and not, judging by Bell's recollections, accurate to within, say, a three-quarters wedge shot. But between the maps and Bell's memory, here is the quickie tour of Bayport Golf Club:

The layout, measuring a shortish 2,248 yards, started with a par 4, 357 yards. It was a dogleg right that crossed what is now Highway 95 and finished at or near the current site of the large Andersen patio door factory building. The second hole, a 412-yard par 5, headed north, along what is now Highway 95, and finished near the current First State Bank & Trust building. The next three holes were on or near the current grounds of Croixdale. The rest of the course traversed what is now a residential neighborhood but never made it all the way up a steep hill that separated the course from a cemetery to the west and the state prison grounds to the northwest. Much of the course played around swamps.

There was no clubhouse.

"They had a little box there with a lock on it, and you'd pay there," Bell said. "But they never collected it — someone was always breaking into it."

That being unsound business practice, the lockbox was retired, Bell said, and greens fees for the public course were collected at the First State Bank of Bayport.

"You had to go to the bank and see Karl LaVine or Happy McPherson to get permission to play," Bell said.

Bell caddied at the course in the early 1930s, during the Great Depression. Asked what he was paid, Bell said: "It all depends on who you had (as a golfer/employer). If you had one of the men who had some money, you might get 50 cents. It was all the way from 35 cents up to 75 cents."

Bell's recall is as sharp as Phil Mickelson's short game. Bell is, in essence, a one-man Bayport historical society. On a one-hour tour from corner to corner of town, he extracts names, faces and places as though today were decades ago. Among the memories: He said legendary coach Bernie Bierman and his powerful University of Minnesota football teams would stay at the White Pine Inn on nights before home games. The inn, listed as "The 19th Hole" on an old Bayport GC scorecard, is now home of the Bayport Public Library.

As for Bayport Golf Club, its exact life span is unknown. One of the sketched historical society maps lists it as "?1922-1934" and the other as "?1921-1935?" It's almost certain that 1934 or 1935 was the course's final year. Bell said the course was shut down when Highway 95 was built through the grounds, though he wasn't certain that was the only reason for the course's demise. "Nobody was playing it," he said. Highway 95 first appears on an official Minnesota highway map in 1934, and Minnesota Department of Transportation documents say construction grading on Minnesota 95 through Bayport began in 1935.

Part of the golf course grounds became a Civilian Conservation Corps World War I veterans camp. The workers, between 200 and 300 of them, helped with soil erosion control and were paid $30 a month plus room, board and clothing, according to the booklet *Bayport: Three Little Towns on the St. Croix* by Hila Sherman.

A few blocks north of Bell's house, the vagaries of researching lost golf courses were on display in late 2012. Knowing next to nothing about Bayport Golf Club, and not yet having met Peanuts Bell, I took copies of the historical society sketches into Bayport, asked around, and ultimately wound up in the living room of Al "Packey" Schultz, the city's former mayor.

So, Mr. Mayor, help me out here, I said. Take a look at this map, if you would. Am I reading it right? I think I am.

Schultz studied the map, which at the time appeared to be geographically accurate and eminently believable.

It sure looks to me, I said to Schultz, like this is where your house is, at 6th Avenue North and 5th Street. And …

The former mayor nodded in agreement.

"We're sittin' right there on whatever hole," Schultz said. He looked toward his wife, Beverly, and two other visitors.

"Well, I'll be damned!" Schultz exclaimed. "Now I can say I lived on the golf course."

Sadly, the map was not a thousand percent accurate. Months later, as Bell and I visited the old Bayport GC grounds, I asked him if Schultz's house was part of the grounds. No, he said confidently, the golf course did not go that far south and west. Even more sadly, Schultz had died three months earlier. I never did get an opportunity to correct myself with him.

Nonetheless, the visit with Schultz was a blast. Among his many colorful stories, he had noted that he wasn't a golfer.

"I only golfed once. That was enough," he said. "It was at Long Prairie, in northern Minnesota. I bought balls, shoes, clubs. I teed off, and, shoosh, the god dang ball went in the pond.

"I got done with the round, and the shoes, the balls, the clubs, they all went in the pond."

THE CITY OF BAYPORT WASN'T ALWAYS KNOWN BY ITS present name. Originally, there were three towns: Bangor, Baytown and Middletown. They were platted as South Stillwater in 1873, and South Stillwater became Bayport in 1922.

CHAPTER 15

Sheared by Sheep

COURSE: NAME UNKNOWN
CITY: SLEEPY EYE
COUNTY: BROWN
YEARS: 1920s

The September 1927 issue of *The 10,000 Lakes Golfer* magazine includes a reference to Ish-Tak-Ha-Ba Golf Club in Sleepy Eye, a city of 3,599 in south-central Minnesota. Ish-Tak-Ha-Ba is not a lost course.

Gary Vait, manager of Sleepy Eye Golf Club, confirmed that Ish-Tak-Ha-Ba and the current Sleepy Eye GC are one and the same. The bylaws of the club, dated March 6, 1927, and including a front-page image of Ish-Tak-Ha-Ba, or Chief Sleepy Eye, confirm this.

But Vait said a woman who used to play the course, Villa Lietz, knew of a Sleepy Eye course that opened in the 1920s. Vait said Lietz, who died on her 105th birthday in October 2011, remembered playing the course as a junior in high school. Lietz was a 1925 graduate of Sleepy Eye High School.

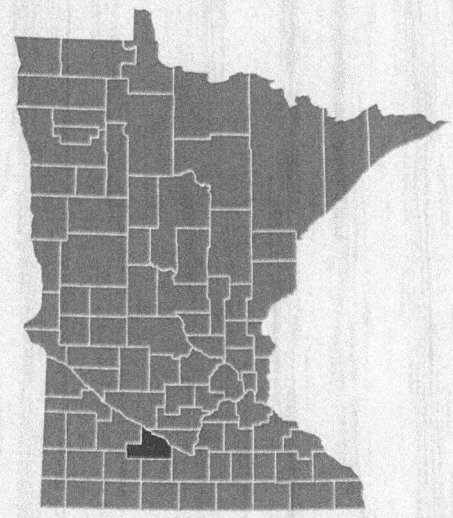

"This course (Sleepy Eye Golf Club) was groomed by sheep, and I suppose the other course was, too," Vait said.

Vait later said the lost course was located on farmland now owned by Gerald Helget, and Helget confirmed that. Helget's property is situated along the Cottonwood River, four miles southwest of Sleepy Eye and 3 ½ miles south of the current Sleepy Eye course.

Sleepy Eye's lost course might have been Blind Hole Central.

"If that was a golf course," Helget said of his rolling farmland, "there were lots of places where you wouldn't see the flags."

CHAPTER 16

Capital Losses

ROADSIDE GOLF CLUB AND MERRIAM PARK GOLF CLUB
CITY: ST. PAUL
COUNTY: RAMSEY
YEARS: 1897–1903; 1900–1906

IN MINNEAPOLIS, A LOST GOLF COURSE, BRYN MAWR, SPAWNED THE ESTABLISHMENT OF TWO ESTEEMED COUNTRY CLUBS, MINIKAHDA AND INTERLACHEN.

In St. Paul, the reverse: one esteemed country club, two lost golf courses.

Town & Country Club, situated just off Marshall Avenue, its clubhouse 500 feet from the Mississippi River, was established in St. Paul in 1893. It is Minnesota's oldest golf course and the second-oldest course in the United States still operating in its original location.

For four seasons, Town & Country Club members had the game to themselves in Minnesota. They did not, however, aspire to keep it that way.

"Town & Country Club began spreading the gospel of golf soon after its own course was complete," Rick Shefchik wrote in *From Fields to Fairways*. "Town & Country Club members established two short-lived courses nearby …"

The first of those was historic in its own right. Its inception was noted in a May 9, 1897, *Minneapolis Tribune* column titled "Notations and Notables of the Social World":

"The St. Paul society girls have taken hold of golf in earnest and have formed a 'Roadside Golf Club' for the furtherance of the sport which they have found as entertaining."

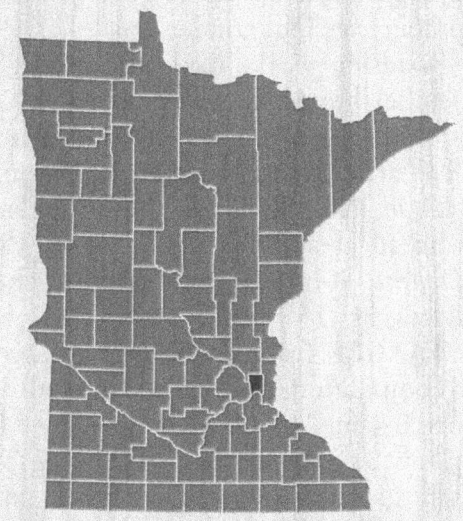

The date is significant. Roadside likely was Minnesota's second golf course, predating the likes of Winona Golf Club (summer 1897), Bryn Mawr (1898) and Minikahda (1898). The only other contender for second-oldest course likely is the Burton Private Course in Deephaven, which dates possibly to 1897 but does not have a verifiable start date.

Just as significantly, Roadside was established primarily as a women's golf club. William F. Peet, a founding member of Town & Country Club, said so in a 1930 letter he wrote to Town & Country's president, Dr. E.L. Kannary.

"The Roadside Club," Peet wrote, was "situated on Summit between Lexington, Selby and the railroad track. This big tract, known as Anna E. Ramsey's Addition, was practically vacant; bare of houses and even streets and was, of course, very close to our residential section.

"A group mostly of women who could not afford the Country Club urged Billy Trowbridge, one of our leading young players, to help them start a club there, which he did with the assistance of our pro and a bunch of our members and it developed into a rattling good golf club with an excellent course."

Roadside was a 12-hole course, its membership peaking at 225 in 1902. Its clubhouse, the *St. Paul Globe* noted in an 1898 article, was "located on Summit Avenue, just this side of the bridge, and is an ideal summer club." The 1901 *Harper's* golf guide listed the club's address as 1195 Summit Avenue.

The *Globe* featured periodic reference to competitions at Roadside, including a "brisk game" in October won by Miss Lillian Stephenson and N.P. Langford, with scores of 118, and a caddies' competition in September won by Paul Newton, with a score of 95.

Roadside was perhaps singular in another respect. Though segregation was U.S. golf's most distasteful characteristic well into the 20th century, a note from the *St. Paul Appeal*, which billed itself as "a National Afro-American Newspaper," implied that Roadside might not have been exclusionary. "Mr. and Mrs. J.H. Dillingham entertained Mr. and Mrs. A.M. Lee and Mr. and Mrs. W.T. Francis at golf, at the Roadside golf links last week," the newspaper reported. Francis was a black attorney in St. Paul, and the Dillinghams were mentioned frequently in *Appeal* stories.

But by 1903, urban growth had squeezed out Roadside Golf Club. "The Roadside Golf Club is no more," the *Globe* reported on April 3, 1903. "The reason for this is that the club no longer possesses links on which to play. … The grading of streets has broken up this stretch of territory and tendered it unfit for golfing purposes."

Less than 10 blocks to the west, however, Town & Country Club members had helped establish another golf course. The *Minneapolis Tribune* of June 17, 1900, handled the introduction.

"The people in Merriam Park have caught the golf fever, have organized the Merriam Park Golf club, and have had links laid out on a tract of ground between Selby and Summit and Prior and Snelling avenues," the newspaper story read.

The story featured something commonplace in 21st-century golf journalism but highly rare in those days: a course review, and not an entirely glowing one at that.

"The worst place on the course for a beginner is off the second teeing ground," the *Globe* reported. "About 12 feet from the tee there is an excavation about 14 feet deep, with a sloping bank on the other side. It is fully 75 feet over the hazard, and the beginners have a hard time to drive the ball over it.

"The first teeing ground is a little too far from the ninth hole, and there seems to be a tendency among the beginners to start and play for the second hole. This might have been avoided by bringing the

Roadside now: The former grounds of Roadside Golf Club in St. Paul's Merriam Park Lexington Hamline neighborhood is now occupied mostly by residences. This one-level house is at 1195 Summit Avenue, the same address formerly listed as the home of Roadside Golf Club.

JOE BISSEN PHOTO

first teeing ground up to the Prior avenue boundary and putting the first hole over to the west."

That same day, the *Tribune* reported that Minneapolis Mayor James Gray had made his golfing debut as a guest of Merriam Park Golf Club. The newspaper delighted in describing Gray's travails.

"He made a very creditable score, 53, that is for the first four holes. They lost count before they made the nine, but the mayor declares his score was 103."

Gray was credited with a nicely lofted, 75-yard drive off the first tee, but on the second hole, the one with the devilish excavation, Gray whiffed off the tee, and "the club kept right on and nearly succeeded in carrying his honor over the bank that overhangs the hard hazard. Then he laid down the club and began to go over himself very carefully, feeling his bones from head to foot."

The next year, 1901, Merriam Park became one of the seven founding clubs of the Minnesota Golf Association. The club's first tournament, the *Minneapolis Journal* reported on Aug. 26, 1901, was won by J.D. Barwise, with a net score of 93. The newspaper reported the course's length as 2,677 yards.

There is contradiction, albeit slight, over Merriam Park's boundaries. Shefchik wrote that the course was situated between Dayton, Fairview, Cleveland and Summit avenues. The *Minneapolis*

Journal reported the boundaries were Summit Avenue on the south, Selby Avenue on the north, Cleveland Avenue on the west, "and extend almost as far as Snelling or Summit avenue on the east." The 1903 *St. Paul City Directory* listed the club's address as the corner of Selby and Prior avenues.

Merriam Park Golf Club's membership peaked at 80. The golf course was gone by 1906. It is listed in that year's St. Paul city directory, but not in the 1907 directory. As with the area formerly occupied by Roadside, houses soon sprang up on the Merriam site.

Today, the two old golf course grounds, the late offspring of Town & Country Club, are occupied by nearly 80 city blocks and more than a thousand homes and small businesses in St. Paul's Merriam Park Lexington Hamline neighborhood.

CHAPTER 17

Nine for Lunch

QUALITY PARK
CITY: ST. PAUL
COUNTY: RAMSEY
YEARS: 1925–UNKNOWN

Almost two decades after Merriam was abandoned, golf re-emerged in the heart of St. Paul, albeit on a much smaller scale.

Quality Park was a nine-hole, par-3 course built on the grounds of promotions and advertising company Brown & Bigelow, at University and Hamline avenues. The course was open to the public and was lighted, allowing for nighttime play. It opened in 1925.

The 1925 book *Tee Party on the Green*, a compendium of information on St. Paul golf courses, noted this about Quality Park:

"A 9 hole Mashie course of 675 yards, owned and maintained by a private company solely for the recreation of employes — this course on the front lawn of Brown & Bigelow is believed to be the first one of its kind in the country.

"Tom Vardon planned the course, and on July 25, 1925, officiated at its opening."

The course featured competitive play: "… August 26th, the professionals of the Twin Cities played 36 holes of match play. Willie Kidd of Interlachen won the match, turning in a card of 103, breaking the course record, getting a 3 under par and making an ace on No. 4."

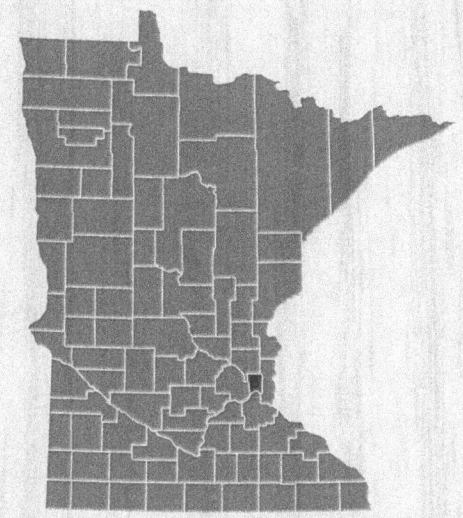

Quality Park also featured informal play: "The course is ideal for noon-hour recreation, as it can easily be played in less than one hour's time. Within one month after the official opening more than 100 employees who had never played the game before, became ardent enthusiasts."

It isn't known how long the course lasted, but it did have at least some shelf life. A two-page photo spread, with a decidedly socialite tone, on a tournament at Quality Park was featured in the Jan. 30, 1928, issue of *The 10,000 Lakes Golfer*. The course, the magazine reported, consisted of "one-shot holes." It featured "bunkers, water hazards, roadways and shrubbery."

Mrs. F.H. Stanchfield covered 36 tournament holes in 118 strokes and was crowned "Queen of the Mashie."

The Brown & Bigelow building, which was completed in 1914 and whose land before that had been occupied by the Lexington Race Track, is gone today, replaced by a Super Target store. Its old front lawn — Mrs. Stanchfield's Mashie Queendom — is now primarily a Super Target parking lot and a Noodles & Company Restaurant.

CHAPTER 18

Thor and Tom's Place

MATOSKA COUNTRY CLUB
CITY: GEM LAKE
COUNTY: RAMSEY
YEARS: 1923-38

Fore! Gone.

Nobody in Minnesota owns the two curiously exceptional connections to golf that Thor Nordwall does.

Connection No. 1: Nordwall once owned the golf club that struck the most famous shot in the history of the game.

Connection No. 2: Nordwall knows a fair amount about a lost golf course.

So, which would you like to find out about first? (Hint: This book is about lost golf courses.)

Oh, fine. Spoilsports. Sit tight, and we'll get to the lost course.

Nordwall was 18 when the PGA Tour made its then-annual stop in Minnesota in July 1939. The St. Paul Open was contested at Keller Golf Course, and Nordwall, who grew up in St. Paul's Payne-Phalen neighborhood, was a summertime caddie at Keller, having "graduated" — his word — from a previous caddieing job at a course north of St. Paul (the lost course … sit tight, I said).

In those days, many of the caddieing jobs at pro tournaments were chosen by lot. Nordwall's lot that week was to tote the clubs of a touring pro named Sarazen.

Gene Sarazen. "The Squire."

"I drew his name. When I pulled him, I didn't know who he was," Nordwall said. "There were a lot of traveling caddies in those days, they would go from tournament to tournament, and this one black guy caddieing, he says, well, you'll have a lot of trouble with that guy. He's a fussbudget, and everything like that. It scared the hell out of me, but it turned out very well."

Sarazen won 82 PGA Tour events, but he did not win that week at Keller. Disgusted with a poorly played approach shot on his final hole of the final round, he slammed his fairway wood back into his bag — headfirst, according to Nordwall's recounting of the event for sportswriter Dave Kindred in a 1999 *Golf Digest* story.

Nordwall said in 2012 that Sarazen "was a cheapskate" with the money he paid his caddie that week, even though in a 1939 recounting by Al Wold of the *Minneapolis Star-Journal*, Sarazen reportedly called Nordwall "the best caddie I've ever had." But Nordwall did receive two golf clubs from Sarazen as remuneration: a 7-iron and the offending fairway wood.

The latter club, as it turned out, was the 4-wood that Sarazen had used to hole out from 235 yards for a double-eagle 2 on the 15th hole at Augusta National en route to victory in the 1935 Masters. Almost 80 years later, "The Shot Heard 'Round the World" remains the most famous blow in golf history.

The 4-wood's provenance has been the subject of scrutiny, but Nordwall's story holds more water than those of the other parties that have claimed to own the Sarazen double-eagle club — Augusta National Golf Club and a person in Japan. Nordwall and his buddies whacked the 4-wood around for a while as youths, and decades later, after Nordwall came to realize he owned golf's equivalent of Bobby Thomson's Shot-Heard-'Round-the-World baseball

Thor Nordwall stands near the site of the second hole at Matoska Country Club in Gem Lake. The par-3 featured a carry across the pond in the background.

PETER WONG PHOTO

bat, he eschewed the tens of thousands of dollars he could have received for selling it and instead donated it to the United States Golf Association Museum in Far Hills, N.J.

But, hey, that's all trivial stuff. On to that lost golf course.

Before Nordwall's matriculation to Keller, he spent his summer days caddieing at Matoska Country Club. Matoska was organized in the fall of 1922, its nine greens laid out late that season. Its membership limit of 50 filled quickly, and it opened as a private club in the spring of 1923 on a plot in what then was White Bear Township and now is the small, bucolic city of Gem Lake. The course bordered Scheuneman Road on the east and the shore of Gem Lake on the west. Matoska means "white bear" in the Sioux language and was and is a commonly used name around the city of White Bear Lake.

The *White Bear Press* of March 29, 1923, heralded Matoska Country Club's inception, even if it did misspell the club as "Motoska" on first reference.

"The establishment of this club is just another step forward for the great White Bear," the newspaper story read. "It is to afford a country club with all its pleasures and conveniences at a moderate cost, and in order to accomplish this the club has incorporated in its by-laws very strict regulations on assments (sic). It is to be nice; it is to be ample, and it is tobe (sic) kept within reasonable cost, and it will unduobtedly (sic) become very popular."

Matoska was born with a pedigree. It was designed by Tom Vardon, the redoubtable head professional at White Bear Yacht Club in Dellwood and arguably one of the two or three most important figures in the first 50 years of Minnesota golf. An English native and the brother of six-time British Open champion Harry Vardon, Tom Vardon recorded nine top-10 finishes in the British Open before moving to America in 1911. He served as professional at the Yacht Club from 1916-37 and instructed Jimmy Johnston, the most celebrated amateur golfer in Minnesota history. He is a Minnesota Golf Hall of Fame inductee.

Vardon also was an accomplished course designer. More than 40 layouts are credited to him, including St. Cloud, Hillcrest, Eau Claire, Southview and Stillwater country clubs and Highland Park, Lake City, Phalen Park, Spooner and University of Minnesota golf clubs. (Not to mention a handful of lost courses.)

Walter Yeager was Matoska's club pro in 1925, the year G.O. House made a hole in one on the 154-yard fifth hole, according to the 1925 book *Tee Party on the First Green*. Yeager was replaced as pro by Archie Houle, who moved from his assistant pro's position at White Bear Yacht Club. Houle broke his own Matoska nine- and 18-hole course records in May 1927 with rounds of 33 and 36 for a 1-over-par 69.

Tee Party listed all 67 of Matoska's 1925 members. They were mostly from White Bear Lake and St. Paul and included A.K. (Arthur) Fillebrown, namesake of the noted Fillebrown House on Lake Avenue in White Bear Lake; C.E. Buckbee, who would become White Bear Lake mayor; and White Bear hockey legend Frank "Moose" Goheen, an Olympian and 1952 Hockey Hall of Fame inductee.

Matoska CC went public at some point, and in 1935, the *White Bear Press* featured a half-dozen short articles about the club. Lovell Ness was the club pro in those days. The newspaper in its April 5 issue publicized a "golf mass meeting" that was to be held at City Hall "in the interests of Matoska Golf Course." On April 12, it was reported that the No. 4 green, which had not been in use for two years, would be used that season. And on May 3, the Press reported what would stand, for better or worse, as one of Matoska's all-time recorded playing highlights:

"Bad weather prevented much playing. Bailey Langhorne made a shot striking a duck in a water hazard on the course."

1935 also was the year Thor Nordwall began caddieing at Matoska. The St. Paul teenager caught a ride at 5:30 every morning from a Summit milk farm "boss" who drove from the intersection of Payne and Lawson avenues, near where Nordwall lived, to the milk farm at the corner of U.S. 61 and County Road E in White Bear Lake. Nordwall walked the remaining half-mile to Matoska, where he earned 50 to 60 cents a loop.

Seventy-seven years and change later, in the fall of 2012, 91-year-old Thor Nordwall catches another ride to Matoska.

Nordwall and I meet for the first time in Vadnais Heights, the city in which Nordwall now lives, and he expresses enthusiasm over a proposal to make the short drive over to the old Matoska grounds, which he says he hasn't visited for years.

Tom Vardon, designer of Matoska Country Club and more than 40 other Midwest golf courses.

BAIN COLLECTION, LIBRARY OF CONGRESS

We drive to Gem Lake, head south down Scheuneman Road and turn right onto the southern section of Hillary Farm Lane.

Nordwall's memory springs into action. "OK, this is the first tee here, and the green backs up against a pond that's probably gone," Nordwall declares.

Nordwall's recall is clear. This is not your stereotypical 91-year-old. He looks at least 15 years younger, maybe 20. He still drives, and he hikes and cross-country skis, no surprise there considering his Nordic roots — he was born in Sprängsviken, a town in central Sweden.

There is no reason to believe Nordwall's recounting is anything other than spot on.

We drive about a hundred feet farther. This is private property, part of an upscale residential development known as Hillary Farm at Gem Lake, and that's why Nordwall has been reluctant to revisit the Matoska site. But I have been given dispensation to visit by the developer, Jim McNulty, so we continue.

The drive through the semi-circle that is Hillary Farm Lane continues, and the synapses in Nordwall's memory continue to spark. He remembers that Matoska's second hole was a par 3 over the corner of the aforementioned pond, which still exists, and that the third hole came back south toward the clubhouse, running parallel with No. 1. The course then headed back north, then west, then south, not far from the eastern shore of Gem Lake.

We are as close as one can get to the lake from Hillary Farm Road. The water, hidden from nearly every other roadway in town, is barely visible to the south, beyond a handful of million-dollar homes.

Fore! Gone.

A folder for prospective Hillary Farm at Gem Lake clients features an aerial view of the development, which coincides closely with the former Matoska Country Club grounds.

"It was intriguing for us to look across the edge of the lake there," Nordwall says, remembering his caddieing days. "I always wanted to crawl through the fence and go look at the lake. It was one of those things, you didn't do those things — 'this is private property.'"

On the other side of the road, Nordwall notices a grove of trees partway up a hill that leads to the former Judson Bemis house, an iconic Gem Lake residence. This triggers another recollection.

"Sometimes you could cut this corner in the proper high trajectory, the big hitters could at the time, and then the green was up toward the house," Nordwall says.

Nordwall is positive there used to be a green back among trees and wetlands along the southwest edge of the course, and he is nothing if not intrepid. We exit the SUV and begin to tromp through the woods. He nearly tumbles on a spongy patch of terra-not-so-firma but regains his footing, while I wonder how I am going to explain to the authorities why I am on private property with a 91-year-old who's being gurneyed out of the woods with a broken hip.

At the edge of the lake, still in the woods but not far from a resident's back yard, Nordwall says he is sure this is where the green once lay. However, we see no remaining evidence of the golf course.

The next day, I return to hike around the property again. I take almost the same path into the woods. But my attention is now turned more toward an old golf course than an old pair of hips, and, not 15 feet from where we had just walked, I see it.

Remarkably, it is plain as day. Tucked into the woods, on Hillary Farm Lot

No. 4, there is an old tee box — a flat, rectangular piece of land, pushed up in front so as to elevate the teeing area, with an old steel pipe, possibly part of Matoska's watering system, sticking a foot out of the ground.

McNulty, the developer, told me weeks earlier that he remembers tee boxes having been graded over during building at Hillary Farm, and this appears to be the only one remaining. As it turns out, this is the oldest clearly remaining landscape element from any lost golf course that I would find in more than six months of hiking through weeds, wetlands, prairies and forests in search of tee boxes, bunkers and greens. That same day, on a different part of Hillary Farm, veiled within a stand of white pine trees that didn't exist when the golf course was active, I come across a series of four small, pushed-up pieces of land, each consisting of fine dirt and/or sand, the tallest about 18 inches high. On one side of two of these dirt hills, there is a slightly hollowed-out area. They are, little doubt, a group of old Vardon-designed bunkers.

Aerial photographs from 1940 bear out suspicions about the old tee box. Wonderful things, these old aerial photographs and the websites that host them. Some allow users to overlay or fade modern-day aerial photos onto old ones. A Ramsey County website enables users to overlay current structures, roads and bodies of water onto the old aerials, so I straddle a span of seven decades as I drop modern-day Hillary Farm onto 1940 Matoska.

The old tee box matches exactly the routing Nordwall described of the dogleg hole — starting with a drive through a chute of trees and up to the corner of the dogleg. The green site for the preceding hole now is likely partly submerged into Gem Lake, also partly the corner of a resident's back yard. Other green sites also are visible on the 1940 aerial map. In fact, Mr. Occupant of 20 Hillary Farm Road, don't be alarmed, but your driveway — and a corner of your garage — are resting atop one of Vardon's old greens. (Please mow daily, sir, if you would.)

By 1938, Matoska had a new name. A White Bear Press advertisement touted the opening of Gem Lake Golf Course. Membership cost was $15 for a single, $20 for a family. Greens fees ranged from 25 cents for nine holes on weekdays to 50 cents for 18 holes on Saturdays, Sundays and holidays. However, no further references to the golf course could be found in the 1938 or 1939 *White Bear Press*, and it's assumed the course closed in one of those years, another victim of the Great Depression.

The Gem Lake name will ring a bell for many area golfers. But Gem Lake Golf Course, nee Matoska, was not the same course as Gem Lake Hills Golf Course, an 18-hole, par-57 layout established in 1955 and still operating just north of the old Matoska grounds. The two sites are almost adjacent. Only an open field and less than 200 yards separate the second fairway on Gem Lake Hills' executive nine from the old Gem Lake GC/Matoska grounds.

Fore! Gone.

JIM MCNULTY, CO-OWNER OF MCNULTY CONSTRUCTION IN Minneapolis and developer of the Hillary Farm neighborhood which occupies the former Matoska Country Club site, grew up next to another lost-course site. His family, including his father, Robert, for five decades owned and managed the former Westwood Hills Golf Course in St. Louis Park.

Clubhouse Conundrum

One of Gem Lake's urban legends — well, it's a suburban legend, really — is that the old Matoska Country Club clubhouse became the residence of one of the city's most prominent citizens.

Urban legends can be entirely true. They can be entirely false. Or their veracity can lie somewhere in between.

In the mid-1940s, Judson "Sandy" Bemis bought 80 acres along the eastern shore of Gem Lake, much of it the former Matoska Country Club property, and named it Hillary Farm. Bemis owned the Bemis Bag Company of Minneapolis. His wife, Barbara (White) Bemis, had grown up in Gem Lake. Judson Bemis built a home at the highest point of the former Matoska CC property, and it's said he occasionally knocked golf balls around his land. The Bemises had a keen interest in horses and built a stable below their home. The stable still stands; it is the sales office of the Hillary Farm at Gem Lake development company. Part of the building is restored to its original "stable" state, with nameplates for two of the Bemises' horses — Second Fiddle and Tiny Tim — hanging on the walls.

As for the Bemis house, its origin is less clear. Was it the old Matoska clubhouse, or wasn't it? The answer isn't definitive. Here is some of the evidence:

- A number of area residents, as well as a recent *St. Paul Pioneer Press* account, said the Matoska clubhouse was the Bemis home, all or in part. Judson Bemis of Minneapolis, son of Judson "Sandy" Bemis, said his father told him part of the golf clubhouse was used for the Bemis house.

- Gem Lake resident James Lindner, in a city history he wrote in 2005, included a footnote from a 2001 interview with Lloyd Labore that read: "According to Lloyd, the former clubhouse stood where Bemis' driveway now stands." That would not be on the exact site of the Bemis house. Labore died in 2012, so his account could not be confirmed or refuted.

- The current owner of the Bemis home, Greg Smith, said in 2012 that he didn't have a lot of confirmed information about the house's origin.

- Ramsey County property records say the structure built on what is now 5

The former stable on the former estate of Judson "Sandy" and Barbara Bemis in Gem Lake occupies part of the old Matoska Country Club grounds. The building is now the sales office for the Hillary Farm development in Gem Lake.

PETER WONG PHOTO

Hillary Farm Road (Smith's address) was built in 1946.

- The Bemis home was built by the construction company Jos. E. Johnson & Son. Joe Johnson of Shafer, Minn., whose father built the home, said it was his belief that the Bemis house was built "from scratch," but he allowed that he didn't have any records to that effect.

- Nordwall, who caddied at Matoska Country Club in the 1930s, said in fairly firm terms that the old Matoska clubhouse and the current Bemis/Smith home are not on the same site. He said the clubhouse was closer to the Bemis/Smith driveway, just off Hillary Farm Road.

- Old aerial photos, viewable on a Ramsey County website, support the recollections of Labore and Nordwall. A 1940 aerial strongly indicates that the Matoska clubhouse was just south of the current Hillary Farm Road — not terribly close to the Bemis/Smith home. The 1940 photo also shows no structure where the Bemis home was eventually built.

Author's conclusion: It's possible some materials from the old Matoska clubhouse were used in the construction of the Bemis home, but it's almost certain the two did not occupy the same site.

CHAPTER 19

Valleys Forged

COURSE: SOUTHVIEW COUNTRY CLUB
(also known as Ironwood)
CITY: MANKATO
COUNTY: BLUE EARTH
YEARS: 1961–84

COURTESY OF DAVE PEHRSON

Fore! Gone.

Hook up the oxygen tanks. Strap on the rappelling gear. We're off to Southview Country Club.

All right, slight exaggeration.

Southview once occupied a small plot on the south side of Mankato. Exaggeration aside, with its wooden steps, its chairlift, its ravines and its 90 feet of elevation change from highest point (clubhouse) to lowest (seventh green), the place had more ups and downs than John Daly's scorecard.

The opening holes on the par-32 course were relatively sedate, except for the possibility of a severely hooked tee shot off the second tee smashing the windshield of a car in the parking lot. Times were different then, former Southview owner Harry Musser said, and offended parties tended not to file insurance claims. "The guy would look at you," Musser said, "and say, 'Oh, don't worry about it; I'll take care of the windshield.'"

But after the early holes ... buckle up.

"On our fourth hole," Musser said, "you'd hit over a ravine to a blind hole, and you couldn't see the sucker. You couldn't see where (the ball) went or anything. And then, (the group on the tee) couldn't tee off until the guy rang the bell. There was a big bell back there (behind the green), bang, bang, bang, and then, OK, we can tee off now.

"On the seventh hole, you had to hit down into a valley, and then you had to go down maybe 150 steps or 200 steps to get to that other level, the lower level. ...

"Then on no. 9, we had a chairlift — just like a ski lift. You'd load four people and their bags on it, go up the hill, and then you'd send it back down."

The cable on the ski lift cost a dime to operate and, it was learned, snapped on occasion, shaking up its riders.

"You'd never find another golf course like this (today)," Musser said, "a golf course with that many goofy things. You'd never find this on a public golf course, too much liability, too much whatever-whatever. (But) the people that played it loved the course. The people that played it just got a kick out of it."

The kicks (and climbs) at Southview started in approximately 1961, when a group of Mankatoans built and opened it. They continued through 1976, when Musser bought the course — he renamed it Ironwood either that year in 1978, depending on whom you believe. And then through 1984, when Musser sold two-thirds of the land for the purpose of residential development.

"We were out there every day," said Joe Oberle of Fridley, who played Southview as a youngster growing up in Mankato. "We'd go out there and play nine holes and have a pop and then go play your Little League game or whatever.

"It was fun. As a kid, it was a perfect challenge for me to go out and learn the game."

Agreed, said Dave Pehrson of Kasota — with an asterisk.

Pehrson, whose father, George, and mother, JoAnn, owned the course in its early days, recalled that Southview "was a golf course that everybody could play.

It didn't matter if you were a zero handicap or a 10. ... Anybody could play with anybody."

But Pehrson acknowledged the quirkiness, too. It once cost a fellow a big, shiny trophy.

The first hole, Pehrson said, was listed as 325 yards on the scorecard but was much shorter. He recalled that during a playing of the Mankato city championship, which was contested over multiple courses, a particularly long hitter came to Southview with the lead entering the final round. But he had never played the course and knew nothing about it. The poor guy pulled out his driver — and blasted his tee shot over the head of a forecaddie, over the first green, over the nearby fourth green, over the fifth fairway, halfway to South Dakota — well, onto the sixth fairway, anyway, at the western edge of the course.

"Needless to say," Pehrson said, "I don't know how big his lead was, but he lost the whole thing on the first side — shot a 48 or something."

Southview's most conspicuous — and penal — features were its ravines, which swallowed balls at will or at whim. Fred Taylor of Mankato, who played and worked at the course, said balls hit into ravines rarely were seen again. Oberle said of the gully on No. 4, "If you made it over, your sense of relief was huge. If you hit it into the ravine, there was no way you'd get it out."

Or, to put it another way:
Quoth the ravine / Nevermore.
Anyway, back to Southview ...

Another golf course staple was Amy. She was a regular at the place in the late 1970s and early '80s, but she never booked a tee time, lugged a cart across the course or cursed a stray shot.

Amy was Musser's dog.

"For the eight years that I had the golf course," Musser said, "I had a Great Dane that was as big as me, and that dog walked the golf course with everybody imaginable. She lived to be 13, and then in 1984, when I shut the golf course down, she immediately got arthritis and died. So there's something to be said for you and me to try to keep moving, go for a walk or something."

Southview likely was built in 1960 and opened in 1961. That was the recollection of Taylor, whose father and mother, Fritz and Alice Taylor, bought it in the summer of 1962, along with Fritz Taylor's sister and brother-in-law, Virginia and Argyle Cole. Taylor said the course lay dormant during the 1962 season.

Ownership changed hands often during Southview's early years. Taylor said his parents sold the club on a contract for deed in 1965 or '66, but "these guys didn't pay their bills or whatnot, so my parents got it back again." The Taylors operated it for another year or two, then sold it to the Pehrsons, who ran it for several years. Musser bought Southview in 1976 and owned it until its closure in 1984.

Taylor got his start in golf at Southview, where he weeded greens for his parents for a quarter an hour at age 5. In his late teens, he joined Musser's employ.

"I was out in Colorado being a ski bum," Taylor said. "Harry got ahold of me out there and said he's got this golf course. He didn't know anything about golf; his background was in food and beverage and dining. I had worked there through high school for the Pehrsons ... and so he called me."

Taylor joined Musser, then soon moved on to Mankato Golf Club, the city's private country club, where he has been employed for 35 years and has been golf course superintendent since 1992.

In its latter years, Southview — by then, it was known as Ironwood — had difficulty finding a niche. "A lot of people want to hit drivers, hit the long ball, and there were only a couple of holes that you could do that on," Musser said. Also, he said, increased competition arose from taxpayer-funded municipal courses in the area.

"So I had to run a real social golf club, a lot of leagues, things like that, a lot of family events, which was OK, but it did get to the point where every year I was probably losing about 10 thousand dollars a year," Musser said.

Musser sold the course to a developer in 1984. He kept one-third of the property, however, and set up shop in a new field. Today, he continues to own and operate Applewood Restaurant and Banquet Center out of the building that used to be the Southview clubhouse.

West of Musser's restaurant, nine homes on Telemark Drive occupy roughly what used to be the six "upper" holes of Southview Country Club. In the back yard of one of those homes, there is said to be a flat piece of land that was the old No. 3 green. Farther north, where Southview's final three holes were, on lower land that included a creek, that land is now wooded and grown over.

Taylor, too, offered fond memories of Southview. "It was affordable," he said. "When the Pehrsons had it, they were very outgoing and had a family atmosphere among the members. I still see people that were among the members, how many years ago, back in the '60s and '70s, and they say, 'Oh, that was such a good time out there.'"

Well, not always. Not for everyone.

"One day we went out with a pair of twins down the street, Richie and Ron," Oberle said. "I'll never forget on the sixth hole, Richie got really mad because he missed a putt; he was struggling. He took his putter and just threw it into the woods — this entire course was surrounded by pretty deep woods — and he stormed off the course. And so the other three of us looked at each other, and 'should we go get it?' I looked at my brother, and he shook his head, no. no. Just leave it there.

"So I'm wondering — the course is gone, but I'm wondering if the putter is still lying in the woods there. I know exactly where he threw it."

OTHER SOUTHVIEW ALUMNI INCLUDE JEFF MARKOW, course superintendent at the ultra-scenic and ultra-exclusive Cypress Point Golf Course in Pebble Beach, Calif., and Larry Cole (son of former Southview owners Virginia and Argyle Cole), senior vice president of business development for noted management company Troon Golf.

CHAPTER 20

Not So Much the Golf Course...

MUDCURA GOLF CLUB
CITY: CHANHASSEN
COUNTY: CARVER
YEARS: 1926–1940s

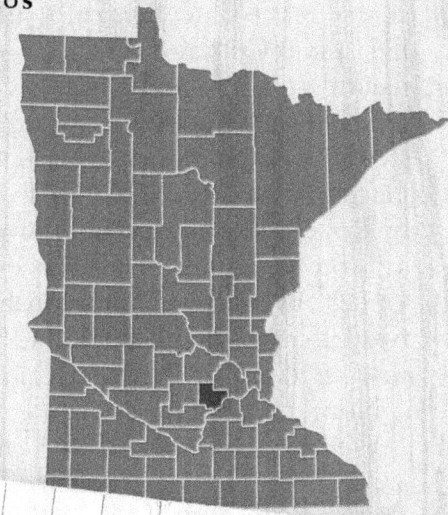

COURTESY OF PHIL KOSTOLNIK

Mudcura Golf Club

SHAKOPEE : CHASKA
MINNESOTA

OFFICIAL SCORE CARD

High heels or spiked shoes absolutely barred from the course

REPLACE TURF

LOCAL GROUND RULES

A ball played through or over any fence or over public highway or outside of bounderies marked by white stakes is out of bounds. Another ball must be played and the first shot counted.

The creek on the 1st, 5th, 7th, 11th, 13th and 17th fairways is a water hazards. Ball may be lifted and dropped on fairway not nearer hole. Penalty one stroke.

A ball lying in a gopher, crab or mole hole may be lifted without penalty and dropped one club length from same.

Lost ball, new ball to be dropped and played from approximate spot where ball was lost. Penalty one stroke.

A ball hitting wires stretched across fairways may be replayed without penalty.

A ball lying within one club length of any fixed obstruction may be lifted and dropped within two club lengths of such obstruction, and not nearer the hole and played without penalty.

Players must not drive from the tee until players ahead are out of range, nor play up to the putting green until the players in front have holed out and moved away.

Players after holing out must leave the green promptly.

Players looking for a lost ball, shall, after a reasonable length of time, signal to the players following them to pass, and having given such signal must not continue the play until these players have played through and are out of reach.

Turf cut or displaced by a player should be at once replaced and pressed down with the foot.

IMPORTANT RULES

Single players must give way to all others. Twosome may pass all other players. Threesome may pass a foursome.

To know and apply the Rules and Etiquette of Golf is the duty of every player. U. S. G. A. and Western G. A. Rules govern all play.

Drop Your Cards in Box at West Entrance of Sanitarium

Hole	Yards	Par	Hdcp.	Self	Ptnr.	Opp.	Opp.
1	132	3	16				
2	338	4	1				
3	252	4	10				
4	263	4	7				
5	141	3	13				
6	293	4	4				
7	132	3	17				
8	338	4	2				
9	252	4	11				
Out	2141	33					

Player
Attested
Date

PLEASE REPLACE TURF

Hole	Yards	Par	Hdcp.	Self	Ptnr.	Opp.	Opp.
10	263	4	8				
11	141	3	14				
12	293	4	5				
13	132	3	18				
14	338	4	3				
15	252	4	12				
16	263	4	9				
17	141	3	15				
18	293	4	6				
In	2116	33					
Out	2141	33					
Total	4257	66					
Handicap							
Net Score							

THIS CARD MEASURES SIX INCHES WHEN OPENED. (STYMIE MEASURE)

Fore! Gone.

The oddest confluence of modern-day Minnesota golf courses and their lost counterparts lies in and around the Carver County cities of Chaska and Chanhassen.

First, the former:

Three modern-day courses in this area boast indisputable stature: Chaska Town Course, designed by Arthur Hills, regarded by many as the best city-owned course in the state; Bearpath, just across the Carver County line in the Hennepin County city of Eden Prairie, designed by Jack Nicklaus and home to some of the state's most affluent residents; and Hazeltine National in Chaska, designed by Robert Trent Jones and reworked by his son Rees, host club for two U.S. Opens, two PGA Championships and two U.S. Women's Opens, and host-in-waiting for the 2016 Ryder Cup.

Now, the latter:

Wedged in among all that eminence are two old courses that are, frankly, about as revered as liver spots.

Tracy D. Swanson, president of the Chaska Historical Society, summarized two Carver County lost golf courses in an email:

"In the Chaska history book *Chaska, A Minnesota River City*, golf was referred to by Chaskans as 'cow pasture pool' because a primitive course was carved out of a community pasture in Chaska in the 1930s.

"Another course just east of Chaska was located behind the old Mudcura Sanitarium, but the same soothing springs that gave cause for Mudcura's existence also contributed to a poor golf course."

Yikes. Don't save a spot for these two in the pantheon of great layouts in Minnesota history.

Lost Course A — let's call it Cowpie Country Club — shall be allowed to fade into oblivion. As for Mudcura, there is further peculiarity — not because of the golf course so much as because of its next-door neighbor.

Mudcura Sanitarium was just north of what is now Flying Cloud Drive and west of Bluff Creek Drive, in southwestern Chanhassen. Its cause was noble. A *Chaska Herald* story reported that the sanitarium, which was said to have opened in 1909, "offered mud baths and respite for those suffering from rheumatism, arthritis, asthma and a variety of skin, kidney and nervous diseases." It also was said to have been an early alcohol abuse treatment facility.

Even before the place opened, however, and certainly afterward, there was oddness.

A detailed history of Mudcura Sanitarium written by Joseph Huber, Michael Huber and Patricia Huber noted that the grounds were situated on 120 acres, half of them mud, that construction on the main building began in 1908, and that by December of that year, "with only the foundation completed, they were calling the facility the Swastika Sulphur Springs Sanitorium. ... When finished it was called Mudcura, even though they still

Mudcura Sanitarium, undated postcard. The fellas on the left are engaged in a game of croquet.

had a decorative Swastika in the main office."

In fairness, it should be noted that the swastika symbol did not come to have negative connotations until it was adopted by the Nazi party in Germany in the 1920s and incorporated into the state flag of Germany after Adolf Hitler's Nazi party gained power in 1933.

During the decades Mudcura Sanitarium operated, there was mud everywhere — and a few dark moments, according to the Hubers' history. A man receiving treatments at Mudcura was nabbed after stealing a $600 diamond in 1921. A June 1925 tornado did $25,000 worth of damage to the property, and sanitarium founder Dr. Henry P. Fischer and his assistant Larry Hunter both suffered broken arms trying to close a second-floor door during the storm. Later that year, a patient's body was found on the grounds; he had presumably slit his own throat with a pocketknife.

Mudcura Sanitarium was sold in 1951 to, according to the Hubers' history, "the Black Franciscans, Order of Friars Minor Conventual, Our Lady of Consolation Provience, Louisville, Kentucky." The place later became known as Assumption Seminary, a seminary college and dairy farm operating in association with the colleges of St. Catherine and St. Thomas from the 1950s to 1970.

After the seminary closed, the grounds lay dormant. Sadly, the main building did not age gracefully, apparently becoming something of a haven for partiers and curiosity seekers, some with a bent for the paranormal.

And eventually, Mudcura Sanitarium was labeled these things:

- Creepy.

- Haunted.

- Hell House.

Yes, Hell House. That appellation was spray-painted on the front of the building, and there are reports of satanic graffiti having been applied liberally to other parts of the abandoned building. There are multiple reports of the building's caretaker chasing interlopers off the property with a shotgun and one report of the caretaker painting over the satanic graffiti with biblical phrases.

"Just thinking about that place gives me the heebie jeebies up my back," wrote one poster on an Internet message board.

At least three websites feature prominent entries on what became the gloomier side of Mudcura. All can be easily accessed through a simple Internet search. Details will not be provided here, so as to spare the faint of heart from a possible case of the heebies, or jeebies, or both.

The Mudcura Sanitarium building burned to the ground in 1997 in a spectacular blaze. The Hubers' history reported that the Chanhassen Fire Department burned the dormitory down as a practice exercise, but others have suspected a more nefarious cause: arson.

Two people who posted about Mudcura on Internet sites graciously offered more information on their visits to the Mudcura grounds vie email but declined requests to be interviewed on the record.

"When it burned down, I nearly cried. It was like I lost an old friend," wrote one, a frequent Mudcura visitor.

"It was definitely creepy," wrote the other.

And this: "My great-grandfather was one of the foremen during its last renovation before being abandoned. He kept extensive journals from his life, and

Aerial view of Mudcura Sanitarium, from postcard dated Dec. 29, 1943. Reverse side of postcard includes the notation "near golf course," and just to the left of the main building is an oval shape that is presumed to be a green.

COURTESY OF JOE HUBER

included a strange comment about the building that said, 'it will be too soon the next time I return to this place.' Also he said many of the workers had very unusual experiences while working on the project. He didn't note in any detail. ... On the night the building burned down, one of my aunts committed herself into religious asylum for protection (which she never explained to anyone) and my other aunt decided to burn my great-grandfather's journals."

The burned-out building stood for a time before it was reduced to rubble, and the rubble was hauled away.

The first mention of Mudcura Golf Course in Carver County Historical Society archives is from an Aug. 19, 1926, story in the *Weekly Valley Herald* of Chaska. The newspaper reported on a match at the course between players from Shakopee and Chaska. Shakopee won the match, 727 strokes to 731. E.G. Darsow had the lowest 18-hole score, an 85. Six of the 17 competitors were doctors. All players had dinner at the sanitarium, and the club was offering memberships for the balance of the season for $5.00 for "Gentlemen" and $2.50 for "Ladies."

A *Weekly Herald* story from April 19, 1928, reported on a meeting at which a membership limit of 85 had been established. "The club is composed of members from Chaska and Shakopee, who are very enthusiastic about their little course which is described by many golf fans as being one of the most sporty in this section."

An old, undated scorecard says Mudcura was a par-33 course. The scorecard lists nine holes out and nine holes in, as would any traditional scorecard for a nine- or 18-hole course. But here's where it gets curiouser and curiouser, as if so much about Mudcura weren't curious enough:

All indications are that Mudcura was a six-hole layout.

On the scorecard, the yardages for holes 1 through 6 are identical to those of holes 7 through 12, and then again for holes 13 through 18. The golfers who filled out the scorecard marked only the first six holes, a logical ending point on a six-hole course. What's more, a 1937 aerial photograph of the area distinctly shows six — no more, no less — small, white circles, identical in appearance to sand greens seen on other aerial photos from the same era. The circles are distinct enough to suggest the course was still active.

The aerial photo contradicts the notion that the golf course was "behind" the sanitarium. Two greens were, but the rest of the course appears to be west of the sanitarium, on both sides of the creek, almost as far south as Flying Cloud Drive.

The creek came into play on two holes, according to the scorecard, and the second hole, a 338-yard par 4 and the No. 1 handicap hole, must have been a beast: Someone named "HHP" took an 11, with no scores higher than 6 on the rest of the card.

The scorecard included this notation: "Drop your cards in box at west entrance of sanitarium."

The likely resting place of part of the former Mudcura Golf Club grounds can be viewed from the Minnesota River Bluffs LRT Regional Trail, by walking about a half-mile west on the trail where it intersects Bluff Creek Drive. The site is nothing more than farmland and

This concrete block, about six inches high, is the only visible above-ground feature remaining on the site of the old Mudcura Sanitarium. Mudcura Golf Course was just to the west of the sanitarium.

JOE BISSEN PHOTO

marshland, with no evidence of golf ever having been played there. "If you like nature, it's worth it just for the view," one of the website posters wrote.

Beyond the newspaper stories and the scorecard, Mudcura Golf Club is barely a footnote in county history. On this author's visit to the Chaska-Chanhassen area, six people were asked about it. Three had heard of the sanitarium, two others of the seminary. None had heard of the golf course.

Today, all that remains of Mudcura Sanitarium are portions of the driveway, angled and leading to a circular slab of concrete that served as a parking area, judging by old aerial photos. Just to the west, in a thicket, is another slab of old concrete, about a foot square and a foot high. And that is it.

The surrounding area, however, is not without modern-day significance. It is the site of Seminary Fen. A fen is a lowland, and Seminary Fen is a calcareous fen, considered one of the rarest ecosystems in the world. A 2008 *Star Tribune* of Minneapolis story covering the dedication of Seminary Fen described this area of the Minnesota River Valley:

"Environmentalists say that only about 500 calcareous fens exist worldwide, with Minnesota home to about 200 of them. … The fens thrive in cold groundwater at the bottom of a slope or bluff enriched with calcium and magnesium."

Limited public access is permitted on 73 acres of Seminary Fen, which is under the supervision of the Minnesota Department of Natural Resources.

You're welcome to walk around in much of the fen. You might discover the scant remains of Mudcura Sanitarium. Maybe, if you're paranormally plugged in, you'll sense the old "Hell House" aura. But Mudcura Golf Club is history. Very little history, actually, but history nonetheless.

THOUGH THE MUDCURA GROUNDS ARE CLOSER TO THE downtowns of both Chaska and Shakopee, they are within the Chanhassen City limits. Two public courses are within 1½ miles of Mudcura: Bluff Creek and Halla Greens.

CHAPTER 21

Bunker Hills, the Elder

BUNKER HILLS COUNTRY CLUB
CITY: MENDOTA HEIGHTS
COUNTY: DAKOTA
YEARS: 1933-42

COURTESY OF PHIL KOSTOLNIK

FORE! GONE.

"We're driving on the eighth fairway right here."
– Don Dostert, piloting his Lincoln Town Car down a Mendota Heights, Minn., street, 2010

DON DOSTERT IS AT THE WHEEL, HEADING SOUTH ON DODD ROAD IN MENDOTA HEIGHTS, JUST NORTH OF MINNESOTA HIGHWAY 110. A VISITOR HAS TAKEN DOSTERT UP ON HIS OFFER TO BE SHOWN AROUND THE GROUNDS OF THE GOLF COURSE HE ONCE KNEW SO WELL.

Dostert turns right on Willow Lane. He looks up the hillside at the brick ranch-style house on the corner.

"The clubhouse was here. It looked a lot like that," he says.

Dostert is playing tour guide because, well, who else could? Is there anyone else around who knows this turf in the same way Dostert does?

Probably not.

Except that Dostert's turf is not just turf anymore. It is sprinkled with driveways and patios and cul de sacs and winding streets.

Dostert tromped up and down the nooks and crannies of this part of Mendota Heights 75 years ago. It was his stomping grounds as a boyhood caddie on the grounds of Bunker Hills Country Club.

No, not *that* Bunker Hills. Before there was the well-known Bunker Hills Golf Course in Coon Rapids, there was Bunker Hills Country Club in Mendota Heights, a popular 18-hole, public, daily-fee course.

The history of Bunker the Elder is sketchy. Dostert, 85, thought the course opened in 1933 or '34. Minnesota golf author Rick Shefchik, in his book *From Fields to Fairways*, wrote that the course was designed by Tom Vardon and opened in 1933. Dostert remembered caddieing at Bunker Hills for about six years and looping there in the state public links championship in 1938. The course was owned by John Dobnor, who at one point asked Dostert to work on the grounds.

"In 1942, World War II had just begun," Dostert said, "and John Dobnor couldn't get anyone to cut the grass. I was just a kid, 17 years old, and the fairways were this thick (he holds his fingers at least two inches apart)."

Bunker Hills fell into disrepair. It closed later in 1942, but Dostert already had begun golfing at Riverview (now Mendakota), just across Highway 110 from Bunker Hills, where he arranged to play for $18 a year. He entered the Marines later in 1942, served in the Pacific, had a bullet pierce his lung and graze his heart in the Battle of Peleliu, spent 14 months in a hospital, was awarded a Purple Heart and received a free membership at Riverview as a military veteran when he returned from the war.

And he got good at golf. Dostert went on to win the 1950 state public links championship and 1964 Birchmont. He was a semifinalist in the 1947 U.S. Public Links Championship at Meadowbrook in Hopkins and captured 17 club championships at Riverview/Mendakota.

But back to Bunker Hills.

"It was a very good golf course — it would be a little short now for today's players," Dostert says as his Lincoln rolls over the next fairway and the next.

The first hole was a 471-yard par 5, running parallel to Dodd Road. The ninth was a formidable par 3 of 211 yards, across a gully and back up to the green. The 14th, a double-dogleg, 555-yard par 5 now occupied by a street known as Ridge Place, "was named one of the best holes in Minnesota by the St. Paul newspaper," Dostert says.

The course measured 6,018 yards and played to a par of 70.

A 1947 aerial photo of Mendota Heights, accessible at historicaerials.com, shows what remained of the outline of Bunker Hills, as well as many of the green sites. The course was bounded in general by Marie Avenue on the north, Dodd Road (Minnesota Highway 149) on the east, Minnesota 110 on the south, and what are now Crown Point Drive and the Interstate 35E corridor on the west. There are no home sites clearly visible in the photograph, and the clubhouse appears to have been razed or removed.

Today, the area is almost entirely residential. A house at the corner of Dodd Road and Ridge Place rests almost precisely on what was the first green, judging by Dostert's description. A house on Wachtler Avenue, near Ridge Place, occupies another green site.

Though Bunker Hills has been closed for 71 years, a portion of it still gets heavy traffic. The course's southernmost green appears to now be occupied by the westbound lane of Highway 110 — yep, they paved paradise in Mendota Heights, too. Just off the green, on what used to be "froghair" and now is the shoulder of the

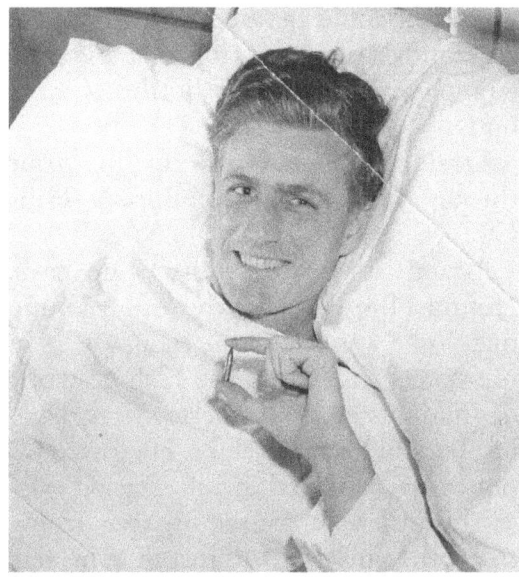

Don Dostert in a hospital bed, displaying a bullet that pierced a lung and grazed his heart in the 1944 World War II Battle of Peleliu, Pacific Ocean.

Don Dostert, accepting the Presidents Trophy at a 1957 awards ceremony at Mendakota Country Club. Dostert's grandson Chris Mulcahy relates the story: "The Presidents Trophy was for the Tournament of Champions. Louie Fischer had a tournament consisting of players who had all won other tournaments that year. That is where my Grandpa was asked to give a speech and said, 'It's about time' and sat down. He didn't like public speaking."

PHOTOS COURTESY OF CHRIS MULCAHY

highway, would be the lost-golf-course redefinition of a collection area: Big Mac wrappers, empty water bottles, Camel butts.

Dostert is wrapping up his tour through the shadows of Bunker Hills CC.

"Want to hear a story?" he says. "Johnny Bloyer, when he was a young man — he was one of the best players in the state — he played the 12th hole one day and missed a putt there. His dad had just bought him new clubs. He tossed his putter up a tree, and then he started tossing his other clubs up in the tree, trying to get the putter down. Just then his dad came by and saw his kid throwing his new clubs up in the tree.

"His dad took his clubs away from him for a week."

At this point, you can almost see Dostert reliving in his mind a pitch shot he might have hit as a 13-year-old, trying to finish his round by noon, when the woman running the clubhouse would ring the cowbell, signaling the end of the day's play for caddies.

"Sure brings back memories," he says, and soon turns back onto Dodd Road, once more leaving Bunker Hills behind.

A version of this chapter appeared in the Summer 2010 edition of *Minnesota Golfer* magazine. It is reprinted with permission of the Minnesota Golf Association. Don Dostert died in September 2011.

DOSTERT TALKED OF ANOTHER LOST COURSE NEARBY, A lighted par-3 course near the southeast corner of Highway 110 and Dodd Road that he said was owned by Louis Fischer, whose farm on the west side of Dodd Road was converted into what is now Mendakota Country Club in the early 1900s. Dostert's grandson Chris Mulcahy said Dostert tried to buy the par-3 course in the 1950s but couldn't get financing. The grounds is now a strip mall.

CHAPTER 22

Park Place, and What a Park

ANTLERS PARK GOLF LINKS
CITY: LAKEVILLE
COUNTY: DAKOTA
YEARS: CIRCA 1923-38

COURTESY OF PHIL KOSTOLNIK

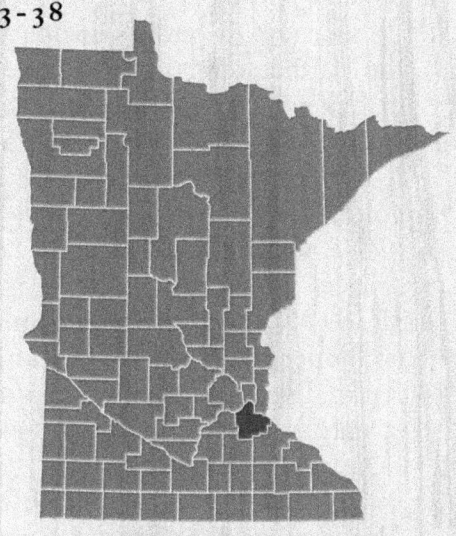

Score Card

No fivesomes permitted. Twosomes has right over threesomes, and threesomes has right over foursomes.

Players must secure a ticket from attendant before starting play, and play off in the order of their ticket number.

Date....................192...

Holes	Yards	Men's Par	Handi-cap	First Op.	2nd Op.	Part-ner	Self	Won X Lost — Halved O
1	225	3	17					
2	340	4	10					
3	250	4	14					
4	265	4	12					
5	345	5	2					
6	205	3	6					
7	165	3	7					
8	135	3	5					
9	380	5	4					
OUT	2310	34						

Replace Turf

Score Card

On Saturday afternoons, Sundays and Holidays only foursomes shall be permitted to play.

Players looking for lost ball shall, after a reasonable length of time, signal to the players following them to pass, and, having given such signal must not continue their play until these players have played through and are out of reach.

Holes	Yards	Men's Par	Handi-cap	First Op.	2nd Op.	Part-ner	Self	Won X Lost — Halved O
10	140	3	18					
11	155	3	8					
12	145	3	9					
13	240	3	11					
14	300	4	3					
15	500	5	1					
16	205	3	16					
17	260	4	13					
18	245	3	15					
IN	2190	31						
OUT	2310	34						
Total	4500	65						

GENERAL INSTRUCTIONS

George O'Rourke, owner of the Antlers Park Golf Links, will not be responsible for the loss or damage to personal property nor for injuries to persons incidental to the game of golf.

Players assume all such risk.

All players should be provided with a bag and at least three clubs.

All players are required to register and pay the link's fee or show season tickets.

Do not drive until players ahead are out of range nor play up to a putting green until players ahead have holed out of range.

High heeled shoes are prohibited.

Golf is a gentlemen's game and all players are requested to be courteous to others at all times.

Replace All Turf

GROUND RULES

Out of Bounds: Across fence on No. 14 and 15 out of bounds. If out of bounds from tee, drive another ball, lose distance. If out of bounds from fairway, drop ball as near as possible where ball went out. Penalty, one stroke.

Lost Ball: No penalty if lost on fairway. If lost in rough or out of bounds, drop as near as possible to where ball was supposed to be. Penalty, one stroke.

Hazards: Trees in all fairways are hazards.

GEORGE O'ROURKE, Owner

FORE! GONE.

T**HE DATE IS, LET'S SAY, 1930. THE CONVERSATION, BETWEEN MINNESOTA GOLF COURSE OWNER GEORGE O'ROURKE AND A VISITOR TO HIS LAKESIDE PROPERTY, IS FICTIONAL BUT ENTIRELY PLAUSIBLE.**

Visitor: Nice place you've got here, George.

O'Rourke: Thank you.

Visitor: The golf course ain't bad, either.

George O'Rourke's property along the southeastern shore of Lake Marion in Lakeville might have been the most popular piece of land in Dakota County in the first third of the 20th century. But golf had little to do with it.

O'Rourke opened his golf course — Antlers Park Golf Links — sometime after 1917, the year he became owner and operator of Antlers Amusement Park. The golf course's reputation is largely unknown, but George's amusement park drew rave reviews.

Antlers Amusement Park attracted Minnesotans and outstaters by the thousands to the then-small town of Lakeville. Antlers ranks alongside Excelsior Park, which lay on the Lake Minnetonka shoreline, and Wildwood, on the White Bear Lake shoreline, as the foremost Twin Cities-area amusement parks in the first half of the 20th century.

"Antlers Park was once home to some of the grandest and most thrilling amusement rides in the upper midwest," proclaims a plaque in the parking lot of modern-day Antlers Park, which occupies much of the old amusement park grounds. "From its opening day in 1910," the plaque continues, "Antlers Park was the center of activity in Lakeville, offering an amusement park, picnic grounds, dance pavilion, lake and many activities."

Ahead to 2012 …

George Warweg's back yard, off 202nd Street West, lies within a hundred yards of the parking-lot plaque. Warweg says he has never read it. He doesn't need written words to recall the spectacle that was Antlers Amusement Park. He can do it by memory.

Warweg is taking a visitor on a drive around all things Antlers on an October day. He pulls up on 202nd Street, not 100 yards west of his house. Just off the street, next door to Warweg's house, is George O'Rourke's old house. O'Rourke occupied it while he owned Antlers, and Warweg lived in the old O'Rourke house for a time after his uncle, George Warweg Sr., bought Antlers Park for $22,000 in 1942.

Warweg pinpoints where the old Antlers Park clubhouse, including the golf clubhouse, once stood — on what is now a patch of gravel just off 202nd Street. The details flow like — well, like the suds once did at Antlers.

"There was an icehouse on the lake and at the clubhouse, for people to cool their beer for the picnics," Warweg says. "There was 10,000 people at the old Dakota County picnics. There was a big basement underneath (the clubhouse) where they stored their extra beer, because they couldn't truck it out."

Warweg vividly remembers the clubhouse, which featured an oak-floored dancing pavilion.

"This lower level had a big kitchen, there was plates, big platters, for these picnics. On the lower level, there were a couple of bars down there, a dining area, it was all cement, a place for people to dance, a place for golf, I suppose for people to pay their dues or whatever, and then there was an upstairs. That must have been for the members only. That had a nice, beautiful bar up there, a nice dance floor, tables all the way around it, then they had a balcony all the way around it on the outside to look at the lake with tables and stuff. It overlooked the lake with a beautiful view.

"I was probably 13, 14 years old, and I thought that bar was the most beautiful thing. It was pretty exclusive, I imagine."

What else did Antlers Amusement Park have? What did it not have?

It had a swimming beach, with 1,000 feet of sandy Lake Marion shoreline, a diving tower and high sliding chute, plus a boat dock with sailboats, rowboats, and canoes available for rental. It had a bathing area that featured 250 individual dressing rooms. It had a children's playground with a miniature operating train and pony ring. It had tennis courts, athletic fields, and a baseball diamond with grandstand. It had a 12-piece orchestra that played dance music in the afternoons and evenings. It had a golf course (yes, we're getting to that). And it had, perhaps most visibly, an aerial swing.

Warweg called the swing a "ferris wheel," which hints at the swing's capaciousness but might not accurately describe its construction and operation. Longtime Lakeville resident Betty Weichselbaum called it a "high tower" with four or five canoe-shaped chairs that twirled.

No doubt, anticipation built when families approached Antlers Amusement Park and saw the aerial swing. And Antlers' original owner made sure they approached — by the traincarful.

Colonel Marion Savage was the original owner of Antlers Amusement Park. In 1907, according to the Antlers Park plaque, Savage "filed articles of incorporation for the Minneapolis, St. Paul, Rochester, and Dubuque Electric Traction Company (a.k.a. the Dan Patch Line) to connect his many business enterprises by rail. The Dan Patch Line was named for his famous racehorse." Dan Patch was perhaps the greatest harness-racing horse of all time; in 1906, at the Minnesota State Fairgrounds, he ran a mile in 1 minute, 55 seconds, an unofficial record that has been matched but never bettered. The horse died on July 11, 1916, and Col. Savage died the next day.

But before that, in 1908, Savage had purchased 40 acres on the east side of Prairie Lake in Lakeville; he and several partners dreamt of building an amusement park along the Dan Patch Line and bringing patrons there by rail. The line went into receivership in 1918 and was reorganized as the Minneapolis, Northfield, and Southern. Under its various owners and names, the line connected residents of such cities as Minneapolis, Golden Valley, Northfield, Edina and Savage, with a spur available for dropping off riders at Savage's Antlers Amusement Park.

Col. Savage was a man with an apparent dash of hubris. He and his horse,

Fore! Gone.

A pond and swamp near the terminus of 199th Street West in the Antlers Park neighborhood of Lakeville. This area likely was on or near the western border of Antlers Park Golf Course. The home in the background almost certainly is on former golf course property.

JOE BISSEN PHOTO

which often accompanied him on rail trips for the purpose of drawing customers to the Dan Patch Line, traveled in two private cars — the horse's was a converted baggage car painted white with gold lettering, and with white-uniformed grooms in tow. Perhaps that was a display of pomposity; perhaps it was a display of Savage's keen marketing sense.

Speaking of excessive pride, another local legend centers on Savage. The Antlers Park plaque claims Savage renamed Prairie Lake after himself — Lake Marion — upon purchasing the park in 1908, although that is disputable: The Lake Marion Association website says the renaming took place in 1946, long after Savage's passing.

Regardless, after Savage's death in 1916, the park went into receivership. Along came George O'Rourke.

In 1917, according to the plaque, "George P. and Catherine O'Rourke purchased Antlers Park at the receivership auction for $16,000. O'Rourke, an engineer with General Electric, which provided the traction engines used on the railroad, is credited with providing the illumination of the park by utilizing one of the electric locomotives from the Dan Patch Line."

This was not O'Rourke's only 500-watt idea. Building a golf course was another.

Details about Antlers Park Golf Links are sketchy and contradictory. Its year of inception is unknown, though a series of photos showing both the golf course and amusement park is dated "circa 1925" by the Minnesota Historical Society. A 1922 *Minneapolis Tribune* story reports a public accountants outing to be held at Antlers Park would include a "one-hole golf contest," suggesting the full course had not yet been built.

The parking-lot plaque claims the golf course lay east of the amusement park, but Warweg says otherwise, and his rendition has more 202nd Street cred than the plaque does. Understand that Warweg is not and never was a golfer — "I don't know how anybody could chase those little balls around," he says — but his memories of the golf course land are clear, and he says with conviction that the course was mostly north, even northwest, of the amusement park and only to a smaller degree to the east. A 1937 aerial photograph of the neighborhood confirms that assertion.

Warweg drives his visitor through the area that used to be Antlers Park Golf Links. It is mostly residential, many of the homes built on land Warweg once owned, but there also is farmland still owned by Warweg. A smaller portion of land remains untouched probably since the course closed — a mix of trees, scrubland, rough paths and lagoons that offers evidence of terrain and features suitable for a high-quality golf course.

The borders of the course, in modern-day geographical terms and as described by Warweg, are roughly 201st Street West on the south, Ipava Avenue on the east, Kenwood Trail (Highway 50) to the north and northeast, and Upper 199th Way West and Jaguar Avenue to the north and west. It isn't believed that the course bordered Lake Marion or crossed north of what is now Kenwood Trail.

Warweg figures most of the neighborhood residents don't realize their back yards and driveways used to be fairways and greens. "They put in the streets" upon development of the area, Warweg says, "and I was farming it, so it looked like farmland."

Warweg says he dug up many trees in rows that he speculated lined the fairways of Antlers Park Golf Links. In an earlier telephone conversation, he had referred to "little places where there were sand traps," and while driving through the current neighborhood, he glances at a house on the corner of Iteri Place and Jaguar Avenue and declares: "Oh, yeah. There was a bunker over in here, a big sand bunker. We couldn't plow it; we had to plow around it. It come right up to the road there."

How many holes at Antlers Park? That's another point of contention. Some websites and publications claim there were nine. The plaque says O'Rourke "built a 9-hole golf course and an 18-hole golf course east of the park." A listing from *Minnesota: A State Guide* in 1938 says Antlers was 18 holes. Weichselbaum, who played the course once as a child, probably in the early 1930s, says it was an 18-hole course — with grass greens, to the best of her recollection. A scorecard from the 1920s lists Antlers as an 18-hole course, par 65, measuring 4,500 yards.

Warweg can't say with certainty how many holes there were. His suspicion is that it was an 18-hole course and that there were plans to expand it to 27, with the additional nine to occupy a small, triangular plot east of the amusement park. Warweg now owns that land; it is a cornfield.

The triangular plot most likely could have accommodated only a par-3 course.

"They had planned on putting more golf course in there," Warweg said. "They plotted it out and put trees in there, but then it went broke. When we came here, a good share of it was plotted out and staked out. I know when my dad came here, he said that's what busted it, that they were putting in a nine-hole course and the recession (Great Depression) hit, and that's what busted it. True or not, I don't know."

Weichselbaum, part of a family that for a century owned and operated the well-known Weichselbaum Resort on the western side of Lake Marion, called Antlers "a beautiful course." She remembers that she played Antlers with a woman who lived on the east side of the lake when she was about 10 or 12, and that "it was a terrible day because I wasn't any good."

Undeterred, Weichselbaum forged onward and still was golfing in 2012, on Thursday mornings, at age 92.

"The golf course was just magnificent," Weichselbaum said of Antlers. "It took a lot of young people mowing — their job was to keep the grass green."

But by the late 1930s, green of a different sort was hard to come by at Antlers. Warweg speculated that the golf course operated through the 1938 season, then closed. In 1939, according to the plaque, O'Rourke sold the amusement park to John L. Lenihan, though Warweg offered a slightly different rendition. "He (O'Rourke) lost the place to Lenihan. Lenihan owned the creamery in Lakeville. Lenihan loaned him money, and Lenihan wound up with the park."

Antlers Park had seen better days. George Warweg Sr. and his wife, Myrtle, bought the park in 1942. Events and forces conspired against them. George Warweg the nephew recalled that George Warweg Sr. re-roofed the clubhouse in the World War II years but couldn't get enough help on the project because so many men had gone off to war. The aerial swing was scrapped and melted down during the war years; the younger Warweg said his uncle donated the metal to the war effort.

The park grounds were mowed with a John Deere sickle mower, the younger Warweg recalled, and beverage sales tailed off because "people would come out here, but they brought their six-packs with them and left 'em in the garbage, so that didn't pay off."

In 1958, according to the parking-lot plaque, "The last owners were Leonard Bentson and wife La Salle. They operated the park for large Twin City company picnics, such as General Mills, Northwestern Bell, American Hoist, and many others."

And in 1974, "The park was sold to the City of Lakeville. At the time of the City's purchase, some of the structures still existed, including the dance pavilion, but have since been removed."

LAKEVILLE WAS A SMALL TOWN WHEN MARION SAVAGE established Antlers Park there in 1907. The city's population was 385 in 1910 and didn't exceed 1,000 until after 1960. By 1970, the population had grown to 7,556, an increase of 718 percent in one decade, and the population in 2010 was 55,954.

CHAPTER 23

The Smell Test

AUSTIN MUNICIPAL GOLF COURSE;
HILLCREST GOLF COURSE
CITY: AUSTIN
COUNTY: MOWER
YEARS: AUSTIN MUNICIPAL 1931–32; HILLCREST 1934–CIRCA 1943

Archives from the Austin Daily Herald
COURTESY OF MOWER COUNTY
HISTORICAL SOCIETY

Fore! Gone.

Some things just don't work well when paired together:
Plaids and stripes.
Tigers and Elins.
Golf courses and sewage disposal plants.

Say what?

Yes, each of those pairings has failed miserably at one time or another. Regarding the latter of the three, the question must be asked: With all due respect, long-gone resident leaders of Austin, Minn., what in the name of Renuzit were you thinking?

Austin, the seat of Mower County, a city of 25,000 near the Iowa border in southeastern Minnesota, has two lost golf courses — one with a solid reputation and rather traditional lost-course history, the other with a more ill-conceived, ill-fated and, well, ill-odored past.

Golf in Austin began in 1919 with Austin Country Club, which opened as a five-hole layout 2½ miles east of downtown. A private course, it was expanded to nine holes in 1920 under the direction of noted course architect Tom Vardon and exists as an 18-hole layout today.

During the 1920s, however, there was no public golf course in Austin. As interest in the game grew, and as the 1930s rolled around, Austinites approached the city council with a request to approve a location for a municipal course. Two sites were proffered: one near Todd Park, northeast of downtown, and the other not quite a mile south of downtown, south of Lafayette Park and across the Cedar River. It was an attractive-enough-sounding site except for one detail:

It was within sight — and sniff — of Austin's sewage disposal plant. Inexplicably, at least with the benefit of 80-plus years of hindsight, this was the site chosen.

"Municipal Golf Course With Six Holes Planned," read the headline in the *Austin Daily Herald* of May 20, 1931, followed by a passage that today seems preposterous:

"The land to the south of the disposal plant is an ideal location for a golf course."

Yeah, right. And the land next to Chernobyl is an ideal location for a bed-and-breakfast.

Favorable though the terrain might have been for a golf course, Austin Municipal, originally a par-20, 1,200-yard layout expanded to nine holes in the fall of 1931, faced a significant, intrinsic, olfactory challenge.

"The main drawback of this location was the odor," wrote Sue Doocy of the Mower County Historical Society in correspondence regarding Austin's lost courses, "but the site was popular, though short lived — a few years."

In fact, more than 100 players played the course on a Sunday in early June 1931, the *Daily Herald* reported, and a concession stand eventually was built near the first tee. The May 20 *Daily Herald* further trumpeted the fledgling course with this: "When the temporary greens are built, the grass mowed, and the holes installed, there will be nothing lacking in golf enjoyment but the attempts at breaking par."

Well, that and the daunting prospect of trying to break par with one hand gripping the golf club and the other pinching shut the nostrils.

Austin Municipal, sad to say, put the "pew" in putrid. Never in golf history was the concept of the word "whiff" more repulsive.

There is evidence that play at Austin Municipal continued in 1932, but no record beyond that is apparent.

Public golf made another appearance in Austin with the founding of Ramsey Golf Club, 2½ miles north of downtown, in 1933. The course, since renamed River Oaks, still exists. Then, in 1934, along came another public course, again introduced in part by the *Daily Herald*, but not without a backhanded swipe at Austin Municipal:

"Austin has been in need of a new public golf course ever since the sport of golf swept through the country approximately five years ago," the *Herald* reported on April 26. "The public course that was built out on the grounds of the sewer disposal was rather haphazardly built, but even the best course in the world wouldn't tempt many golfers with such an odor as prevails the grounds."

So as Austin Municipal wafted off into oblivion, its niche as Austin's home of public golf was supplanted by Ramsey and the other new layout, Hillcrest Golf Course, 1½ miles west of downtown, next to U.S. Highway 16, on a plot known as the Banfield property.

"Perhaps it will not be an A-1 course the first season," the *Daily Herald* reported of Hillcrest, "but in the following seasons it will develop into one of the finest public courses in Southern Minnesota." The newspaper reported that Hillcrest was "beautifully situated among rolling hills, surrounded on two sides by a thick evergreen grove, and in the near vicinity of the winding turtle creek."

Indeed, Hillcrest became a course of solid repute.

"It was a very good golf course. Everybody that was a good golfer played there," said Kenneth "Pinky" Erickson, 86, who knows a thing or two about good golfers. Erickson twice played in the St. Paul Open, a former PGA Tour event played at Keller Golf Course, and he might have been an even better teacher than player, having instructed the likes of Austin native Jon Chaffee, a Minnesota Golf Hall of Fame member who boasts three top-10 finishes on the PGA Tour.

Erickson remembers having caddied at Hillcrest but offered no memories of having played there. Asked how much he was paid for caddieing, he replied, "Not very much. About enough for pop and candy."

Erickson's older brother Don, 87, offered similar memories. "No," he said when asked whether he had played the course, "but I caddied on it. My brother (Ronald) was champion of that course for two or three years."

Don Erickson said the caddieing setup at Hillcrest was similar to that at Austin Country Club, where he had more vivid memories of looping in the 1930s.

"A lot of times, there'd be 150 caddies waiting out there," he said. "For many years, we'd all gather around there. Whether we'd get a chance to caddie or not, we'd all be waiting out there for a chance to get 25 cents for a round of golf."

A series of archived clips from the *Austin Daily Herald*, forwarded by the Mower County Historical Society, provided further glimpses into the history of Hillcrest Golf Course. A May 19, 1934, story was particularly revealing:

"The yell of 'fore' will resound over the fairways of the newly constructed Hillcrest Public Golf Links tomorrow as course officials open the links for the season's play. ...

"The course, organized for the benefit of local golfers, was formed by a group of Austin linksmen who coupled their efforts with Alex Taylor, Country Club pro, in completing the project. The workers have been lauded for efforts on what is termed one of the finest natural courses in southern Minnesota."

"... The course is situated one mile west of Austin out Oakland avenue by Turtle Creek."

This article also reported that Hillcrest had sand greens, 30 to 40 feet in diameter, and was designed by Taylor. The first club president was Herman Heinl. Par was 36, and the course measured 3,104 yards. Don Erickson said the sand greens later were converted to grass.

A *Daily Herald* advertisement from April 18, 1936, promoted the opening of the course for play that season. Fees were 25 cents for nine holes, 50 cents for all day. Yearly memberships cost $12 for gentlemen, $15 for families, $5 for ladies and $5 for schoolchildren. "Get your golf supplies here," the ad read, and included promotion of equipment available at the clubhouse: Hagen International Tom-Boys, woods marked down to $6.95 from $13.50 and irons marked down to $4.95 from $8.00, plus Hagen Honey Center Balls marked down to 50 cents from 75 cents.

An ad from May 9, 1941, listed Jim Vacura as Hillcrest's "professional instructor." Vacura was another well-known figure in Austin golf history. A 1999 online obituary for Vacura said he was an employee of Austin's Hormel Company for almost 49 years, that he co-founded and designed Ramsey Golf Course, and that he set a nine-hole course record at Austin Country Club.

The exact year of Hillcrest's demise is unclear, though it almost certainly was during the World War II years. A 1956 *Daily Herald* retrospective on the history of Austin's golf courses reported of Hillcrest: "Lisle Phillips was manager until the project was abandoned in 1942. Although a short course, it was considered sporty and difficult with deep hills contributing natural hazards."

But a 1942 booklet promoting the city of Austin, again provided by the Mower County Historical Society, indicated Hillcrest was still in operation: "Hillcrest Golf Course one mile west of Austin on Highway No. 16 is a beautiful 9-hole course. ... Tourists are especially welcome to stop for a picnic lunch or a few hours recreation." And a 1943-44 Austin-Mower County directory lists Hillcrest Public Golf Club, with L.J. Phillips as manager.

Though Hillcrest has long since closed, it still gets heavy traffic, in a manner of speaking. On the western outskirts of Austin, a short stretch of Interstate 90 runs "diagonally" and briefly cuts through what was the northwestern section of Hillcrest. To the east of the interstate but west of Turtle Creek, a residential development covers most of the rest of the old Hillcrest property. One home in that development belongs to Pinky Erickson, who knows he lives on the old golf course grounds but can't pinpoint exactly what hole his house is on.

"That's a good question; I always thought it was on Number 7 or 8," he said.

AUSTIN IS THE BIRTHPLACE OF TWO FAMOUS NATIVE Minnesota golfers. Tom Lehman, the 1996 British Open champion who has been player of the year on the PGA Tour and Champions Tour, was born in Austin in 1959 but grew up in Alexandria, Minn. Lee Janzen, who won the U.S. Open in 1993 and '98, was born in Austin in 1964 but grew up in Baltimore and Tampa, Fla.

CHAPTER 24

Ya Gotta Wonder, Part II

MEMORIAL GOLF COURSE
CITY: MANKATO
COUNTY: BLUE EARTH
YEARS: 1942–43

THE INTELLECTUAL ACUMEN OF THE FOLKS IN AUSTIN WHO DEEMED IT WISE TO PLACE A GOLF COURSE NEXT TO A SEWAGE PLANT IS MATCHED IN MINNESOTA LOST-COURSE HISTORY ONLY BY CERTAIN FOLKS IN MANKATO — AND WASHINGTON, D.C., TOO. IN 1942, THESE FOLKS LATCHED ON TO A PIECE OF LAND THREE-QUARTERS OF A MILE SOUTH OF THE MINNESOTA RIVER AND OPENED A NINE-HOLE MUNICIPAL COURSE CALLED MEMORIAL. CONSTRUCTION WAS DONE BY WORKS PROGRESS ADMINISTRATION LABOR.

One problem:

"It was built on a slough," said Ken Bohks of Mankato, former owner of Minneopa Golf Course in Mankato. "Any ball hit approximately 30 or 40 yards high, when it came down, you couldn't find it. It was buried in the ground."

Anybody care to guess the shelf life of this swamp thing?

"I don't think it lasted a year," Bohks said.

Bohks was close. By August 1943, a public meeting had been called to discuss the fate of the "flooded, weed grown municipal golf course," as the *Mankato Free Press* described it. A city tractor twice had been stuck on the course, and three greens had been flooded out.

By 1944, Memorial Golf Course had by all indications gone, well, down the drain. In its place today are Mankato West High School athletic fields, Stoltzman Park and a large, unoccupied area south and southwest of the park.

CHAPTER 25

Fearsome Foursome

COURSE: MAPLE GROVE GOLF ACRES
CITY: HERMANTOWN
COUNTY: ST. LOUIS
YEARS: 1972-81, 1984

J IM WOLLACK'S GOLF COURSE IS GONE. HECK, JIM IS, TOO. BUT HIS GIRLS DID BOTH OF THEM PROUD.

Wollack's four daughters kept plenty occupied in the late 1970s and early '80s at their dad's little complex, if that is not an oxymoron, in the Duluth suburb of Hermantown.

Kim, go fire up the deep fryer. Michelle, go cut the greens. Christina, go pick up the range balls. Tricia, go rake the traps.

The Wollack girls did all of those things, and more, at Ye Olde Sawmill restaurant and Maple Grove Golf Acres, Jim Wollack's par-3 golf course, driving range and miniature golf course.

All four Wollack girls worked for Dad at one time or another. During the 1984 golf season, all four were in their father's employ. Kim, the oldest, was 17. Tricia, the youngest, was 12. (Wollack's son, J.W., was a mite on the young side to operate machinery, heavy or otherwise. He was 2.)

"We'd get up in the morning, work for a while, go rake sand traps ... get golf balls out of the pond, so many different things I can remember that we did," said Michelle. "We learned how to run the cash registers, to greet people — customer service."

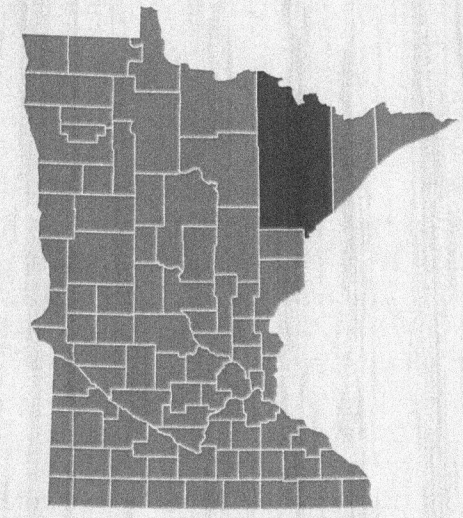

Ah, but the Wollack girls did more than work. They could play, too.

In the early 1980s, as girls golf was emerging as a Minnesota high school sport, Kim, Michelle, Christina and Tricia Wollack made Hermantown High School a perennial state-tournament entrant. All four were accomplished players. Michelle finished second in the 1984 state high school tournament; Christina went on to play for the University of Minnesota, where she was an academic All-Big Ten selection in 1994; and Tricia also played college golf.

Fore! Gone.

The Wollack sisters, Kim (top) and (left to right), Christina, Tricia and Michelle, in 1984 at the Maple Grove Acres par-3 course owned by their father, Jim.

DULUTH NEWS TRIBUNE *PHOTO*

Christina honed her skills on a hole in back of the Wollacks' home at Maple Grove Golf Acres. "I would just go out and hit ball after ball, and I'd try to hit the green," she said. "Eventually, I did."

Michelle got better in part by playing No. 7, which she called the best hole on the course. "You had to go cross a creek that ran on both sides, and the green was just over the water's edge," she said.

Maple Grove Golf Acres was at the corner of Maple Grove and Haines roads in Hermantown, at the city's border with Duluth. The par-3 course opened in 1972. Jim Wollack originally intended to operate a bar as part of the golf course, said his widow, Pat Wollack, "but he bought the Haines Road Building Center because the golf balls were going over into that area."

The building became a restaurant — Ye Olde Sawmill, where Kim was a waitress and cook. The other girls worked mostly at the golf course. Christina remembered customers being amused by the sight of young girls making change at the cash register, mowing the greens and riding fairway mowers. She also remembered "how nice and well kept it was. My dad treated it like another child."

Maple Grove Golf Acres was, in fact, a four-season business. "I remember in the winter we had a golf tournament in the snow; we would clear paths," said Michelle, who also noted that Christmas trees were sold on the grounds.

Jim Wollack shut down his par-3 course, driving range and miniature course in 1981 over a long-running dispute with the city of Hermantown over sewer lines and property tax assessments. He reopened the golf business in 1984 but put it up for sale later that year.

Today, the grounds is mostly a Sam's Club, with other businesses also in place. But Jim Wollack's golf complex hadn't closed without his girls acquiring a notable work ethic — or maybe it was a work/play ethic.

"At our golf course it was really fun, because without my dad having us do all that stuff, we wouldn't be the workers that we are today," said Michelle Wollack Tessier, who still lives in Hermantown and is a secretary at the University of Minnesota-Duluth. "In families that have businesses, I can see a difference in how they work. They have pride, and they want to get things done right."

CHAPTER 26

The Old College Try

ST. JOHN'S GOLF COURSE
CITY: COLLEGEVILLE
COUNTY: STEARNS
YEARS: CIRCA 1926-33

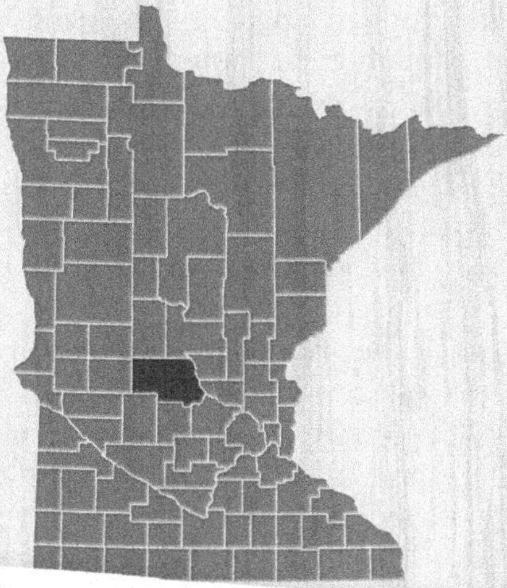

Golf on the St. John's campus.
COURTESY OF COLLEGE OF ST. BENEDICT/ ST. JOHN'S UNIVERSITY

Fore! Gone.

OHIO STATE UNIVERSITY HAS ITS SCARLET COURSE. JACK NICKLAUS PLAYED THERE AS A BUCKEYE BEFORE GOING ON TO WIN 18 MAJOR CHAMPIONSHIPS.

The University of Minnesota has its Les Bolstad Course. Tom Lehman played there as a Gopher before going on to win a British Open.

And St. John's University had its … well, we don't know that its golf course ever had a proper name, and we highly doubt, even though the Johnnies have had accomplished golfers past and present, that anyone who ever played it ever rose to the stature of a Nicklaus or Lehman.

But give the Johnnies the credit for the old college try.

The recorded history of golf in Collegeville, Minn., home of St. John's University, begins with an entry in the April 2, 1925, issue of *The Record*, the school newspaper.

"Golf is also being taken up by some," the newspaper reported. "The little white pellets may often be seen flying around the lower campus pursued by enthusiasts of the great old game. Who knows but that St. John's may put in a golf course in the near future?"

A month later, *The Record* felt further emboldened to push for a campus course.

"Near the thriving village of Flynnville and close to the shores of the lowly Watab," the newspaper reported on May 7, "stretches a verdant pasture surrounded by many trees. Just one small corner of this spacious expanse of terra firma would serve as one of Minnesota's most scenic golf courses."

The Watab also is known as Stumpf Lake, at the western edge of the St. John's campus.

By April 1926, golf was being played on campus, according to Dunstan Tucker and Martin Schirber, Benedictine monks and St. John's professors who in the late 1970s compiled *Scoreboard: A History of Athletics at Saint John's University*.

"The site of the new course was the area north of the lower campus," Tucker and Schirber wrote. "Every afternoon, a cavalcade of students with caddies, bags and camp followers wend their way to the hills. The present course is in an ideal location and with some improvements can easily be the best desired."

The presumed improvements came on the heels of an October 1926 visit by Archie Houle, assistant professional at the White Bear Yacht Club and brother of St. John's football coach Bill Houle. *The Record* reported that Houle "laid out a golf course for St. John's last Tuesday."

An aside about Houle: *The Record* also reported that it was the fifth course he laid out that season, an assertion that seems debatable. His name cannot readily be found in any other reference to golf course design. If he was involved in other projects, it's reasonable to think it might have been as an assistant to his boss at White Bear Yacht Club, Tom Vardon, the club pro who designed more than 40 courses in the Upper Midwest.

In any event, judging by the brief course description in *The Record*, Houle was a practitioner of penal golf course design. "The first, second, third, fourth, and ninth holes all have water hazards 'twixt tee and green' and placed where they can do the most harm to the unwary golfer," *The Record* reported.

A Sept. 22, 1927, *Record* story indicated an oddity — the likelihood that the Collegeville course originally was constructed with grass greens and then converted to the sand variety. "The sod has been cut away for new sand greens which will replace the old grass greens," the newspaper reported.

Tucker and Schirber's compilation indicated that golf was first played as a varsity sport at St. John's in 1928, but they noted that records from that era were sketchy. "The impression," they wrote, "is that the Golf Club was a smooth working organization, with golfers competing against one another rather than seeking opponents outside the St. John's circle."

As was the case at so many courses built during the prosperous 1920s, the organizers and practitioners of golf at St. John's hardly could have anticipated their course would have a short shelf life.

The section of the Tucker-Schirber compilation that covers St. John's golf from 1931-33 speaks to the golf course's demise:

"Around 1931 the Great Depression began to make its effects felt in all colleges in some way or another. At St. John's its effects were especially experienced in a decline of interest in golf. Moreover, drawbacks to the St. John's golf course became more apparent as the golfers became better acquainted with the new courses that were springing up in the smaller towns throughout the state.

"George Durenberger (former St. John's athletic director) has vividly described the drawbacks: the first was the fact that the course had been superimposed on the St. John's cow pasture. When the herd began to be increased in size in the early '30s, a handicap that at first was little more than a bothersome hazard suddenly became a major problem. Big George describes the situation:

"One of our first major problems was that the cows somehow developed a liking for standing on the greens; cow droppings, plus hoof marks, made putting somewhat difficult. Someone came up with the idea of installing fence posts around the greens with a single strand of barbed wire. This kept the cows off the greens, but it still posed a new problem for the golfers approaching the green. Special ground rules had to be worked out.

"Another problem was the vast accumulation of leaves from the nearby hardwood trees, especially in spring and fall. As someone said at the time, 'A golfer spent one hour golfing and two hours looking for the ball among the leaves.'

"A third problem, a serious one, was the close proximity of the fairways to one another. On several of them a slice or hook could easily cross an adjoining fairway, thus providing a dangerous physical hazard. Not a few players had been struck with golf balls over a season. Finally, when the Depression had touched bottom in 1933 and student interest in golf had reached a deep low, the administration decided to abandon the course as a safety measure."

The closure of the golf course perhaps factored into a last-place finish by the Johnnies in the 1934 conference tournament. In the ensuing two decades, St. John's either did not field golf teams or met with modest success at best.

In 1955, an attempt was made to regenerate a campus golf course. The site, it was reported in *Scoreboard*, was the picnic area across the Watab. Durenberger and Tucker were principals in the revival effort, as reported in *Scoreboard*: "For the past three months small crews of frustrated lumberjacks, faculty, collegians and a smattering of preps have been seen carrying axes, saws and other paraphernalia to the pasture area west of the Watab."

Durenberger was then quoted:

"Work progressed slowly but surely. The workmen brought along their chain saws and opened up a fairway through the woods, though much of the area was clear. My son David (who later became a U.S. senator) remembers the Durenberger family out on the course evenings picking up stones, brush, etc.

"Then came the letters. One said that God had been good to St. John's for ninety-nine years and we must not do anything to offend him. Another wrote that golf was a game only for the wealthy people, so we would be doing our students an injustice, since most of them are poor, by creating an interest and skills for a game economically beyond their means. Another objected to the picnic area: 'If we permit this to happen, the grounds will be surrounded by women in short skirts.'

"Some of this rubbed off on Abbot Baldwin, as I was instructed to stop the work on the course for the sake of peace, and we did."

Father Wilfred Theisen, a professor emeritus in physics who spent 47 years teaching at St. John's, also participated in the revival effort and recounted the story much as Durenberger did. "The abbot found out about the course and made us quit," Theisen said in a 2012 telephone interview. "We cut down a few trees, and that was about it."

More details on the St. John's golf course can be found in *Scoreboard: A History of Athletics at Saint John's University*, by Dunstan Tucker and Martin Schirber (viewable in full on the Internet).

THE ST. JOHN'S GOLF TEAM WAS AFFORDED ACCESS TO St. Cloud Country Club in 1959. The Johnnies didn't win their first Minnesota Intercollegiate golf championship until 1968, and not again until 1999. But they have won 10 MIAC titles since 1999 and won NCAA Division III national championships under coach Bob Alpers in 2007 and 2008.

CHAPTER 27

Uphill Climb

HILLSIDE GOLF COURSE
CITY: ST. CLOUD
COUNTY: STEARNS
YEARS: 1930-45

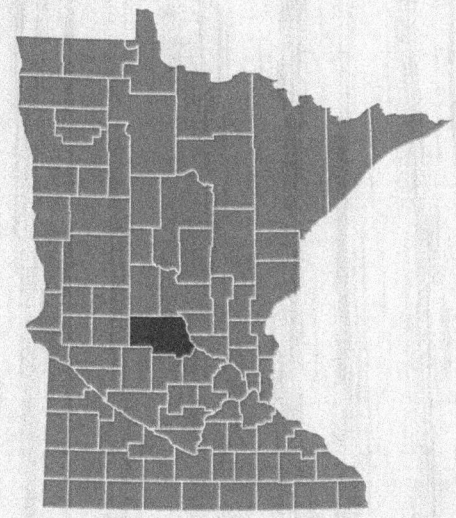

GOOD IDEA. BAD TIMING.

When Mayor J.H. Murphy and Commissioner John Zeirten on the morning of Jan. 14, 1930, cast the deciding votes to approve the construction of a municipal golf course in St. Cloud, they could not have known their city and their nation was in the infancy of an economic depression that would last 10 years, and that a war lasting another five would follow, both events conspiring to abduct cash-paying golfers from cash-requiring golf courses.

In their defense, Hillside Golf Course had a run that lasted a decade and a half. But, as with so many lost courses, the 1930s and early 1940s were too heavy a cross to bear.

St. Cloud in the 1920s was, relatively speaking, golf-poor. Golfers with sufficient means could join St. Cloud Country Club, established in 1919, but there was no municipal course available for play in a city with 15,873 residents at the start of the decade and 21,000 at its close.

As 1930 opened, however, the votes of Murphy and Zeirten carried a motion to lease 87 acres and build a municipal course in the southern part of the city. An adjacent 23 acres of city-owned land would provide enough space for an 18-hole course, if warranted.

"The property," the *St. Cloud Times* reported on Jan. 14, 1930, "is a portion of the Atwood farm, lying just west and adjoining the Great Northern Osseo line, and lying to the south of and adjoining the cemetery road."

The plot that would become Hillside Golf Course was on the south side of St. Cloud, a mile west of the Mississippi River.

The *Times* stated the case for construction of the course, reporting the city planned to build a large reservoir on Calvary Hill, immediately northwest of

Fore! Gone.

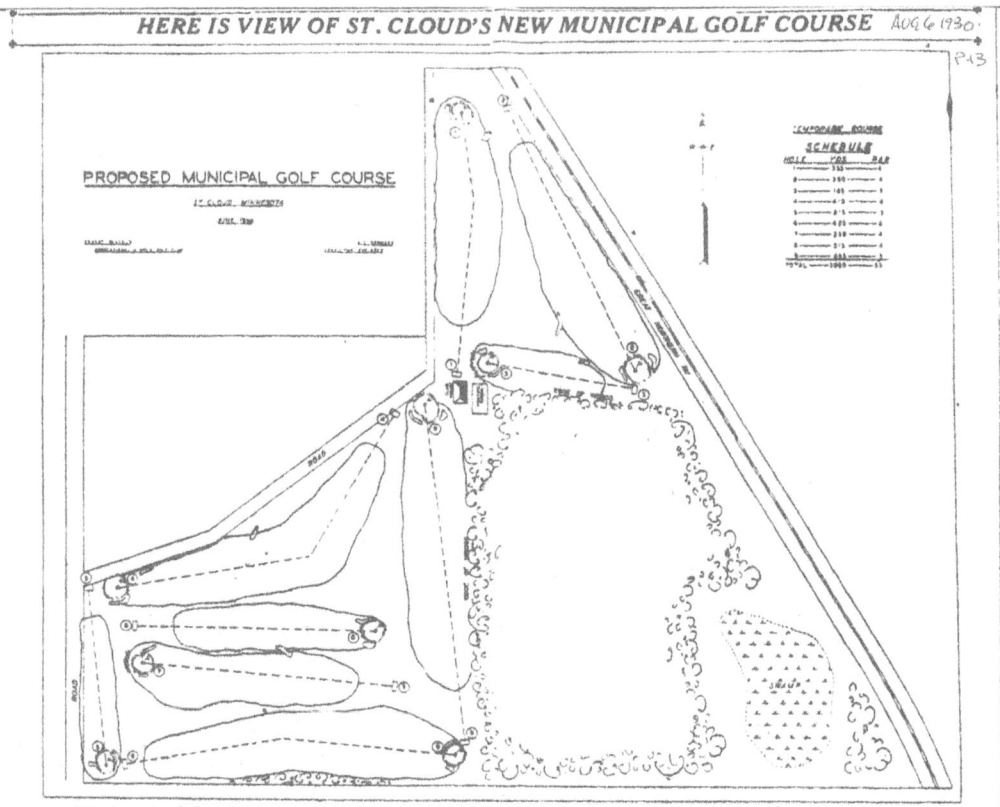

Layout of Hillside Golf Course in St. Cloud, from the St. Cloud Times *of Aug. 6, 1930. Caption below diagram read: "The first nine holes of the proposed 18 hole municipal golf course here were completed recently and the course is now open to the public. A club house has been erected where clubs may be rented. A driving green has been opened just across the road from the club house where instruction is given by Dick Strobel, former Central Minnesota champion."*

COURTESY OF STEARNS HISTORY MUSEUM

the golf course, that could be used for irrigation. The newspaper also reported that the city had received favorable reports on the viability of other municipal courses in Minnesota, including those in Winona and Duluth.

A large *Times* advertisement touted the nine-hole course's opening on July 26, 1930. Opening-day golf privileges were free of charge, and a season pass could be had for $5. Two days later, the newspaper reported that 400 golfers turned out for the first two days of play at Hillside. Larry Rieder displayed his proficiency with a 1-under-par 33.

On Aug. 6, 1930, the *Times* published a map of Hillside Golf Course. The clubhouse was at the intersection of what is now Traverse and Woodhill roads. The first hole ran north along

Washington Memorial Drive, the second south along Roosevelt Road. The par-3 third returned to the clubhouse, and the remaining six holes were south of Traverse Road, east of Cooper Avenue and north of 22nd Street. (An excellent look at the golf course grounds in 1938 can be seen by going to the Minnesota Department of Natural Resources Landview map web service.)

By 1931, the golf course had expanded. "... a fine sod has developed," the *Times* reported. "It is entirely a finished course, comprising 12 holes, and the persons playing there are having their fun."

The next documentation of Hillside available from the Stearns History Museum doesn't come until 1936 and implies that the course had changed ownership or management. "The Allen Atwood course is operated privately," read an entry published in 1936 by the Greater St. Cloud Committee of the Chamber of Commerce and Federal Writers Project. The course's location as described in the entry matches that of Hillside.

Allen A. Atwood is a notable name in St. Cloud history. He was a Kiwanis Club president and is the namesake of St. Cloud State University's Atwood Memorial Center, having been an early advocate for a student center on the campus.

In 1937, the course again underwent change. "New Hillside Golf Course to Be Completed Soon at Cost of $12,000," read a banner headline on Page 14 of the July 16, 1937, *St. Cloud Times*. Ownership of the course was only implied in the story, which said the course "will be run as a public institution and the management has promised rates comparable with municipal courses in the state."

Most notably, the 1937 changes included a redesign of the course, under the direction of Hugh Vincent Feehan, "prominent landscape architect and golf course builder from Minneapolis." Feehan designed Virginia Municipal Golf Course in northeastern Minnesota and Gall's (now Manitou Ridge) in White Bear Lake. The *Times* story also credited him with designing Detroit Country Club in Detroit Lakes — the architect of that course's original layout is not mentioned on the club's website — and "the Rochester Country club." The latter reference is perplexing at best; Harry Turpie did the original Rochester Golf & Country Club design in 1915, and the famed A.W. Tillinghast presided over a makeover in the mid-1920s.

Feehan was a notable landscape architect, though. His work includes O'Shaughnessy Stadium and Athletic Field at the College of St. Thomas in St. Paul, 1908-11, and a 1933 design of a master plan for the International Peace Garden near Dunseith, N.D., at the geographic center of North America.

At Hillside, Feehan's redesign featured six all-new holes and rerouting on the remaining three. "Although the layout was designed for the average golfer," the Times reported, "the typography (sic) of the course is such that it will test the ability of the best players with its shots over a lake, rolling fairways and countless sand traps."

Feehan appeared to have a thing for sand. The 1939 aerial photo does indeed show signs of close to a dozen bunkers.

A name from Hillside's earliest days re-emerged in the Times coverage. An ad in the June 29, 1938, edition touted the completion of the new course and clubhouse, with watered bluegrass fairways and bentgrass greens, and noted that Larry Rieder — the man who shot the 33 on opening weekend — was the Hillside golf professional and manager.

"Increased interest in golf is foreseen in St. Cloud," the 1937 *Times* article stated, but Hillside did not last for a decade after that. There is no specific mention of its passing in the Stearns History Museum files, but there is no listing for Hillside Golf Course in the 1946 St. Cloud telephone directory, after listings were included in the 1944 and '45 directories.

Much information about Hillside Golf Course was obtained from the vertical files at the Stearns History Museum in St. Cloud.

THE 1930 REFERENCE TO "CEMETERY ROAD" IN RELATION to the Hillside Golf Course site is made because two cemeteries are nearby. North Star Cemetery is immediately west of the golf course grounds, and Calvary Cemetery is immediately south.

CHAPTER 28
Road Trip

NOPEMING PRIVATE GOLF COURSE
CHIPPEWA NATIONAL FOREST
COUNTY: ITASCA
YEARS: CIRCA 1925–72

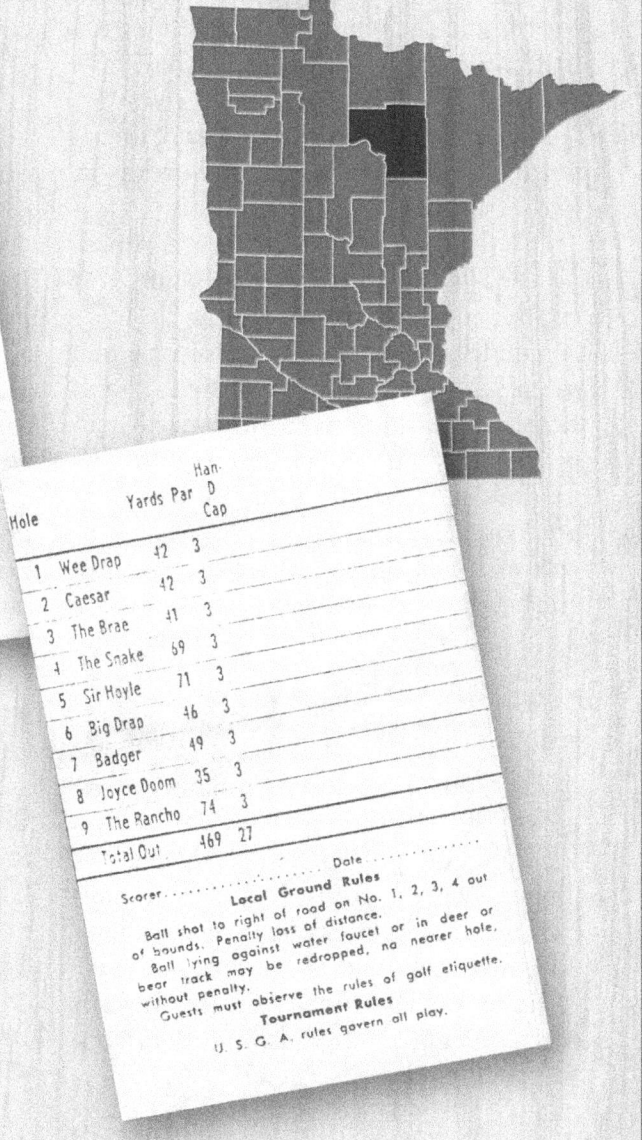

Fore! Gone.

The voicemail message is replayed, and it's all the convincing I need: "My name is Bill Yourd; I work for the Chippewa National Forest. You had left a message inquiring about the golf course at the Joyce Estate, and I do have a little bit of information about that, but not much.

"Apparently there was a nine-hole pitch-and-putt golf course at the Joyce Estate, constructed probably in the '20s, '20s to '30s, and it's since been grown over and looks kind of like an opening in the woods, but if you want a little more information than that, give me a call."

No need, Bill. I heard you say "opening in the woods," and that clinches it. Road trip.

Fill the gas tank. Point the compass north. I will play the Joyce Estate golf course, come hell or high grass.

The folks at the national forest email me a scan of an old scorecard, and it reveals something even more road-trip promising: The Joyce Estate is Minnesota's shortest and most unusual lost golf course.

The totals on the old scorecard are correct:

- Nine holes.
- Par 27.
- 469 yards.

Yes, 469. There is no missing digit before the "4."

Modern-day courses have par 4s longer than the entire Joyce Estate layout. You can't even break a sweat walking 469 yards, can you?

Holes on the old Joyce Estate golf course averaged 52 yards. In order, from first to last: 42 yards, then 42, 41, 69, 71, 46, 49, 35 and ... drum roll for the beastly closing test ... 74.

With yardages like that, and considering I haven't broken 40 for nine holes since disco died, I *need* to play this course.

Yep, road trip.

I must confess; this idea is a ripoff — a low-budget ripoff of my favorite golf book: *Around the World in Eighteen Holes*, by Tom Callahan and Dave Kindred, two sportswriters who in the early 1990s embarked on a four-continent, 21-nation odyssey in which they wrote about playing real, live golf courses in places like Iceland and Nepal and dealing with real, live hazards like crocodiles and, literally, sacred cows.

Anything Callahan and Kindred can do, I can do ... well, not half as well. Still, I'm undaunted. I'm headed north, anticipating my primary hazards at the Joyce Estate will be less imposing than Callahan and Kindred's. Best guess: knee-high fescue, knee-high mosquitoes and no cart girls.

My destination is the western shore of Trout Lake, 20 miles north of Grand Rapids, near the southern border of the Chippewa National Forest. (Marcell, 15 miles to the northwest, is the town closest to the Joyce Estate.)

The Joyce Estate was established in 1917 by David Gates Joyce of Chicago, whose family fortune was derived in part from lumber taken from northern Minnesota via the Itasca Lumber Company. The Joyces carved a leviathan estate out of the northwoods: 4,500 acres on 11 lakes, 26 miles of shoreline, 40 buildings, private telephone line, tennis court and airplane hangar.

Construction on the estate continued through 1932. The main portion of the complex, on a peninsula on Trout Lake, featured Adirondack-style log work. The primary grounds included a Main Lodge, two main sleeping cabins, bath house, playhouse, root cellar, pump house, gun house, laundry, barbecue pit and ice house. The "Cabins on the Hill" housed the butler, maid, seaplane pilot and the Joyces' daughter, C.B. Inland was a greenhouse. The recreation area featured a tennis court, trap house and the ever-so-humble nine-hole golf course, complete with clubhouse and pumphouse. The course is said to have been built in about 1925.

The Joyces named their estate "Nopeming," which in Ojibwe means "place of rest." In other words, if you weren't busy at the Joyces' place working on your backhand, brushing up on your short game, oiling the guns, watering the plants, grilling some dogs, burying tongs into a block of ice or unloading the seaplane, you could get some R&R.

The Joyces worked, played and rested at Nopeming for 5½ decades. After Beatrice Joyce Kean, once rumored to be the third-wealthiest woman in the world, died in 1972, the Nature Conservancy bought the Joyce Estate for $2 million in 1973. Ownership was transferred to the U.S. Forest Service in 1974, with the mission of preserving the estate as a refuge and historical site.

At the entrance to the Joyce Estate.
JOE BISSEN PHOTOS

There is no readily available evidence that the golf course was ever played after 1972.

Until now.

The trip I am about to make, from the northern Twin Cities suburbs, will cover 222 miles. The first 219, courtesy of Buick and Minnesota Department of Transportation asphalt, turn out to be a breeze. The last three, after entering the Chippewa National Forest and

The one remaining green site at the Nopeming Golf Course, Joyce Estate.
JOE BISSEN PHOTO

parking at the trailhead to the Joyce Estate, will consist of a healthy walk through the woods, three miles in and three miles out.

Feet, don't fail me now. Here we go.

Not 150 yards onto the trail, I gingerly step around the largest pile of animal feces I have ever seen. It is, I must say, the Grand Teton of turds. This backwoods jewel was deposited either by a bear, a moose or Sasquatch from the Jack Link's commercials.

I am undeterred, more or less. The rest of the walk is uneventful and in fact serene, featuring an occasional glimpse of lakes plus encounters with only three other human beings: a couple from Kenyon, Minn., who had the foresight to navigate the trail via bicycle and a local man, recently retired, who oddly enough doesn't think I'm batty when I tell him I want to re-create a round of golf on the Joyce Estate course.

At the end of the hike in, there is a clearing, and the main grounds beckons. The setting is spectacular, with Trout Lake on three sides and a forested hillside as backdrop. It's easy to see why David Joyce set up 4,500 acres' worth of camp here. About one-third of the original structures are still standing, including the Main Lodge.

The golf course is around a bend, about a quarter-mile back, actually, northwest of the main grounds. It's inaccessible, at least in 2012, via the shoreline or through a hoped-for "shortcut" through the woods. That brilliant idea produces only a dead end and a slightly twisted ankle. A retreat back to the main trail leads to another opening in the woods, and there it is:

Nopeming Private Golf Course.

Well, what's left of it.

What's left is one green, inappropriately named, considering it is yellow-brown at the end of a dry Minnesota summer. But it is absolutely, positively

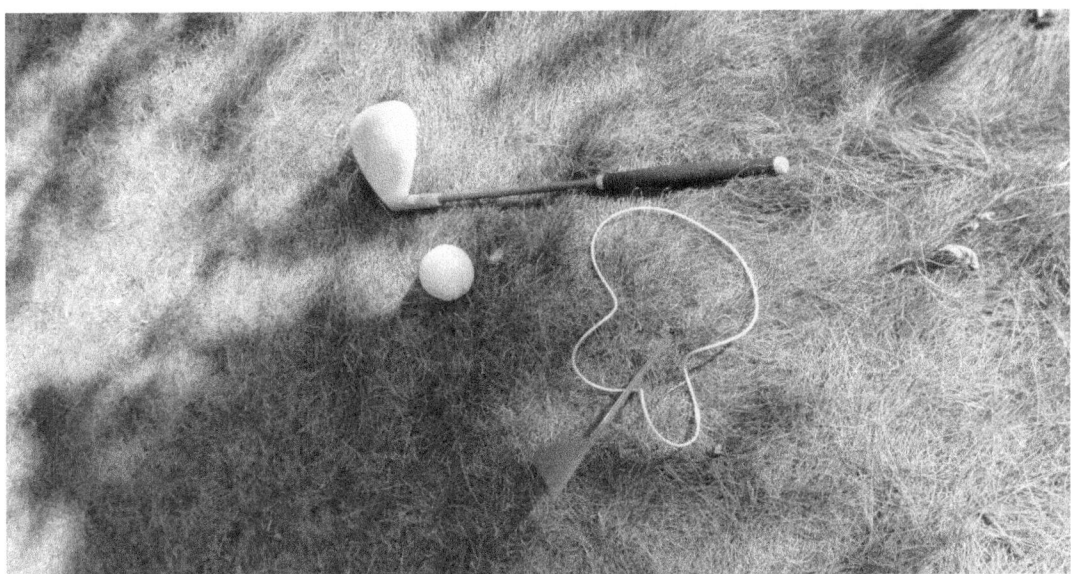

Majik Big Golf — the author's weapons of destruction in the re-creation of the Joyce Estate golf course.
JOE BISSEN PHOTO

an old golf green — the most unmistakable lost-golf-course feature I have seen in my first 2½ months of exploring old sites. Built in the classic style of the early 20th century, the green is round, about 60 feet in diameter, resting on a small shelf, sloped back to front, with an "entryway" guarded by what was a small pot bunker on the left and what might have been a larger bunker or a very small water hazard on the right.

The rest of the course? Lost. Gone, and surely forgotten. Everything is overgrown with sumac, underbrush and trees. A 20-minute walk reveals five other carved pieces of land that surely were green sites or tee boxes. But, to my chagrin, there is no way to reconstruct all nine holes of the Nopeming Private Golf Course, and, it would seem, no way to re-create a round of golf.

But — ha! — I have anticipated this, based on Yourd's "kind of like an opening in the woods" comment. I have purchased new golf equipment, just for this rough-and-tumble occasion.

Nopeming Private, meet Majik Big Golf.

"Supersized Two Player Golf Action!" it says on the box. "Manufactured by EastPoint Sports." Contents: two supersized golf clubs with handles that extend to 30.25 inches; two inflatable, vinyl golf balls, 3.5 inches in diameter; two target rings, two target flags and two super sized golf tees.

Yes, it's a kiddie golf set. For ages 6 and up.

Ask me if I care.

Perhaps by luck, perhaps by planning, this golf set is perfect for the 2012 incarnation of Nopeming Private. The balls will sit up in the long grass and are playable from just about anywhere. The only problems are that the target rings won't take a proper circular "golf hole" shape, and the flags can't be planted in the rock-hard ground. (Can't figure out

Postcard image showing the clubhouse for The Nopeming Private Golf Course on the Joyce Estate. The clubhouse was built around 1925 but no longer exists.

why the Forest Service staff hasn't aerated lately. You should do it at least once a year, you know.)

Tee time has arrived. Given the fact that only one green is playable, my only choice is to play to it nine times from different starting points. Call it Nopeming: The Redesign. USGA Rules of Golf apply, except when I say they don't. For instance, any shot that so much as touches the target ring shall be deemed to have been holed out.

No. 1: A reasonably easy opening hole seems in order: 19 yards, no hazards, hole location in back of green. I visualize my shot, wind up … and, with a hollow, resonant thud, the kind you get when you nail one of those giant plastic baseballs with one of those giant plastic bats, I hit it stiff. Two feet from the flag. Easy birdie. I might be 1,653 miles from PGA Tour headquarters, but I can sense my Champions Tour player's card at this moment being prepared.

No. 2: Emboldened, I design a more challenging test — beneath the branches of a large pine tree and over a picnic bench, with a second picnic bench a potential hazard on the right. 27 yards. … Tee ball hits leg of picnic bench. Second shot hits leg of other picnic bench and rolls behind me. After three shots into the front and side bunkers, I make an 8. I might be 1,653 miles from PGA Tour headquarters, but I can sense the folks who were preparing my card now erasing furiously.

No. 3: Tee shot over former pot bunker. … After two shots, I'm within five feet of the target ring. But my putt, headed straight and true, is stopped by a stick-like weed growing on my intended line. Bogey 4.

No. 4: At this point, I remember that the Joyces, on the old scorecard, have named all of the holes. Nos. 1 through 3 were Wee Drap, Caesar and Brae. No. 4 was The Snake. I decide to try to make the rest of my holes match the character of the Joyce names, so I plot a 54-yard route along a winding path. A healthy swing is required to clear a sumac patch. … Club breaks in downswing; ball goes nowhere. I will play a mulligan. (Hey, my course, my rules.) Well-struck mulligan clears sumac but still is unplayable, leading to double-bogey 5.

No. 5: Sir Hoyle on the original design. No amount of creative thinking can re-create that. Redesigned hole is 28 yards, teeing off from a sandbar. It's an almost impossible shot that must clear the elevated back of the green. … With original club retired, replacement club strikes a shot to the front of the green, then on. And the damn stick-weed gets in the way of the putt again. Bogey 4.

No. 6: Big Drap ("drap" is Scottish for "drop." Note to Tiger Woods, re: 2013 Masters: Guess what "illegal drap" means in English?). Considering the green is the highest point within 100 yards in any direction, there's no way to replicate a "big drap." I find the only higher spot — the base of a pine tree in back of the green, nine yards from the target ring. … It's a gimme hole. Birdie 2.

No. 7: Badger. All I can think of is to find the spot closest to Wisconsin and hit from there. … Teeing off from the shore of Trout Lake, with one foot in the wet sand, I make a bogey 4.

No. 8: Joyce Doom. Surmising with absolutely no basis in fact that the Joyces were mortified by the pot bunker to the left of the green, I design a 24-yard hole with a tee shot that must clear the bunker. … I execute a remarkable strike that lands on the green. In the process, the backing on my replacement club — thunk! — snaps off. Still, feeling refortified, I line up the birdie attempt … and get the yips, three-putting for a bogey 4.

No. 9: The Rancho. At 74 yards, this was the longest hole on the real Joyce Estate course. I settle on the longest navigable route possible — 58 yards, from the edge of the woods and cutting through a narrow, sumac-lined trail. Third shot bounces off a fire pit, leading to a triple-bogey 6.

Still, my final score is, in my eyes, a beauty: 39.

I gather my golf set — I don't think the national forest folks want their trashcan littered with it — and begin my three-mile walk back toward civilization. Assuming I don't meet Sasquatch en route, it's been a wonderful road trip. Thank you, David Gates Joyce.

THE CHIPPEWA NATIONAL FOREST WAS ESTABLISHED IN 1902. It covers 666,623 acres in the northern Minnesota counties of Cass, Itasca and Beltrami and contains more than 1,300 lakes.

CHAPTER 29
Minneapolis Mystery

BRYN MAWR GOLF CLUB
CITY: MINNEAPOLIS
COUNTY: HENNEPIN
YEARS: 1898–1910

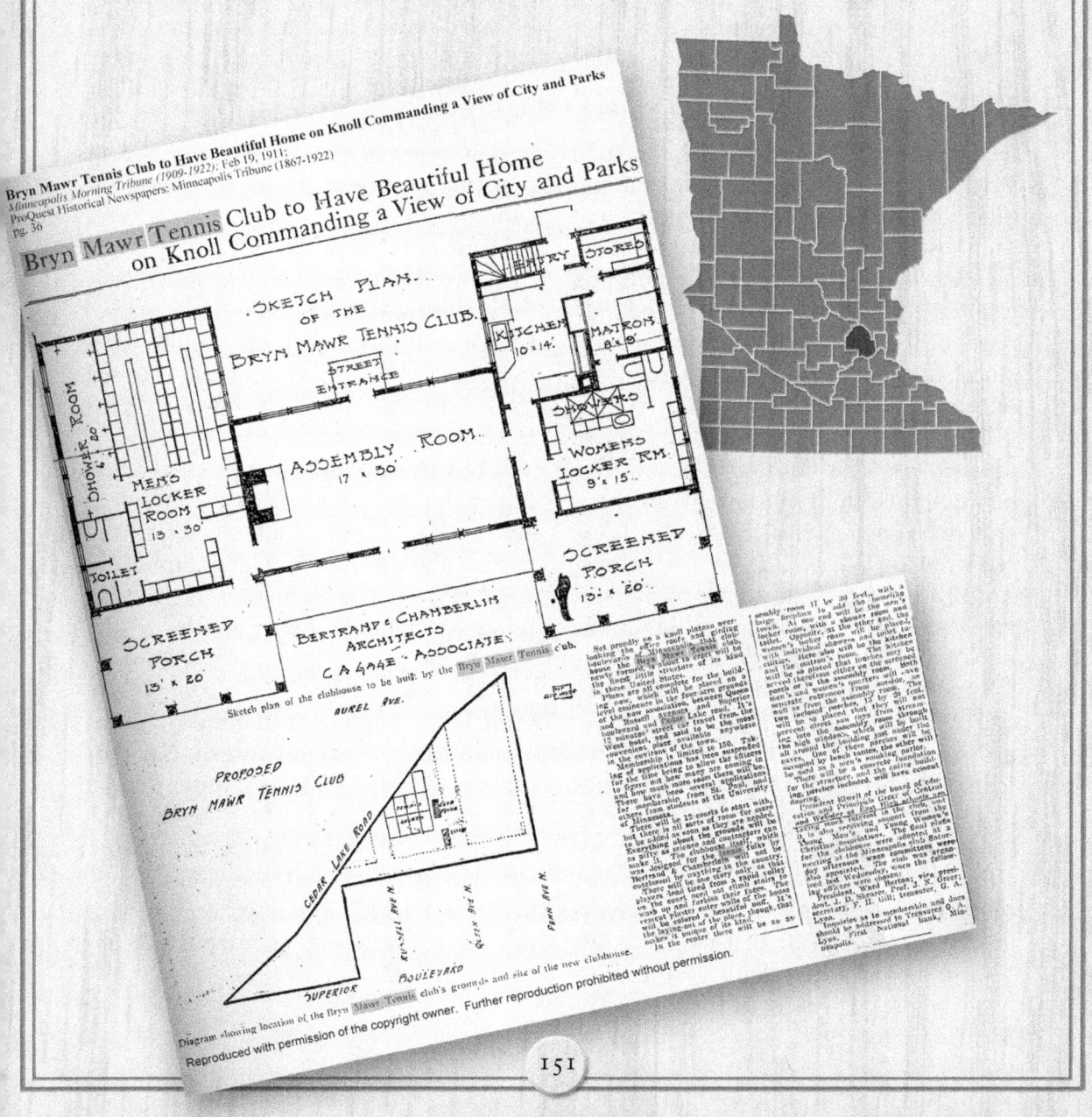

Fore! Gone.

T**he haystack is the city of Minneapolis. The needle is Bryn Mawr Golf Club. The mission is to locate the needle.**

Just to be clear, the mission is not to *describe* the needle. It is to *locate* it.

Where, exactly, was Bryn Mawr Golf Club? This is the grassy-knoll mystery to top all mysteries among Minnesota's lost golf courses.

Get out your Minneapolis map.

Much of Bryn Mawr's history is public record. It was Minneapolis' first golf club, originally formed as the Minneapolis Golf Club in 1897 but renamed Bryn Mawr Golf Club the next year and officially established during a meeting at the West Hotel. "Twenty or more of the men who are enthusiastic over golf and want links near at hand met for the purpose of forming a Minneapolis golf club," the *Minneapolis Tribune* reported on April 23, 1898.

The private, nine-hole golf course opened less than a month later. "The new golf links in Bryn Mawr, Minneapolis, will be open today," the *St. Paul Globe* reported on May 7, 1898. "A professional has been secured in readiness to give lessons and supply everything in the way of clubs, balls and implements. The 200 membership limit has been attained, and the club begins with flourishing prospects."

In 13 years and two incarnations, Bryn Mawr's membership rolls featured some of Minneapolis' most prominent citizens, its grounds witnessed play by the some of the most skilled players in Minnesota golf history, and its demise — make that demises, plural — gave birth to two nearby country-club courses, Minikahda and Interlachen, that are among the most estimable in the state.

No attempt will be made on these pages to reconstruct the definitive history of Bryn Mawr GC. That has been done, in the form of a two-part blog entry posted in 2010 by Minneapolis author and city parks historian David C. Smith. It is a thorough, engaging recounting that can be viewed at minneapolisparkhistory.com.

Smith, to this point, has come closer than anyone to identifying the exact location of the old Bryn Mawr golf course. Other attempts have been roughly akin to trying to hit a bull's eye on a dart board from 50 yards. Into a headwind. With foam darts.

A history of Interlachen Country Club reports that the Bryn Mawr club was in "north Minneapolis." That's technically true, but just barely, and, geographically speaking, imprecise. Sort of like identifying Missouri as being in the Milky Way Galaxy.

Some have speculated Bryn Mawr Golf Club was in the Parade Stadium area, near the southwestern edge of downtown Minneapolis. Nope; missed by a mile (literally, not figuratively).

Some believe the course was in the current Bryn Mawr Meadows Park. Getting warmer. But the best guess is that the course was never part of the current Meadows.

Minneapolis Mystery

Just above Penn Avenue and a hedge trimmed to read "Bryn Mawr" west of downtown Minneapolis, the grounds of the former Bryn Mawr Golf Club sweep down a hill, affording a partial view of the downtown skyline.

PETER WONG PHOTO

To be more precise, and to do it in terms that make the most modern-day sense, try this: Imagine you're driving on Interstate 394, just west of downtown Minneapolis, and you take the Penn Avenue exit. Go north a block or two, not quite to Penn Avenue's intersection with Cedar Lake Road.

Look to your left. That's the old Bryn Mawr course.

Look to your right. Yep, that's it, too.

There are, admittedly, no guarantees of this. Hours of research revealed no specific, incontrovertible evidence of the *exact* location of the Bryn Mawr course. But a series of clues present a strong case:

- The name itself. Obviously, Bryn Mawr Golf Club was in Minneapolis' Bryn Mawr neighborhood (stop saying "duh"), near the western edge of the city, about three miles west of downtown. In Welsh, Bryn Mawr means "big hill." And a big hill rises from east to west in that neighborhood.

- Smith's blog entries, Part One. He offers this quote from the 1898 *Minneapolis Tribune* story: "The grounds proposed are in Bryn Mawr and the high land west, ideal in location and well adapted to links, with sufficient hazards to make the game interesting."

- Addresses (brace yourself; this gets complicated). The original clubhouse,

The Laurel Triangle, at Laurel and Oliver avenues and Cedar Lake Road in Minneapolis' Bryn Mawr neighborhood, likely is on the grounds of the former Bryn Mawr Golf Club, near the old first and second holes.

PETER WONG PHOTO

Smith reported, was at 95 Elm Street, a street that later was renamed Morgan Avenue North. This address, bordering Bryn Mawr Meadows Park, is south of Cedar Lake Road and north of what was then Superior Avenue, which roughly served as the corridor for U.S. Highway 12 and then Interstate 394. In the early 1900s, Superior Avenue was the north-south dividing line for Minneapolis street addresses in that part of town.

Bryn Mawr Golf Club closed up shop following the 1898 season, with much of its membership moving 2½ miles south to found The Minikahda Club, but by August 1899, Bryn Mawr had reopened, with new membership. The next year, plans were drawn up for a new, $2,000 clubhouse. A Minneapolis city directory from 1905 lists the new clubhouse address as 97 Oliver Avenue North.

That address, and the building at that address, are defined in more detail through the 1903 *Minneapolis City Atlas*. The building, shaped roughly like a Chevrolet insignia, occupied a lot across Laurel Avenue from what is now known as the Laurel Triangle (the original building no longer stands). This address is almost a quarter-mile away from Bryn Mawr Meadows.

- Smith's blog entries, Part Two. He reported that Bryn Mawr's first tee was west of the original clubhouse, the first green was on the east side of Cedar Lake Road, and the second

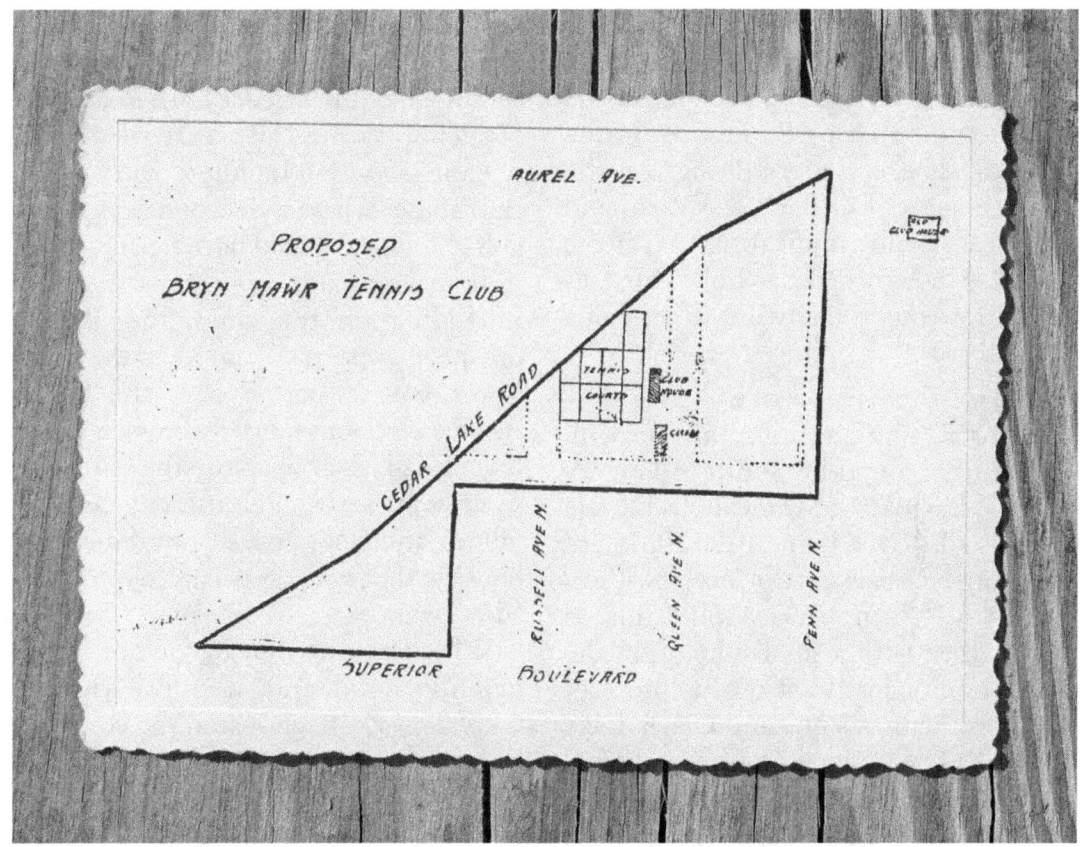

This sketched map, published in the Feb. 19, 1911, Minneapolis Tribune, offers a strong indication of the location of Bryn Mawr Golf Club.

green was across Cedar Lake Road and a small pond.

- Elevation. An April 13, 1902, *Minneapolis Tribune* story describing the neighborhood included this mention: "On the further side of the Bryn Mawr golf links is a large water tower, having a capacity of 53,000 gallons." The implication was that the tower was near the western edge of the golf course. (It would not have been the Kenwood water tower, which was larger, was on the other side of Superior Avenue and was built in 1910.)

Water towers are almost without exception placed on high points of cities or neighborhoods, and the highest point in the Bryn Mawr neighborhood is south of Cedar Lake Road, near the intersection of Russell and Mount View avenues — again, likely on or near the old golf course grounds.

- Etc.: A 1909 *Minneapolis Tribune* story reported that the Bryn Mawr golf grounds bordered on Superior Boulevard (also known as Superior Avenue).

- Development. The 1903 Minneapolis atlas, as well as city directories and *Dual City Blue Books* from the same time period, show empty land, save for one or two small buildings, in an area roughly bordered by Oliver Avenue on the east, Cedar Lake Road on the north, Upton Avenue on the west and Superior Boulevard on the south. There were buildings on the north sides of Cedar Lake Road and Laurel Avenue, indicating that if the course did cross Cedar Lake Road, as Smith wrote, it likely did so only in a small area.

- And the three pieces of evidence closest to a "smoking gun," if you will: The first, found by Smith in January 2013, is a map of Minneapolis bicycle paths, displayed in the 1900 edition of *Hudson's Dictionary of Minneapolis and Vicinity*. "Bryn Mawr Golf Club" is identified with a small square on the map, on or just west of the intersection of Penn Avenue and Cedar Lake Road. The square on the map was placed just north of Cedar Lake Road.

The other strong pieces of evidence take the form of *Minneapolis Tribune* stories from Feb. 17 and Feb. 19, 1911, the year after the final season of golf at Bryn Mawr, after the pressures of city growth pushed club members to build a new golf course 5½ miles to the southwest, in Edina, where Interlachen Country Club was established. The first story reported the organization of the Bryn Mawr Tennis Club, with plans to build 12 courts and a $5,000 clubhouse. "Option on the old Bryn Mawr Golf club grounds has been taken," the newspaper reported. Two days later, the *Tribune* revealed the tennis club's location in a story titled "Bryn Mawr Tennis Club to Have Beautiful Home on Knoll Commanding a View of City and Parks."

The story featured an architect's drawing of the tennis clubhouse, plus a map of the clubhouse and tennis club's grounds. The lion's share of the grounds occupied a triangle south of Cedar Lake Road, west of Penn Avenue and east of Russell Avenue — with a building marked "old club house" where the second Bryn Mawr golf clubhouse would have been.

To make a long, long, long story short: In adding up the clues, the likeliest prospect appears to be that the Bryn Mawr course started near the Oliver Avenue clubhouse, briefly crossed Cedar Lake Road, then swept up the hill to the southwest, across Penn Avenue, to the hilltop, and played back toward the clubhouse in the area now occupied by Mount View Avenue.

Which means that if you are in the neighborhood and stop by, say, the Cuppa Java coffeehouse at the corner of Penn Avenue and Cedar Lake Road, you most likely are on the old golf course grounds.

Cuppa Java is where I met Smith in the fall of 2012; we walked down toward the old clubhouses and came to a general agreement that Bryn Mawr Golf Club occupied that neighborhood.

Smith, in researching the club's history, was most impressed by its founders.

"What was neat about it," he said, "was that the original Bryn Mawr was created by people who created everything else in the city. They were trying to create a better city, for the most part, and were trying to have a little fun, too."

Smith named names in his "Bryn Mawr I" blog entry. "The list of the first 200-plus members," he wrote, "reads like a who's who of early Minneapolis society: Pillsbury, Peavey, Heffelfinger, Jaffray, Rand, Lowry, Bell, Dunwoody, Christian, Morrison, Koon, Loring."

Jaffray was Clive T. Jaffray, who won a Bryn Mawr club tournament in June 1899 with a score of 85. He went on to help design and construct Bryn Mawr's first successor, the Minikahda Club; won the State Amateur and Trans-Mississippi championships in 1906; and served on the United States Golf Association's executive committee. Heffelfinger was, presumably, Frank Totton Heffelfinger, president of Minneapolis grain giant F.H. Peavey & Company and the father of Hazeltine National Golf Club founder Totton P. Heffelfinger.

In 1900, Marvin Watson was hired as a part-time instructor at the reincarnated Bryn Mawr club. He was the brother of Willie Watson, who was both the Minikahda professional and a prominent golf-course architect whose designs or design contributions include Interlachen, Minikahda and dozens of top-flight courses in the western United States. Willie Watson also was said to have served as a Bryn Mawr instructor.

A 1900 newspaper story lauded Bryn Mawr for having greens "as flat as a billiard table," a description that would be considered less than flattering today.

Another noted figure was Bryn Mawr's child prodigy. "Harry G. Legg won the driving contest with the remarkable distances of 247 and 248½ yards, beating any drive that has ever been made by any of the Minneapolis golfers," the *Minneapolis Tribune* reported on June 28, 1903, in covering a competition at Bryn Mawr. "Mr. Legg is but 16 years of age, and has already evinced qualities which will surely make him one of the greatest golfers of the younger generation."

Prescient. Legg went on to win 10 State Amateur titles, five Trans-Mississippi titles, the Western Amateur in 1919 and the State Open, as an amateur, in 1925.

Speaking of heroic efforts by Bryn Mawr golfers, the *Tribune* related one in its Aug. 26, 1900, edition, in the marvelously florid newspaper writing style of the day. "Broke Up Golf Game," read the headline.

"On the road that crosses the Bryn Mawr golf course directly in front of the second hole, a number of laborers have been employed for the last few days removing the black dirt from the side of the road and carrying it away for use on lawns.

"Yesterday afternoon, while the Bryn Mawr-Minikahda match was going on, Ole Johnson, teamster, was discussing the quality of dirt with a fellow laborer whose duty it is to assist in loading Johnson's wagon.

"Johnson was sitting under the bank in the shade, and expressing himself not very favorably upon the quality of the dirt. He for one could see no reason why their employers should send them to carry away such poor stuff.

"The dirt stood these derogatory remarks until it lost patience, and then quietly slid down from its resting place and enveloped Johnson in a loving embrace.

"At least it is supposed that Johnson was under the pile, but the only visible part of him was a boot. Even this was covered with loose dirt. Seeing the predicament of his friend, the helper sent up a mighty cry for help."

The *Tribune* reported that C.S. Alberts and G.S. Shroyer (whose name was spelled "Schroyer" in the next sentence) rushed over, grabbed shovels and extricated Ole Johnson from his earthen predicament.

"… in a short time the badly frightened Johnson was breathing the pure Minnesota ozone," the story continued.

"He thanked his rescuers, and set to work loading his wagon, but it is a 10 to one bet that when he has any more mean remarks to make about the dirt along that road he will secure a strategic position in some friendly tree."

NOT ALL OF BRYN MAWR GOLF CLUB HAS DISAPPEARED. Property records at the Minneapolis Public Library relate the history of the 24-foot by 45-foot "second" clubhouse at the former 97 Oliver Avenue North address (now 412 Oliver Avenue South). In 1910, the clubhouse was moved to 103 Penn Avenue North (now 248 Penn Avenue South). In 1955, that building's foundation became the foundation for a telephone exchange building, while the clubhouse was moved to 1800 Mount View Avenue. In 1970, the building at the Mount View address — the former clubhouse — was torn down. But the foundation presumably remains in place at 248 Penn Avenue South, the site of a Qwest Communications branch office.

CHAPTER 30

Hot, Toasty Leftover

GREEN LAKE COUNTRY CLUB
CITY: SPICER
COUNTY: KANDIYOHI
YEARS: 1917–UNKNOWN

ABOVE: *Green Lake Country Club clubhouse, date unknown*
COURTESY OF KANDIYOHI COUNTY HISTORICAL SOCIETY

RIGHT: *A part of the golf course at Green Lake Country Club, Spicer, Minn.*
COURTESY OF PHIL KOSTOLNIK

Fore! Gone.

THE NEXT TIME YOU'RE IN THE WEST-CENTRAL MINNESOTA CITY OF SPICER, POP INTO ZORBAZ ON GREEN LAKE FOR A $2 TACOZ AND $3 TAPZ NIGHT (THE 19TH LETTER OF THE ALPHABET IZ ZTRICTLY FORBIDDEN ON A ZORBAZ MENU), STROLL ON OVER TO ONE OF THE LARGE BRICK FIREPLACES, AND OFFER A TOAST TO THE PLACE.

You're on the 19th hole.

The nearest operative golf course is three miles away, but still, you're on the 19th hole. And those fireplaces have been toasting buns for nearly a century.

The Zorbaz building, or part of it anyway, is the former clubhouse for Green Lake Country Club, an 18-hole golf course that was part of a thriving resort-and-recreation area in the first part of the 20th century.

Written and oral accounts of Green Lake CC paint an unclear picture of the place, unfortunately. One website places the club's year of inception as 1912. Other sources date the club to 1917, including *The American Annual Golf Guide* of 1926 and a *Minneapolis Morning Tribune* story from May 24, 1917, headlined "Willmar Club Plans Nine-Hole Golf Course." (The newspaper reported the course by name — Green Lake Country Club. Willmar and Spicer are nine miles apart.)

Membership in the club at its opening cost $100; that included the use of tennis courts and swimming facilities on the nearby Green Lake beach. The course opened as a nine-hole, par-35, 2,956-yard layout with sand greens; it was expanded to 18, still with sand greens, in 1923. A 1925 golf directory listed A.A. Anderson as club president and D.N. Fallman as chairman of the greens committee, though that almost certainly would have been D.N. Tallman, a Willmar resident who made a fortune in banking, lumber and development, lost it all early in the 20th century, took up golf at 50, and became a champion player and later president of the Minnesota Golf Association.

Green Lake Country Club's history is addressed in the book *History of Green Lake in Spicer*, published by the Kandiyohi County Historical Society. The golf course, the book reported, "ran east and west from the Kandiyohi road to present Highway 23 and south towards Alvig Slough." A par-5 hole is said to have run along the current Highway 10, across from Green Lake.

"The club became a favorite meeting place and served full meals as well as sandwiches, soft drinks, and ice cream cones," the book continued. "Pop and near beer were sold for a nickel a glass."

But by the mid-1930s, the golfing and social scene along the southwestern corner of Green Lake had changed. The book attributed a decline to the effects of the 1930 opening of Willmar Golf Club, seven miles southwest of Green Lake CC; the Great Depression; and the death of Russell Spicer, an original trustee of Green Lake CC and the son of railroad builder John Spicer, for whom the city of Spicer was named.

The exact closing date is, again, a subject of conjecture. One source says 1936;

another says "the late 1930s." Spicer native Jim Saulsbury says his recollection is that the course was open through 1944 or 1945.

In any event, Saulsbury knows about the old Green Lake CC clubhouse, which became the country club's most enduring feature.

"That was my home," said Saulsbury, who now lives in nearby New London. "My dad bought that in 1946. It wasn't a golf course then, but the bar and everything was still intact, and we lived there."

Saulsbury's father was Guy Saulsbury. "He paid $25,000 for the dance hall, clubhouse and land that included 1,500 feet of shoreline," said Jim Saulsbury, who noted that his father did not buy any of the golf course land.

Some townsfolk apparently were skeptical of Guy Saulsbury's purchase. "Never figured he'd be able to pay for it," Jim Saulsbury said. "He got it done. My father got everything done."

Guy Saulsbury became best known as the proprietor of Saulsbury Antiques. "It probably was one of the largest antique businesses in the United States," Jim Saulsbury said. "He bought antiques from all over the world. That's what went into the clubhouse."

Saulsbury operated his antique business on the shore of Green Lake until the 1970s, then moved it. The old clubhouse still stood, though it had gone through some changes. "I remember the bar. Hauled it out to the dump," Jim Saulsbury said.

The old clubhouse became the Safari South Restaurant, then Melvin's On the Lake, and now is Zorbaz. The old Green Lake Country Club fireplaces still generate warmth, even if it is now via electricity rather than woodburning.

GREEN LAKE, AT 5,560 ACRES, IS THE LARGEST LAKE IN Kandiyohi County.

CHAPTER 31

Unfulfilled Promise

ROYALHAVEN GOLF CLUB
CITY: HUGO
COUNTY: WASHINGTON
DATES: 1969–72

THE BEST MINNESOTA GOLF COURSE EVER? MANY CANDIDATES: HAZELTINE, INTERLACHEN, MINIKAHDA, THE QUARRY, THE WILDERNESS, WINDSONG FARM, A DOZEN MORE.

The best Minnesota golf course never? Much shorter list. Royalhaven might be the one and only.

Royalhaven might be the state's best course never, because Larry Furlong never built it, at least not fully. He wanted to, though, and his dang-I-almost-did-it golf course had the makings of a beauty.

Royalhaven was to have occupied a plot at the rural southern edge of the city of Hugo, between 125th and 132nd Streets North, just west of Sunset Lake. The area is pastoral, out-of-the-way, 2 ½ miles from the nearest significant roadway, U.S. Highway 61, and even farther from the nearest downtowns, Hugo and White Bear Lake.

There is no signature golf course feature on the property that Furlong and a handful of partners in his venture bought in 1969 — no sandswept, fauxlinksland hillocks, no boundless, glimmering lakeshore on which to take a golfer's breath away for a minute or 20.

What the Royalhaven site had, though, was a little bit of everything — enough to have made the sum likely far greater than any part would have been.

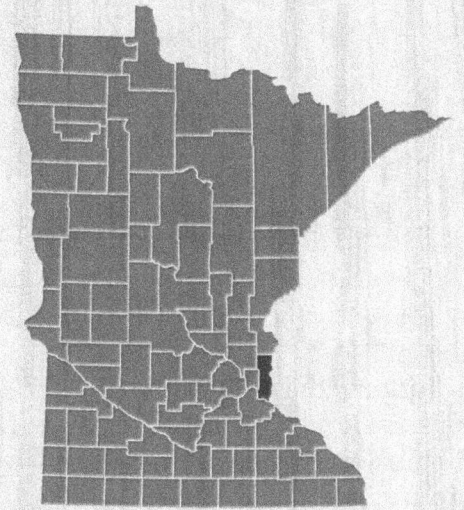

Royalhaven had as its base a rolling piece of land, not so flat that it's uninteresting and not so severe that it would attract bighorn sheep. The land is framed in some places and dotted in others by pine, spruce, maple, oak, willow, apple, birch and more — a melting pot of Minnesota arbor. Six lagoons, a corner of Sunset Lake and one narrow valley would have contributed to the variety and potential of the site as a golf course.

Add the right course architect to the mix, and you'd have a winner.

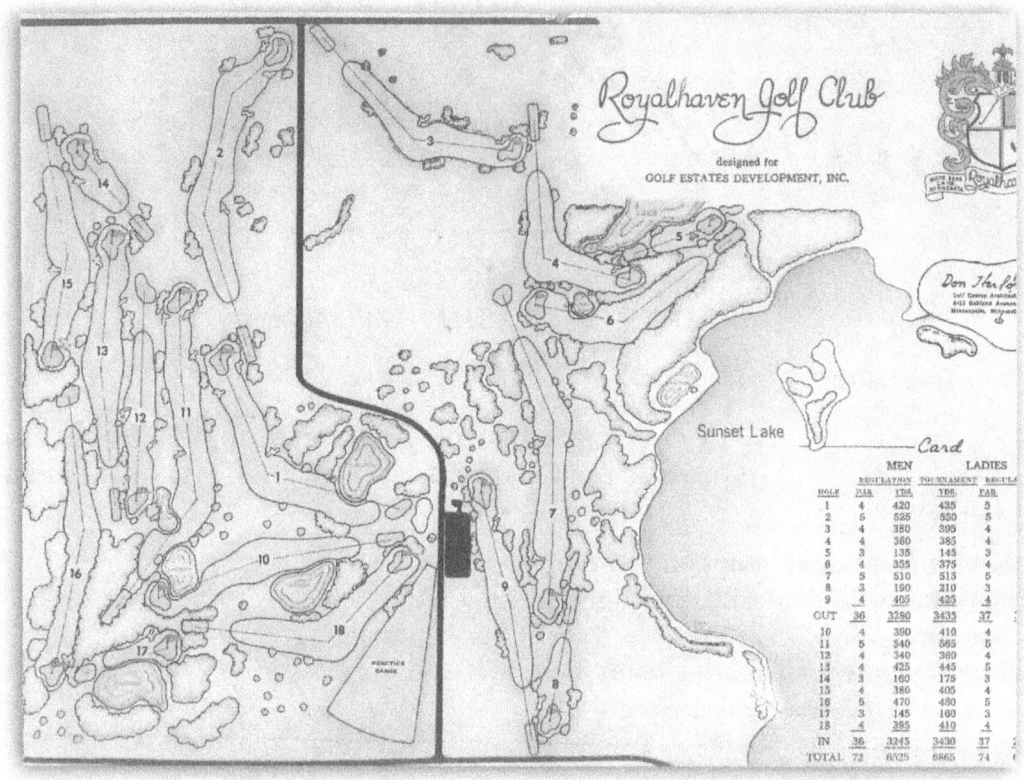

Architect's drawing of Royalhaven Golf Club
COURTESY OF DOROTHY FURLONG

Furlong, the principal partner in Golf Estates Development, Inc. brought Don Herfort on board to design Royalhaven. Herfort, who died in 2011, was not the second coming of Donald Ross, but he wasn't a finger-painter on a canvas of poa annua, either. He knew his way around a golf course blueprint. He was a member of the American Society of Golf Course Architects and was said to have designed or contributed to the design of more than 140 courses in the Upper Midwest, including Indian Hills, River Oaks and Pebble Creek in Minnesota and New Richmond in Wisconsin.

Coincidentally, as Herfort was sketching out Royalhaven's 18 holes, he also was designing a private course three miles to the south, Dellwood Hills. That course opened in 1970. Royalhaven met a different fate.

"In '69 or '70, this (recession) hit. Everything went under," said Furlong's widow, Dorothy Furlong, who lives in a house on Sunset Lake, near what was to be the golf course. "He (Larry Furlong) could not get any loans or funding. The deep well was already dug, and so they kind of had to backtrack and say, we can't build a golf course."

Dellwood, said Furlong, was able to get its feet on the ground partly because it had deeper financial backing. The Furlongs eventually joined Dellwood, and their daughter Kris biked there to hit balls. She got good at the game, played for the University of Minnesota, became the first woman to work as a pro at Minneapolis Golf Club and spent 10 years as pro and manager at Oneka Ridge in White Bear Lake.

As good as Larry Furlong's golf course promised to be, its name was, according to Dorothy Furlong, less than awe-inspiring.

"They named it Royalhaven, and that just freaked me out," she said. "(I thought) Oh, it should be some Indian name, you know, like Big Chief or something — I don't know. But Royalhaven? Oh, well."

Oh, well — Dorothy Furlong painted the golf course's name anyway on an 8-foot sign that stood on the golf course grounds before the project was abandoned in 1972.

Furlong said she believed Royalhaven was intended to be a public course. Larry Furlong owned 21 fuel oil stations in the northeast metro area, so the golf course did not signal financial demise for him.

"We didn't go broke or anything," Dorothy Furlong said. "He didn't make as much money as he might have, but by selling lots and so forth (we didn't lose a lot), and his business was doing well."

Royalhaven investors were given the opportunity to purchase lots on the property for $2,000 apiece, but Furlong said only one or two did. The Furlongs remained in their house on the shore of Sunset Lake, where they would stage picnics and baseball games.

The old golf course land was sold in stages. Larry Furlong, who died in 2004, eventually sold what was left to a company that subdivided the land. Today, the grounds mostly hosts small farms, hobby farms or middle-class homes with relatively large lots.

Plans for Royalhaven Golf Club are examined in July 1969 on the proposed site. Among those pictured are course architect Don Herfort, left, and developer Larry Furlong, right.

ST. PAUL PIONEER PRESS PHOTO

But Royalhaven is not gone. Not completely.

At the southeast corner of the intersection of Henna and 132nd Street, a tee box is clearly visible. It points southeast, and a line of trees defines what would have been the left edge of a hole.

This would have been No. 3, a dogleg-left, 380-yard par 4. Dorothy Furlong has kept a sketch of the course with Herfort's routing, so it's possible to merge the 1970 plan with modern-day reality. A good drive today off the old tee box would sail over the current landowner's garage. A sliced drive might bounce off the guy's front steps — or forehead, if he were sitting on the front steps.

The landowner, incidentally, says he used to hit wedges and short irons on his property, heading back to the tee area to hit longer shots. He knew the area was a former golf course-in-waiting but did not, until the fall of 2012, know he had been hitting balls off an actual teeing ground or that his back yard was an intended landing area.

Further east, at the edge of the Royalhaven property, the extreme dogleg-left par-4 fourth and 135-yard fifth holes were to be guarded along the left side by a corner of Sunset Lake. Ahead is the site of the seventh fairway, which was to be a 510-yard par 5. It cuts through a valley; llamas now graze on part of the lland there. Back on the west side of Henna, the second fairway cuts through what is now a barn and grazing area for two horses, one of them a 35-year-old palomino.

Another sign of what was to be Royalhaven: At the end of the second fairway, now partly occupied by a garage, rests an old green site. The shape of the green is not discernible, but it is next to a small stand of pine trees that also is shown on the course map. Planted into a hole in the ground is 10-foot-tall piece of PVC pipe that the landowner says has been in place for years, since before he moved in. It looks to clearly be a stake signaling to the builders of the golf course that this is where the second green was to be built.

It's worth pondering what a viable Royalhaven might have done to the area's golf landscape. Within nine miles of the Royalhaven site, there are 14 golf courses. Six of them (Applewood Hills, Loggers Trail, Oak Glen, Oneka Ridge, Sawmill and Tanners Brook) are public layouts that opened after the Royalhaven project failed, raising the question of whether all would have been established or remained viable had Royalhaven gotten off the ground, much less fulfilled its considerable potential.

DOROTHY FURLONG GAINED A MEASURE OF FAME IN February 2011 when she remarried, exchanging vows with Charlie Hall. The two shared a connection as former royalty of the St. Paul Winter Carnival; Furlong was crowned Aurora, the Queen of Snows, in 1955, and Hall was Boreas, the carnival king, in 1983. The two had been acquainted through their Winter Carnival connections, and after Hall's first wife, Ceil, died in 2010, they became reacquainted. A romance blossomed, leading to a marriage that was featured by the likes of the *Minneapolis Star Tribune*, *St. Paul Pioneer Press* and *New York Times*.

CHAPTER 32

Urban Hotbed

**FELDER'S GOLF CENTER
CITY: PLYMOUTH
COUNTY: HENNEPIN
YEARS: CIRCA 1958–1987**

At the southeastern corner of the city of Plymouth, there once was an odd combination — one of Minnesota's most unadorned golf courses operating as part of one of Minnesota's busiest golf venues.

The venue was Felder's Golf Center — par-3 golf course, putting green, driving range and miniature golf course. A 1977 *Metropolitan Area Golf Course Directory* listed Phil Hurrle as its professional.

Take it from here, Phil.

"Dean Felder (the golf center's owner) was a corrections officer in Minneapolis," Hurrle said. "The course was built by inmates.

"It was a very simple layout but the only one of its kind around. It had just push-up greens. The land was all peat, so there were good growing conditions, but they just pushed up some dirt and cut the greens. The holes ranged from 50 to 90 yards."

The main attraction was not the plain-Jane golf course. It was the driving range.

"It was busier than hell. Busy all the time. The guy (Felder) had a gold mine there," Hurrle said. "It was fairly close in (to Minneapolis), and there just weren't any driving ranges around at the time."

Hurrle, who gave lessons at Felder's from 1973-77, reaped at least a small cut of the financial action.

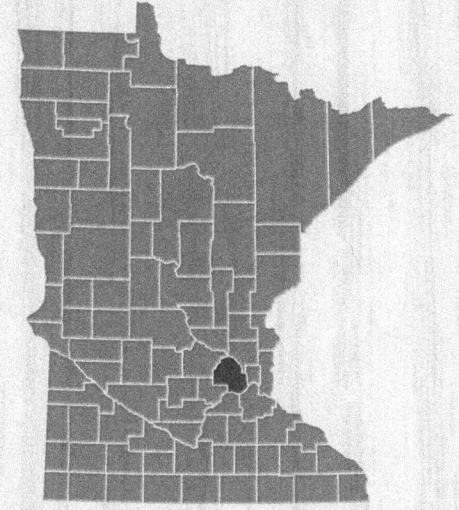

"I was giving lessons for $8 for 20 minutes. One day I gave 21 lessons," he said. "I had nothing to do but stand and give people lessons on the lesson tee.

"There was a lot of poor people who took lessons from me. They would say, 'I don't have a pen or anything to write a check,' so I said just leave the money at the clubhouse — and nobody stiffed me, not once."

The address of Felder's Golf Center was listed as 10354 Highway 55 in a golf guide and 10324 Highway 55 in a golf magazine. Hurrle's recollection was that the course was near Winnetka and Boone avenues, but the golf guide's addresses more closely match a plot a bit to the west, near the northwest corner of what is now the intersection of Minnesota 55 and U.S. 169. Aerial photos from 1969 and 1977 indicate the same. The golf guide noted that "Bassett Creek winds its way through the flat terrain of the course."

The golf magazine note — from Herb Graffis' column in a 1967 issue of *Golfdom* — hints that the golf center was around well before Hurrle arrived on the scene. "Sonny Ryan and Dave Felder are in their ninth year together at Felder's Golf Center, 10324 Olson Hiway, Minneapolis, and have a new pro shop, have enlarged the range to 60 tees and added a new iron practice area."

By 1983, the business was listed as Ford's Golf Center in the Minneapolis telephone directory. It was listed that way through the 1988-89 Minneapolis Yellow Pages but was not listed in 1989-90.

CHAPTER 33

Buried Treasure

WABASHA GOLF CLUB
CITY: WABASHA
COUNTY: WABASHA
YEARS: 1927–CIRCA 1942

TOP: *The old plastic tee Pete Riester found on the former Wabasha Golf Club grounds.*

BOTTOM: *A foursome of Wabasha Golf Club golfers included Charlie Theismann, left, and Harold Schierts, second from right. Theismann won the club championship in 1939 and '40 and Schierts in 1941 and '42, possibly the final four years of the course's existence.*
COURTESY OF MARY ANN STOGSDILL

Fore! Gone.

GOLF BALLS NEVER WERE A CASH CROP FOR PETE RIESTER, BUT HE STILL HAD A FEW BOUNTIFUL HARVESTS.

Riester owns the Mississippi River bottomland in southeastern Minnesota that 80 years ago was the grounds of Wabasha Golf Club. "When the land was plowed, we used to find quite a few balls in there," he said.

The golf balls are gone, plowed up or sucked under, perhaps literally six feet under — subterranean spheres pulled this way and that by river seepage just under the surface of Riester's land.

Almost all signs of Wabasha Golf Club are gone, too. *Almost* all …

"The last thing I found was in 1997 — a tee," Riester says in a phone interview in early 2013.

A couple of months later, Riester shows the tee to a visitor. It's a peculiar item: two pieces of soft, yellow plastic molded together, looking at once exactly like a golf tee yet nothing like any other tee commonly produced in the past 50 years. Because it isn't made of wood, it survived more than 50 years without decomposing in Riester's loam.

A lost golf course can't be reconstructed from one pointy piece of plastic, but the tee is a starting point. The surroundings offer a further portal to Wabasha Golf Club, vintage 1930.

Wabasha Golf Club lay four miles south of Wabasha and two miles north of Kellogg, just off the "old" U.S. Highway 61, now known as County Road 30. The Mississippi River was two miles to the east, with bluffs on the Minnesota side rising practically out of the course's front yard and bluffs on the Wisconsin side 3½ miles away but plainly visible.

The clubhouse was on relatively high ground. It stood about 50 feet from where Riester's house now stands; he had the building's crumbling foundation removed when his house was built. Part of another foundation, perhaps from a storage shed or outhouse, remains at ground level a few hundred yards to the north.

Water must have been a significant feature at Wabasha Golf Club. A 1939 aerial photo shows a creek or wetlands meandering through the course's mid-section, with at least three green sites plainly visible. Today, the only permanent water feature is a pond below Riester's home; everything else is farmland. Still, the entire area is subject to seepage from the Mississippi River, and the waterways can re-emerge as puddles and ponds when the river swells — or as an inland sea when the river floods. Certainly, there were days when it would have been easier navigating Wabasha Golf Club in wading boots than in spikes.

Riester, who is in his mid-50s, knew a bit about the course's routing based on secondhand knowledge. The first hole, he said, proceeded north, along high ground. The rest of the course was on lower ground, with the seventh hole as a northern border, the eighth as an eastern border and the ninth as a southern border. All other holes lay within those perimeters.

Wabasha Golf Club was established in 1927, set off to a lurching start in terms of publicity by the state's most prominent golf publication. "Wabasha Golf Club course opened June 19," read an entry in the August 1927 issue of *The 10,000 Lakes Golfer.* "90 members. On Hwy 3, about three miles south of Winona."

Yes, the entry read "Winona." Brain cramp by the magazine, no doubt. Winona is in the next county south of Wabasha.

Another listing came courtesy of the 1930-31 *American Annual Golf Guide*: "Wabasha Golf Club, four miles from the city, greenkeeper T. Gilsdorf, greens fees 50 cents per day, 95 members, visitors welcome."

One prominent club member was Charles V. Theismann, a co-owner of Andy's Hardware in Wabasha and former city treasurer. Theismann won club championships in 1939 and 1940, said his son, Pete, of St. Cloud, before joining the service during World War II. Pete Theismann still owns the old club-championship trophy with his father's name on it.

Wabasha Golf Club was closed by the time Charles Theismann returned from the service, but he remained an avid golfer and in the mid-1960s helped establish Coffee Mill Golf Club (now The Bluffs at Coffee Mill), atop the river bluffs overlooking Wabasha.

Theismann first made his way to Wabasha GC as a caddie, said his daughter, Mary Ann Stogsdill of Maple Grove.

"He walked from town, the west end of town, to the golf course," Stogsdill said. "He got a quarter for caddying nine holes. ... His mom would pack him lunches; he used to get brown sugar sandwiches, and those were his favorite."

Pete Riester, whose farm occupies the former Wabasha Golf Club. Riester is standing near the site of the former clubhouse; the pond in the background was part of the course. Its water level rises and falls with the changing levels of the Mississippi River, two miles east of his farm.

JOE BISSEN PHOTO

Pete Theismann noted that his father also caught and drowned gophers at Wabasha Golf Course to make extra money, and that he once caddied for Patty Berg in a Twin Cities tournament.

Stogsdill said she believed Wabasha Golf Club closed in the World War II years, when "there were no men around to play the course." The Theismann trophy hints at the same notion. After Theismann's club championships, Harold Schierts won titles in 1941 and '42 — but there are no names on the trophy after that date.

A 1947 aerial photo strongly indicates Wabasha GC was no longer operating at that time — most of the property is tilled, the wetland area is only a narrow

Looking out over the bulk of the former Wabasha Golf Club grounds, with the Mississippi River bluffs on the Wisconsin side in the background.

JOE BISSEN PHOTO

Wabasha Golf Club clubhouse, 1938

COURTESY OF MARY ANN STOGSDILL

stream, and there are no green sites or hole routings evident.

Only one source contacted had any firsthand knowledge of Wabasha Golf Club. The Wabasha County resident did not want his name mentioned — imagine that, a lost-course Deep Throat — but did pass along a few comments.

The Wabasha course, he said, had four grass greens and five sand greens and "was a nice golf course."

Deep T. also passed along nuggets about courses in the Lake City area. He said Lake City Golf Club, now on the north end of town, originally opened in 1927 on the south end of town, on the National Guard grounds known as Camp Lakeview. When the Guard came to Lake City to train for six weeks each summer, he said, "They couldn't hardly golf there."

Also, Monsieur Throat debunked a report that there was a golf course on the McCahill Farm near Lake City. The "golf course" actually was only a three-hole layout, "a "knock-around thing," he said, in the late 1930s, perhaps as late as 1940. He said there later was a driving range on the property that turned into a cabbage patch.

CHAPTER 34

Jewish Forerunner

NORTHWOOD COUNTRY CLUB
CITY: NORTH ST. PAUL
COUNTY: RAMSEY
YEARS: 1915-45

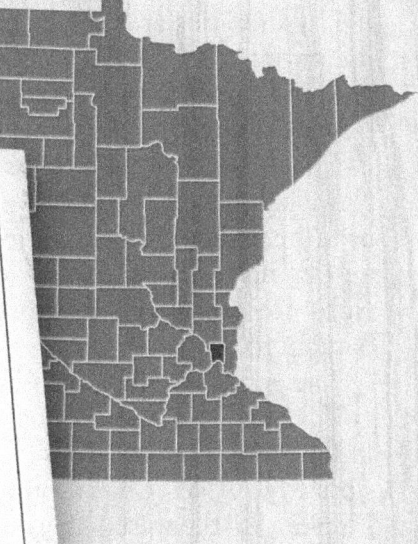

COURTESY OF DAN GOODENOUGH

Fore! Gone.

Hillcrest Golf Club, established in 1921 at the very northeast corner of St. Paul, was long recognized as the Twin Cities east metro's Jewish golf club. The designation wasn't inaccurate; it just didn't tell the whole story.

Before Hillcrest, there was Northwood.

Northwood Country Club, a mile northeast of Hillcrest in the city of North St. Paul, predated Hillcrest by six years and was not only the first Jewish golf club in the east metro but in all of the Twin Cities area. In fact, it took an intertwining of the fates of Northwood and Hillcrest for the latter to even become a Jewish club.

There is irony in the very phrase "Jewish golf club." There might not ever have been such a designation in Minnesota had the state's earliest private clubs not excluded Jews from its membership rolls.

The genesis of the Twin Cities' Jewish golf clubs — Northwood and then Hillcrest on the east side of the Mississippi River, Oak Ridge Country Club in Hopkins on the west — was addressed in the 2012 book *From Fields to Fairways: Classic Clubs of Minnesota*, written by Rick Shefchik. Although Jews, Shefchik wrote, rarely were hired in many traditionally Anglo-Saxon controlled industries, they were successful in others. "A private golf club was not beyond the financial reach of the Jewish community," Shefchik wrote.

Twin Cities Jews organized a social organization known as the Calumet Club in Minneapolis in 1908, Shefchik wrote, which led some Calumet members to consider organizing a Jewish golf club. Calumet golfers were loosely organized into two groups: a Minneapolis group that favored establishment of a Jewish golf club near the University of Minnesota's St. Paul campus and a St. Paul group that favored a parcel of land in North St. Paul owned by Charles Strauss.

The two groups split, most likely in 1914, and Strauss' property became Northwood Country Club the next year. (The Minneapolis group established Oak Ridge in 1920.)

Northwood's inception was noted in a *North St. Paul Sentinel* story from April 30, 1915. The newspaper reported that contracts had been let for "a large club house to be built on their (Northwood's) property on Oak Hill." The building, it was reported, was to be 40 by 83 feet, with a 23 by 40 "ell."

"Each Saturday and Sunday," the newspaper continued, "a number of golf enthusiasts come out to the links and try out the different approaches."

No course architect was mentioned, and in fact no mention of one could be found in any archived material. The clubhouse architect, on the other hand, was quite known. A 1915 issue of *The American Contractor*, a publication that essentially listed plans and specifications for buildings across the country, included this entry: "Golf Club House: 1 sty. & bas. $20M. North St. Paul. Archt. C.H. Johnston. …"

C.H. Johnston was Clarence H. Johnston, a famed and prolific Minnesota architect. He was the state's official architect from 1901–31, and his edifices

Northwood Country Club, circa 1917, from the scrapbook of former Northwood pro Andy Dewar.
COURTESY OF DAN GOODENOUGH

included Glensheen Mansion in Duluth, Central High School in St. Paul, more than 40 buildings on the two University of Minnesota Twin Cities campuses, Williams Arena, the Minnesota State Fair grandstand, and dozens of homes and mansions in St. Paul's Summit Hill neighborhood. He also was the father of Harrison R. "Jimmy" Johnston of St. Paul, the 1929 U.S. Amateur golf champion.

Clarence H. Johnston wasn't Northwood's only connection to the well-heeled of St. Paul. Samuel Dittenhoefer, president of the Golden Rule Department Store in St. Paul, later to become Donaldson's, was listed as the owner of "Northwood Golf Club" in the *American Contractor* entry. His home at 807 Summit Avenue in St. Paul was designed and built by Johnston in 1906 and today is considered one of the city's most historic mansions. Dittenhofer (more commonly spelled that way) and his wife, Madeline, entertained author F. Scott Fitzgerald there.

Some of Northwood's founding fathers are listed on the Oak Ridge Country Club website, and many, in addition to Dittenhofer, had estimable professional backgrounds. Isaac Rose, Dittenhofer's brother-in-law, was a co-owner of Rose Brothers Fur Company. Ben Baer was president of two St. Paul banks. William and Leo Goodkind were officers in Mannheim Brothers Department Store.

Northwood was a nine-hole course with grass greens. Andy Dewar was the first club professional, judging by an entry in *The American Annual Golf Guide* of 1916 and confirmed by a 1917 scrapbook of Dewar's now owned by Dan Goodenough of Edina. Dewar, one of the organizers of the Minnesota Section of the Professional Golfers' Association, served at the North St. Paul course through 1920.

Northwood measured 3,362 yards, making it the longest among Minnesota lost golf courses from the first half of the 20th century. The par 5s were brutes: No. 5, nicknamed "The Oaks," measured 570 yards, and No. 8, "White Gate," was 545.

By 1926, Willard Crummy was the pro and visitors were charged $1 a day for playing privileges. In 1927, Joseph Benson was the greenskeeper.

Northwood's boundaries, based on a 1940 aerial map and translated to modern-day geography, included Holloway Avenue on the south, McKnight Road on the west and Helen Walkway (which is a path, not a street) on the east. There was no single northern border. One hole was near the corner of McKnight and Skillman Avenue; another tee or green was near Eldridge Avenue and Amy Circle; a third section was near Shryer Avenue and 1st Street North. A water hazard in that third section is gone today, reoccupied by Ryan Avenue, four front yards and three houses. The current Northwood Drive cut through the heart of the golf course grounds, and the current Northwood Park, including a water tower at the northern edge of the park, was part of the country club property. The clubhouse was on Northwood Avenue, between Skillman Avenue and 2nd Street North.

The 1925 book *Tee Party on the Green*, a guide to the St. Paul area's private courses, listed Ira S. Baer as club president. His father, Ben, one of the Northwood founders, died in 1921, judging by geneaology records. *Tee Party* listed all 156 club members, with hometowns and addresses, including Dittenhofer and his wife. The large majority were from St. Paul, most living in the prosperous Summit Hill neighborhood.

As for competition, Crummy shot a 75 for the best score in a Scotch foursome match on May 21, 1925, and Miss Mildred Wolfe won the A.N. Rose cup tournament on Aug. 29, shooting a course-record 43, even par for women, while playing out of the first flight.

Personal recollections of Northwood are hard to come by. In early 2013, Ernie Christiansen, 88, of Oakdale passed along a couple of memories of his days caddieing at Northwood, likely in the late 1930s or early 1940s:

"It was a nice course, kept up real good by the Jewish people," Christiansen said. "It had a clubhouse and dining area — a big dining room for big occasions."

Christiansen's recollection was that Byron Hadrath was a club officer, and he remembered one incident with a former club president (Christiansen did not remember his name):

"They threw him in the pond when the caddies were on strike," Christiansen said. "I remember throwing him in because he weighed about 400 pounds."

Christiansen said the president was angry over the incident "a little" but that the tactic worked. "We got raises," he said.

Bob Neumann of White Bear Lake similarly shared memories of caddieing at Northwood at age 12 in 1938. He recalled caddieing for prominent figures in Twin Cities businesses: the Cardozos, who owned a Minneapolis furniture company; the Kleins and Applebaums, who were in the grocery business; and Sam Fisher of St. Paul, founder of the Fisher Nut Company.

The next question was perhaps too obvious. When you caddied for Fisher, Mr. Neumann, did you work for peanuts?

"Probably," Neumann said with a laugh. "We probably made 50 cents if we were lucky."

Neumann, a North St. Paul native, said Northwood "was a nice course back then. I can remember one year, a fellow had an airplane and landed there on the golf course. We pushed the plane to where he lived and into his garage."

The fellow's name was Billy Diamond, and he was flying a Piper Cub, Neumann said. "He landed on No. 2 — it was a long hole right along the (east) edge of the course."

Down the road, Hillcrest had opened in 1921 as a private course. The club had no Jewish ties at the time; in fact, it had no official ties to Northwood other than proximity. But the clubs' fates still would be braided.

Though Northwood had 180 members in 1930 and '31, both it and Hillcrest soon encountered financial difficulties, presumably brought upon by the Great Depression. Hillcrest's problems were persistent — from the late 1920s onward, after it expanded to 18 holes, it shifted from private to public multiple times, and it closed during the World War II years, its grounds serving as grazing land.

Northwood's financial straits probably were no less substantial. The 1940s brought on tumult for the North St. Paul club. Northwood was listed in the 1940 North St. Paul telephone listings but not in 1941, and no mention of the club could be found in spring or summer issues of the *North St. Paul Courier* from those years. The course was renamed Woodlawn and sold to a developer in "the early 1940s," according to a city of North St. Paul publication. The 1942 phone listings included a "Woodlawn CC" but no Northwood. Neither of those titles is found in the 1943, '44 or '45 phone listings.

A few sources offered recollections of the area, sometimes sprinkled with guesstimates. Frank Fiorito, a former Hillcrest pro, suspected that the Northwood course closed in 1942 or '43. Paul Anderson, a North St. Paul native and president of the North St. Paul Historical Society, similarly said he believed the course closed during the World War II years.

In any event, Northwood and Hillcrest had their fateful convergence in 1945. Shefchik explained in *From Fields to Fairways*:

"Despite having a fine Tom Vardon golf course that had been strategically tweaked by A.W. Tillinghast, Hillcrest continued to struggle financially through the Depression and the war years. But in 1945 a new Hillcrest was born; the club was sold to a group of businessmen, some of them former Northwood members, and reorganized as the Jewish club of St. Paul."

Northwood's demise, however, cannot be tied up that neatly. The city of North St. Paul publication says the city obtained part of the Northwood course in 1946. The 1947 St. Paul phone listings include "O'Brien's Northwood Country Club" under its golf course heading, yet Ramsey County property records show home construction in the Country Club Heights section of North St. Paul beginning in 1947, and a 1947 aerial photo shows nearly a dozen homes along Northwood Avenue.

A longtime east metro golf figure said the Northwood course was still open in 1948, but Anderson remembered walking across the grounds in that period — 1948, he recalled — and said the course was closed.

Mixed into this soup of factoids, and perhaps fictionoids, it is certain that another incarnation of Northwood

Country Club endured for almost three more decades. As houses sprouted all around, the Northwood clubhouse stood and was reopened, likely in 1949, still as Northwood Country Club but in the form of a restaurant and supper club.

The restaurant featured dancing as well as dining. A 1950s menu featured a New York sirloin steak dinner for two at $7.50. One of the reborn Northwood Country Club's best-known figures was John Heimel, who became manager in 1952 and owner in 1953. Heimel always greeted guests with "Happy New Year," according to a 1991 obituary.

On June 1, 1976, Northwood Country Club burned to the ground. A newspaper clipping at the North St. Paul Historical Society reported that the fire caused a "total loss" estimated at a quarter-million dollars. The supper club never reopened; its address is now occupied by two homes on a knoll on Northwood Drive. The last-known standing relic from the golf course was its caddie house, which stood in what is now Northwood Park. The caddie house was moved to Colby Hills Park, at the southwest edge of North St. Paul, before being razed in 2009.

Down the road at Hillcrest, golf continued, though Hillcrest's identity as a "Jewish club" had faded by the end of the 20th century, Shefchik wrote in *From Fields to Fairways*. In 2010, the club was sold for $4.3 million to the Steamfitters Pipefitters Local 455 in St. Paul.

NORTH ST. PAUL'S BEST-KNOWN LANDMARK IS NOT A GOLF course, current or lost (there are no current courses within the city limits). Best known is its Snowman, a 44-foot-tall sculpture near downtown, just off Minnesota Highway 36. The Snowman's smile is 16 feet across.

CHAPTER 35

Striking View

JAKE'S / MISSISSIPPI GOLF COURSE
CITY: COON RAPIDS
COUNTY: ANOKA
YEARS: 1931–36

GOLFERS LOVE LISTS. THEY LOVE TO READ ABOUT THE TOP 100 GOLF COURSES IN THE U.S., THE BEST 18 HOLES IN THE TWIN CITIES OR THE 10 CRAZIEST MINI GOLF COURSES ON EARTH (YES, THERE REALLY IS SUCH A LIST).

We're not offering a list of best holes at Minnesota's Lost Golf Courses, because, well, the holes are *lost*, silly. Who knows what they looked like?

But if we did have such a list, we surely would, even if it is sight unseen, throw in Nos. 5 and 6 at Jake's Golf Course. (We'd have to dock points for the sand greens, but hey, you can't have everything.)

Lewis O. Jacob, aka Jake, opened his golf course on Aug. 4, 1931, on farmland he owned in Anoka Township, now Coon Rapids. He enlisted the help of a British golfing friend, Harry Edmonds, in laying out the course, according to a 1992 story by Peter Bodley in *ABC Newspapers*.

Say this for Jake and Harry: They knew where to plant those flagsticks.

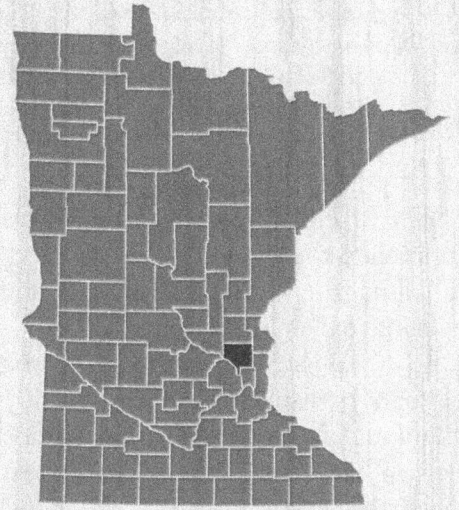

The first four holes at Jake's Golf Course, also known as Mississippi Public Golf Course, covered mostly treeless and relatively flat land, judging by elevation maps and a pre-1950 aerial photo. The holes' only distinguishing features are the modern-day sites they occupy: the first tee was near the intersection of Crooked Lake Boulevard and 109th Avenue Northwest, the second hole cut across a corner of the Mississippi Elementary School grounds, and the fourth ran south along Mississippi Boulevard.

Ho-hum. But when golfers reached the fifth tee, they got a look at Jake's Big, Watery Payoff.

The fifth and sixth holes bordered the Mississippi River. It must have been a spectacular stage — the river, lying 15 feet down an embankment, forging a path more than 220 yards wide, lazily but inexorably heading south toward the Coon Rapids Dam, two miles downstream.

Fore! Gone.

The back yard of the home of Jerry and Susan Koch of Coon Rapids, on Mississippi River Boulevard, lies along the shore of the Mississippi River and is the former site of the fairway or perhaps left rough of the fifth hole at Mississippi Golf Course. The hole was 502 yards, a par 5 for men (or Gents, as the scorecard referred to them) and a par 7 for women (or Ladies).

JOE BISSEN PHOTO

You wouldn't have to be a golfer to appreciate the scene.

"I imagine back to that time, and it must have been pretty picturesque," said Amy Norquist, who, with her husband, Nathan, owns a home with a back yard that abuts the river and once was a fairway on Jake's Golf Course, just ahead of the sixth tee.

Norquist said the riverside's current denizens include fox, deer, eagles and raccoons. If that's true today, it certainly was true, and probably then some, 70 years ago, before homes lined both sides of the Mississippi.

The fifth hole at Jake's was a par 5 for "gents" and a par 7 for "ladies," according to an old scorecard, featuring a 502-yard riverside stroll. The sixth, a par 4/5 of 330 yards, also headed north along the river, possibly through a grove of trees, judging by the aerial photo.

The Norquists aren't golfers, but they have a connection to the old golf course. They live in the house Jacob built next to the river in the 1950s, almost two decades after Jake's Golf Course had closed. The Norquists had heard about the old course from Lee Swisher, Jacob's daughter, who lived nearby, also on Mississippi Boulevard.

Swisher fell ill in early 2013 and was not available to be interviewed, but in 1996 she had talked at length about the golf course with Bill Peterson, a former member of the Coon Rapids Historical Commission. Peterson produced a booklet on Mississippi Golf Course, an almost grail-like document for someone who might be interested in the then-and-now of old golf courses.

Peterson's booklet includes a playing history of the course, a copy of an old scorecard, two 1936 season tickets (for gents and ladies, again) and two other remarkable pages: a property/plat map of the golf course area, with a routing of the course drawn upon current property and street lines, and a listing of each tee box and green site alongside its 1996 street address:

"1st Tee … 10908 Dahalia (sic) St.
"1st Hole … 2981 108th Lane …
"5th Tee … 10510 Miss. Blvd.
"5th Hole … 10660 Miss. Blvd. …
"9th Tee … 2972 108th Lane
"9th Hole … 10908 Dahalia (sic) St."

Peterson's entries on the course history, which he credited to *ABC Newspapers*, included notations that the course had sand greens, dues were $1 a month at the outset and that women were allowed to play free on Wednesday afternoons. The course's original length when it opened on Aug. 4, 1931, was 1,992 yards, though it was later lengthened, and the scorecard listed the length at 2,961 yards.

"The very day after the course opened," one entry reads, "Young Bill Mathey sank his drive on the 133 yard 11th hold (sic) for the first hole-in-one on the new course."

Jake's patrons were afforded the privilege of pull-hooking balls into the Mississippi for only five full seasons. The course's last year of operation was 1936. Its viability no doubt had been compromised the year before, when the city of Anoka voted to build a golf course, with Works Progress Administration support. That course, known then as Greenhaven and now as Green Haven, opened in July 1937.

L.O. Jacob, meanwhile, built a legacy beyond the confines of his golf course. On his farm, he raised cattle, hogs, sheep, 500 chickens and 1,000 turkeys, according to the May 29, 1992, obituary of his wife, Ethel. Jacob was credited with introducing new techniques for farming and irrigation in the Coon Rapids-Anoka area. He also was a teacher, football coach and former school board member for whom L.O. Jacob Elementary School in Coon Rapids is named.

L.O. Jacob died in 1959.

JAKE'S WAS NOT THE FIRST LOST GOLF COURSE IN THE Anoka-Coon Rapids area. Sue Austreng of *ABC Newspapers* wrote of two others in a May 2012 story:

"Anoka's first golf course was located on property now known as Goodrich Field with the first tee in the neighborhood of the entrance of the Anoka junior high school on Fourth Avenue. Several fairways crossed each other 'making for an interesting, but very hazardous layout.' … Anoka's second golf course was called Parker's Golf Course and was laid out on property owned by Sam Parker, laid out on the former Akin property at the foot of Third Avenue and west to the Rum River."

CHAPTER 36

Memory Serves

MOUND GOLF COURSE
CITY: MOUND
COUNTY: HENNEPIN
YEARS: CA. 1929–1940s

The Mound '29ers, on the grounds of Mound Golf Course.
COURTESY OF WESTONKA HISTORICAL SOCIETY

FORE! GONE.

CONSIDER A SMALLISH PLOT OF LAND IN MOUND, A CITY OF 9,000 ON THE NORTH SHORE OF LAKE MINNETONKA. THIS LAND, APPROXIMATELY 500 BY 600 YARDS IN AREA, IS A HALF-MILE SOUTHEAST OF DOWNTOWN AND JUST NORTH OF COOKS BAY. IT IS JUST OFF SHORELINE DRIVE, THE MAIN DRAG THROUGH TOWN.

Now imagine the 1930s version of this plot, and imagine that it's mounted directly atop the 21st-century edition.

What do you get?

You get a tee shot on No. 1 at Mound Golf Course that sails past Mount Olive Lutheran Church. A putt on No. 4 that rolls down a hallway in Shirley Hills Primary School. An approach shot on No. 7 that flies — Fore! Duck! Hold the anchovies! — straight over the pick-up counter at Domino's Pizza.

So it is when old meets new on the former site of Mound Golf Course, a nine-hole, public layout from the 1930s and '40s. The old golf course is largely unknown in Mound, though a couple of former city residents remember.

"I could almost walk you to the holes; it's changed a little, but not a lot," said Daryl Blatzheim.

"It started out as a six-hole golf course, and it was all sand greens," said Blatzheim's brother Bob.

The Blatzheims are two of nine sons of Ed Blatzheim, former manager of Mound Golf Course (there were two Blatzheim girls as well). Six of the brothers helped their father on the golf course. Bob, a longtime Edina resident who now lives in Punta Gorda, Fla., and Crosslake, Minn., started caddieing on Mound Golf Course at age 11.

"The third hole was real long, and right in the middle of it was an alfalfa field. All the balls ended up in there mostly, and they (golfers) had a hell of a time finding 'em," Bob Blatzheim said. "There were a lot of woods going around the corner to the ninth hole, and a lot of balls ended up in the woods back there, too."

The course's modern-day boundaries are roughly Shoreline Drive on the north, Hidden Vale Lane and the eastern edge of the Shirley Hills school property on the east, Bartlett Boulevard on the south, and Wilshire Boulevard on the west. About half of the former golf course is now occupied by the Shirley Hills school and grounds.

If it's a guided tour you want, Daryl Blatzheim is your man.

"I know the layout (even though) I was just a little kid" when the course operated, said Daryl, now of Robbinsdale.

Play along, and see if you can break par.

"That church (Mount Olive) down below is the first hole," Daryl Blatzheim said. "(No.) 1 went east, or a little southeast, then 2 went along that road going to Spring Park (Bartlett Boulevard) … and there's trees there; it's almost like you could walk there and the green would still be there.

"Then 3 had a hill going along toward where that school is now, and you kind of had to hit it to the right a little bit. You'd go west, or southwest a little bit. Four went up right to where that school is. Five was a little par 3 down where that hill is, going west again from that school. And then 6 went over towards the water tower (among homes at the northeast edge of the course). I don't know whether that was a par 4 or 3; I think it was a 4 but could have been a long 3.

"Then along that road (Shoreline Drive) that used to lead right to Mound, I know they've changed that road a little bit, that road straight up toward the American Legion, that would have been the seventh hole right along that road, and then 8 was a little par 3 that went over the hill going back south again. And then 9 went along the woods and made a right turn down to the right of the clubhouse."

Dang. I don't know about you, but I developed this damnable slice, hit three O.B. and shot a 47. Almost put out a church window on the first hole.

Mound Golf Course was originally owned by Frank Yost, the town pharmacist, and E.C. "Doc" Mitchell, the town doctor. It was expanded from six holes to nine shortly after it opened, and the sand greens were converted to grass. The course was not long, Daryl Blatzheim said, with the closing hole, perhaps 475 yards, the longest. The clubhouse, he said, "was just a little shack."

An early reference to play at the course, from the 1932 April/May issue of the *Mound Laker* newspaper, was passed along by Pam Myers of the Westonka Historical Society in Mound. "Last Sunday quite a crowd turned out to play at Mound's nine-hole golf course," the story read. "... A charge of 25 cents is asked on week-days and 35 cents on Sundays."

The course can plainly be seen on an old Lake Minnetonka aerial map made available through the Westonka Historical Society, and its boundaries can be seen on a 1933 plat map of Mound's water system. But few other references to the golf course's playing days could be found. Two historical society photos show a group of men called the '29ers at the course. The '29ers Club, organized in 1929 and originally consisting of 29 members, promoted events in the Mound and North Shore area.

The course was sold in its later years, two sources said, though they didn't recall with any certainty the name of the new owner. It presumably lasted into the 1940s, though there is no listing for it in the 1945 or '46 area telephone directories. The course was gone by 1952 at the latest, when Shirley Hills Primary opened and the land around the school — the former golf course — had been graded and finished.

The June 1942 issue of the Laker proclaimed that "The Mound golf course will prove a financial success and is here to stay."

Sure. And Dewey will defeat Truman, too.

MOUND IS THE ORIGINAL HOME OF TONKA TOYS, FAMOUS for its pressed steel trucks of the 1950s and '60s. The company is now a division of Hasbro.

CHAPTER 37

Playing with Conviction

STILLWATER PRISON
CITY: BAYPORT
COUNTY: WASHINGTON
YEARS: MID-1970s

A LOST GOLF COURSE BUILT ON A SWAMP (MANKATO). ANOTHER BUILT NEXT TO A SEWAGE DISPOSAL PLANT (AUSTIN). A THIRD PLAYING AROUND A FAIRGROUNDS GRANDSTAND (ROSEAU).

Weird, weird, weird. But nothing beats this on the Lost Golf Course Bizarre-O-Meter.

A blurb in the December 1974 newsletter issued by the Minnesota Golf Course Superintendents Association ratted out this curiosity:

"Do you have or know where a used but still usable Greens' Mower can be located that the owner would donate to a worthy group (minimum security inmates at the Stillwater State Prison). They have or are building a 4-hole golf course and need this equipment."

Who knew the "correction" in "correctional facility" had anything to do with the adage about weakening the grip to correct a hook?

Yes, a golf course on prison grounds. It happened. In fact, the "4-hole golf course" reference was understated. In the mid-1970s, the Stillwater State Prison featured a nine-hole course.

The intent, Jerry Murphy insists, was decent.

Murphy, who lives in Inver Grove Heights, was the longtime course superintendent at Somerset Country Club in

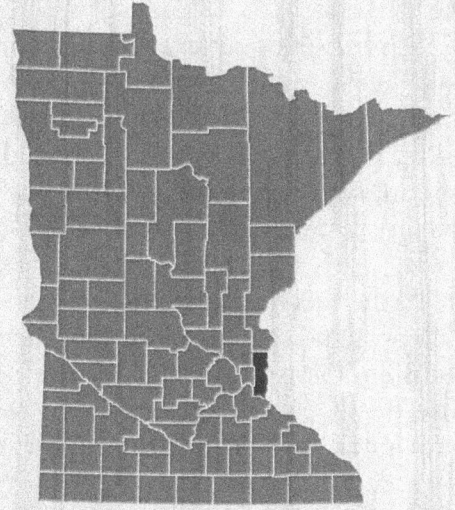

Mendota Heights and a leader in the superintendents association. He also volunteered with minimum-security unit prisoners nearing their release dates.

"I took one of the prisoners one time to one of the golf course superintendent meetings. There was a purpose for that," Murphy said. "I said, how many of the inmates that are ready to be released, how many of those folks do you think would be interested in learning a little bit about golf? He said, well, I don't know, but I imagine it would be a number."

Murphy talked with the assistant prison warden, who talked with the warden, who, Murphy said, gave his blessing to building a small golf course near the prison grounds. The project began with three or four holes but was expanded to nine. As Murphy recalled, the course lay on the grounds just to the south and west of the entrance to the minimum security unit. (Though the prison is named Minnesota Correctional Facility-Stillwater, it is in Bayport. The location of the makeshift prison course, coincidentally, is less than 500 yards from the site of the lost Bayport Golf Club of the 1930s.)

"A number of different golf courses came across with enough material to do this," Murphy said. "We got flags, flagpoles, cups, plastic pipe for sprinkling system, some seed and mowers and all that good stuff, and we went up and laid it out.

"In the meantime, we talked to some club pros and came up with some sets of clubs and assistant pros and they said, sure, we'll come out and teach these guys how to golf, and that was how it all came about.

"It was quite successful for quite awhile. I think it folded after a number of years when the original group that was interested kind of let it go."

The project, Murphy conceded, did not gather universal support. "We did have a few of the guys in the golf industry who said, yeah, well, we'll see if it will work or not," Murphy said.

A follow-up article on the project, printed in the March 1975 superintendents newsletter, reported that the golf/prison project "is part of an overall rehabilitating program. It is not restricted to various forms of recreation with a Country Club atmosphere. ...

"This program is designed to help them (prisoners) prepare for their return to a normal happy life."

George Jennrich of Plymouth, former superintendent at Woodhill Country Club in Wayzata, spent some of his weekends installing an irrigation system and building greens on the site.

"I didn't have any reservations," Jennrich said. "They did it to give the guys some work, because everybody who goes to jail is supposed to work. I didn't think it was a bad idea or good idea. I don't know if it was to rehabilitate people or not."

Jennrich did allow that the experience could be, well, unusual. He toured the locked-down portion of the prison and had lunch with the inmates. One day, he grubbed alongside T. Eugene Thompson, who was convicted of the 1963 "murder of the century" in Minnesota for hiring a man to kill his wife, Carol Thompson, during a St. Paul home invasion.

"I sat next to him," Jennrich said of T. Eugene, "and he never said a word. ... It was kind of an experience."

Once in a lifetime. In an effort to find out whether anyone on the state side might remember the prison course, Minnesota Department of Corrections spokesman John Schadl was contacted. He sounded taken aback at the notion of something as oxymoronic as a prison golf course.

Times have changed, Schadl said firmly.

"That absolutely couldn't happen today," he said.

CHAPTER 38

Scotsman's Craft

CHISAGO GOLF CLUB
CITY: CHISAGO CITY
COUNTY: CHISAGO
YEARS: 1920–CIRCA 1943

Chisago Golf Club championship trophy from 1936, won by Barton V. Lundquist, owner of Chisago Lakes Distributing in Chisago City.
COURTESY OF DONNA LUNDQUIST COLBERT AND CHISAGO CITY HERITAGE ASSOCIATION

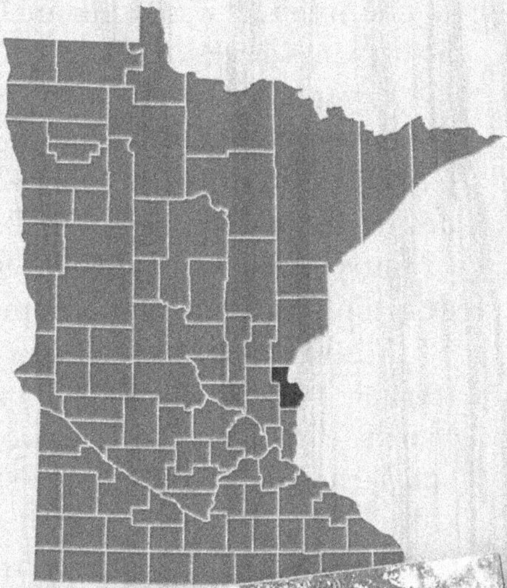

Postcard, appears to be dated 1927. Caption reads, "Golf Links Chisago City, Minn."
COURTESY OF PHIL KOSTOLNIK

Fore! Gone.

Among Minnesota's 80-plus lost golf courses, only six have what might be considered "architectural chops." That is, only a half-dozen were verifiably designed by prominent golf course architects. Five were Tom Vardon designs: Bunker Hills in Mendota Heights, Matoska in Gem Lake, the original Ortonville Golf Club, Quality Park in St. Paul and Westwood Hills in St. Louis Park.

The sixth featured a curious melding of golf course and high-profile architect.

The architect was William D. Clark, a Scotsman who came to Minnesota in 1917 by way of Omaha, Neb., to serve as the club professional at Minneapolis Golf Club in St. Louis Park. Clark went on to design the highly regarded Oak Ridge Country Club in Hopkins, as well as designing or contributing to the designs of Minneapolis city courses Gross (earlier named Armour), Columbia, Wirth (earlier named Glenwood Park) and Meadowbrook (Southwest).

In 1920, Clark added another course to his portfolio. At a glance, the course appeared "un-Clarklike." The layout originally consisted of only six holes, it featured sand greens, and it was not located in the Twin Cities area. The course was Chisago Golf Club, on the south side of Chisago City, a city 40 miles northeast of Minneapolis and at the time listing 422 residents.

Moira F. Harris described the genesis of the municipal course in her book on the history of Chisago City, *By The Shores of Ki-Chi-Saga*. Attributing the information to the *Chisago County Press* of May 10, 1923, Harris wrote:

"J. E. Vanstrom and a committee of local businessmen organized the Chisago Lakes Golf Club in 1920 on a forty-acre spread leased from the Chisago Land Company. The course was designed by W.D. Clark, a golf course architect from the Superior Golf Club in Minneapolis. ... The course was located on the east shore of Green Lake near the swimming beach."

(The mention of "Superior Golf Club in Minneapolis" might puzzle some. Superior Golf Club eventually became Brookview Country Club — renaming golf courses apparently was a cottage industry in the Twin Cities — and now is Brookview Golf Course, owned and operated by the city of Golden Valley. It, too, was designed by Clark.

(Also, there is conflicting information over the exact name of the Chisago course. It is most commonly referred to as Chisago Golf Club, but some publications called it Chisago Lakes Golf Club.)

Harris, who lives in North Oaks, said in 2013 that she remembers having walked across the old Chisago Golf Club grounds as a girl spending summers in Chisago City. Another Chisago City native, B.J. Muus, grew up just across Old Towne Road from the course and did Harris one better.

Muus recalled having played the course in its final years, perhaps 1942 or 1943, "at which I was only 6 or 7. I went over there and played it a fair amount.

You can barely call it playing, but I walked it and hit the ball.

"It was a beautiful golf course. ... Nine holes, sand greens, oily, short, but a full-scale golf course," said Muus, who lives in Auburndale, Fla. "As I recall, it was a (par) 34. Very nice."

Clark's six-hole design was expanded to nine holes in the spring of 1935, according to the Chisago City website. (Harris, in her book, reported that par after the expansion to nine holes was 33.)

The first hole, Muus said, was a par 5 of about 440 yards along Old Towne Road. "Then it wound around the lake. I know my dad was upset when it closed — even then me, too, as small as I was. ... It had lots of trees, beautiful trees, was a really nice course, too doggone bad."

Muus also recalled the clubhouse.

"It had one of those real little clubhouses; you didn't even go inside," he said. "You could walk in there and get a bottle of pop; it was the size of one of those real little gazebos."

Yet not everything about the golf course was modest. In its own way, it had "chops," too.

Chisago Golf Club was something of an adjunct to the Dahl House, billed by the owners as "Minnesota's Finest Summer Resort." Frank Dahl built the resort in 1891 along the western shore of Chisago Lake, and as the area north and east of Minneapolis and St. Paul became prime recreational country in the late 19th century, business at the Dahl House boomed. Dahl developed a reputation for "honesty, integrity, friendliness," according to a Chisago City Heritage Association website entry, and was visited by the likes of the Hamms, the famed St. Paul brewers, and the family of St. Paul railroad magnate James J. Hill.

In 1920, Frank Dahl retired and sold the Dahl House to a group of 20 men, 17 from the Twin Cities and three from Chisago City. The year coincides with the opening of the golf course — though it's possible that was not mere coincidence.

Charles Gramling, a Chisago City pharmacist and treasurer of the Chisago City Heritage Association, passed along much information on the Dahl House and the 1920 founding of the golf course and suggested a connection between the two that's hard to dispute.

Among the new Dahl House ownership group was Frank G. Danielson, who owned a drugstore on Central Avenue in Minneapolis and was at one time an Interlachen Country Club member. The resort's new manager, Thor Follestad, also was well-acquainted with golf. He had built a reputation as manager at Town & Country Club in St. Paul, home of Minnesota's first golf course.

The Dahl House and Chisago Golf Club were about 600 yards apart, the former on the east side of Old Towne Road and the latter on the west. Resort guests were afforded playing privileges on the course. Harris wrote in her Chisago history book that the golf club held annual tournaments for men and women, and that greens fees were 25 cents.

In 1925, according to notes compiled by Town & Country Club and published in the book *Tee Party on the Green*, Town & Country Club member N.P. Langford "established a new record for the six-hole course at Chicago (sic) City. Langford made the six holes in 22 while the former record for the course was 23."

The golf course served briefly as a multipurpose sports venue. Allen Holmgren, a 1939 graduate of Chisago Lakes High School, remembered that his high school football team practiced on the grounds in the summer of 1938 and played home games there that fall. "That was the only flat piece of land available," he said.

The 1930s brought on hard times for Chisago Golf Club. In 1934, a group of local businessmen took over operation of the course, according to a 1982 story in the *Chisago County Press*. Harris wrote that in 1939, the Chisago Land Company forfeited the golf course land to the city for delinquent taxes. The city operated the course briefly, but, according to the Chisago City website, "With the enlistments after the start of the war in the early 1940s, there were not enough golfers to hold interest."

The land was sold in the 1940s to The Board of Christian Service, owners of Chisago City's nursing home. In the 1980s, the same organization, then known as the Board of Social Ministry, constructed Point Pleasant Heights, a townhouse and apartment complex, as part of its expansion of senior living choices. The golf course, though long gone, received a posthumous tribute in the form of the neighborhood's street names — Fairway Lane and Ironwood, Greenway and Eagle drives.

THOR FOLLESTAD, THE FORMER DAHL HOUSE MANAGER, had another connection to a lost golf course. Starting in 1925, he was the manager of the noted White Pine Inn in Bayport, which is advertised on an old Bayport Golf Club scorecard as "The 19th Hole."

CHAPTER 39

Short Hitter

**CHISAGO LAKES PAR 3
CITY: LINDSTROM
COUNTY: CHISAGO
YEARS: 1963-65**

In an earlier era, before there were business plans, mission statements, consulting firms and befuddling terms like eco-efficiency, there were guys who just wanted to open golf courses.

Guys like Connie Gustafson.

Gustafson — officially, he was Conrad E. Gustafson — opened Chisago Lakes Par 3 Golf Course on June 8, 1963, on the western edge of the east-central Minnesota city of Lindstrom. Gustafson was the principal of Lindstrom-Center City High School, also known as Chi Hi, and had an interest in golf.

"He put this golf course on what was a farm field," said his daughter, Mary Lynch of St. Croix Falls, Wis. "I don't know if he was just scratching an itch or why he did it, but it didn't stay open very long, so I don't think it was very lucrative."

As with many small-town courses, there was a seat-of-the-pants element to Chisago Lakes Par 3. Forget the Titleist sales reps; forget the state-of-the art Toro machinery.

"He had an old World War II Jeep that he hooked up rotary mowers behind," Lynch said, "and he'd mow the grass with that outfit. I learned to drive in a Jeep; that was kind of cool … stick shift, you know, on the floor."

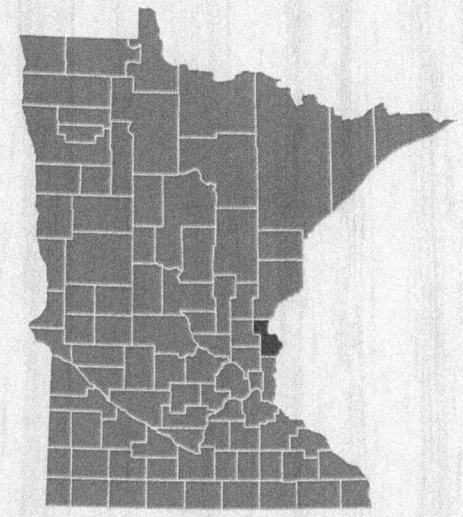

It seems fair to say Gustafson probably didn't have big plans for his golf course. In fact, there really was nothing big about Chisago Lakes Par 3. It was Herve' Villechaize with fescue.

"The holes were all pretty short," said Keith Carlson, the fifth-term mayor of Lindstrom who played the course as a teenager, "except for the ninth hole, where you could hit a full shot, maybe 120 yards."

All of the other holes were less than 100 yards, Carlson said.

If Gustafson didn't offer much in terms of his course's length, he didn't ask much, either, in terms of its price. Greens fees were 50 cents for the first nine holes, Lynch said. That made the course popular among young people, though Carlson allowed that "I probably never played the golf course after I got a driver's license."

Chisago Lakes Par 3 closed in 1965, and Gustafson opened a mobile home court on the property, Elms Estates, that still exists today, along Lake Boulevard. "It's very tiny," Lynch said of the mobile home court, "so you can see how small the golf course was."

CHAPTER 40
The Iron Game

CHISHOLM PUBLIC GOLF COURSE
CITY: CHISHOLM
COUNTY: ST. LOUIS
YEARS: 1927–CIRCA 1941

IRON ORE MINING WOULD SEEM TO HAVE NOTHING TO DO WITH GOLF — EXCEPT THAT ONE INVOLVES IRON AND THE OTHER INVOLVES IRONS.

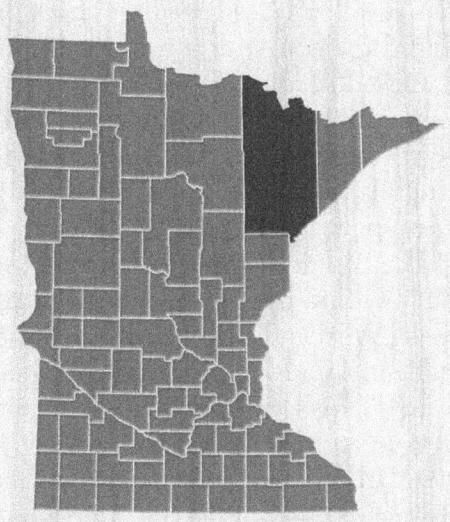

Yet in a sense, even if tangential, iron ore mining did have something to do with golf in the northeastern Minnesota city of Chisholm.

Chisholm's first major resource was timber. Beginning in the 1880s, lumbermen harvested pine and birch trees from what is now the town site. About the same time, prospectors discovered hematite, a valuable mineral, in the northeastern Minnesota earth. Iron ore mining soon became the bedrock for early 20th-century growth and development in a 150-mile arc from Crosby to Ely that came to be known as the Iron Range.

Chisholm lay in the heart of the Mesabi Range, one of the three ranges that make up the Iron Range. European immigrants migrated to the area to work for the mines, exponentially increasing cities' populations. By 1910, Chisholm, incorporated as a village only nine years earlier and devastated only two years earlier by a fire that nearly wiped it off the map, boasted a population of 7,684. By 1920, the population had risen to 9,039.

By 1927, with the Iron Range economy still steaming along and having helped build a vibrant Chisholm, townsfolk sought to add a new feature to their landscape.

"The organization of a golf club at Chisholm is assured," reported the June 1927 issue of *The 10,000 Lakes Golfer*, "following the visit of Leigh Simms, Minneapolis, who assisted local players in laying out a nine-hole course."

The magazine's next issue reported that the Chisholm golf course would be ready to open by July 4. It would consist of nine holes, "1 mile from the city," and would be supervised by the American Legion post.

The golf course lasted less than two decades, and, judging by more than a half-dozen telephone calls placed to residents of the area, almost no one remembers it.

Almost.

"I remember the course," said Bill Loushine, 91. "I golfed on it probably a couple of times, but none of us had golf clubs. It was just (for) the elite in town."

Loushine, a retired educator who still hunts deer and golfs, said the Chisholm course was in the northwest part of town, on a level parcel. He said he thought he played the course around 1935 and that it closed before World War II. He remembered that it was near 13th Street Northwest, that a creek ran through the grounds, and that a man named Grams might have been the manager.

The course might have lasted at least partway into the World War II years. A 1941 Works Progress Administration guide to Minnesota Arrowhead Country listed "Chisholm Public Golf Course," with an address of 8th Avenue North. A 1942 Iron Range telephone directory, however, does not list the course.

Loushine said that after World War II and the golf course's closure, the land was to be used for veterans' housing, but that financing fell through. He said in the late 1950s, when the land belonged to Chisholm's housing authority, the Junior Chamber of Commerce sought to revive the golf course in bits and pieces — two or three holes a year. "It's too bad that didn't materialize," he said.

Also, Loushine said, he recalled someone hauling sod off the golf course grounds, and that he stopped the fellow and procured 1,500 yards of sod to be used along the shore of Longyear Lake in Chisholm.

Chisholm no longer has a golf course. The nearest is Hibbing Municipal, six miles to the south, where Loushine still plays. With the heyday of iron ore mining having long since passed, Chisholm's population has dropped by almost half since 1920; the city had 4,976 residents in 2010.

A 1941 aerial photograph, viewable through the Minnesota Department of Natural Resources' Landview website, reveals more about the course. It was indeed in the northwestern corner of town. A driveway and building along Eighth Avenue Northwest, just south of 13th Street Northwest, were the only signs of development in the immediate neighborhood, and the building presumably was the golf clubhouse.

Perhaps 200 yards west of the clubhouse on the aerial map is a series of three white, round dots — almost unquestionably the site of sand greens. (Another longtime Chisholm resident, Michael Valentini, said it was his understanding that the course had sand greens.) A fourth such dot is plainly visible southeast of the clubhouse, and at least two other dots, slightly fuzzier on the photograph, also are not far from the clubhouse.

Loushine said the old golf course lay on what is now a recently developed subdivision, west of Eighth Avenue and along 12th and 13th Streets, and the aerial photos bear that out. Though it isn't clear whether the course crossed north of 13th Street, it does not appear to have stretched as far northwest as Calvary Cemetery. Most notably, in comparing the 1941 aerial with modern-day Chisholm, a significant portion of the old golf course was on what is now the grounds of the Range Center, a facility for people with developmental disabilities. The southeasternmost green on the golf course, mentioned above, appears to have been almost exactly at the eastern edge of the Range Center's main parking lot.

If you drop a ball on that spot today and try to replicate a putt from 80 years earlier, be advised that parking lots tend to run significantly faster than sand greens.

LEIGH SIMMS, WHO HELPED PLAN THE CHISHOLM COURSE, was a talented player out of the Midland Hills and Columbia courses in the Twin Cities in the 1920s and was a prominent figure in the formation of the Minnesota Public Golf Association in 1922.

CHAPTER 41

Take it from Dad

BEMIDJI MUNICIPAL GOLF COURSE
CITY: BEMIDJI
COUNTY: BELTRAMI
YEARS: 1920s–EARLY 1940s

KATIE PETERMEIER OF GRAND RAPIDS EMAILED WITH A REPORT OF A COURSE HER FATHER, LYLE OFTEDAHL, TALKED ABOUT.

"I'm not sure what the name of the course was, but my dad told a story about a course that was just south of Bemidji by Lake Plantagenet where he won his first golf tournament. It had to be in the late 1920s or early 1930s, since my dad was born in 1919. He said he won the tournament with a 5-iron and a putter and broke the putter before he finished the round. He ended up winning a set of golf clubs!"

New clubs, eh? Had to be tough retiring that do-it-all 5-iron …

Months later, Petermeier emailed again, noting that her sister recalled that the course was on or near the "Fenske Farm."

Indeed it was. The course, Katie, was Bemidji Municipal Golf Course, and it was a real, live, actual layout, despite the mild protests of a Bemidji city employee who said she had never heard of such a place and expressed doubt that it ever existed.

Bemidji Municipal is mentioned in a handful of old books and newspapers, including a listing of Minnesota Arrowhead golf courses in the July 10, 1937, *Winnipeg Free Press*. It was not quite as far

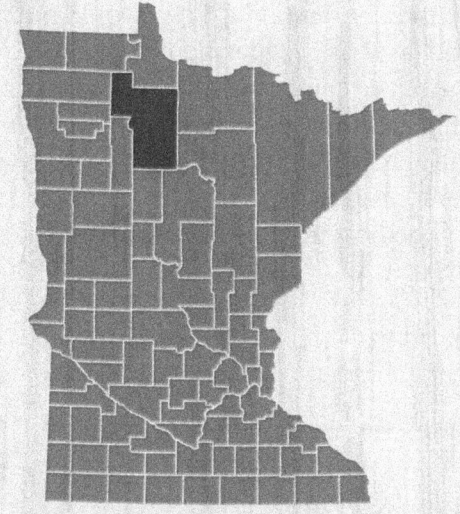

south of Bemidji as Lake Plantagenet, but that was the correct general direction: It was about 2½ miles south-southeast of downtown Bemidji.

And, yes, it was linked to the Fenske name.

Edwin Fenske and his brother Walter for most of the 20th century owned and farmed land south of Bemidji, just west of U.S. Highway 71. They also operated the well-known Fenske Dairy out of the same site, starting in 1951. The original Fenske farmland was adjacent to Bemidji Municipal, and the Fenskes bought the golf course land after the course closed. Edwin Fenske's widow, Audrey, 93, said the course was closed by the time she married into the family in 1942, though the course still is listed in the 1942 Bemidji city directory — but by 1946, the course was no longer listed.

Audrey's sons Harold and Gerald had heard about the former golf course.

"My dad said for years and years when they farmed the land, they'd find golf balls," said Harold Fenske, of Nebish.

"They used to always have a five-gallon pail on the tractor seat," said Gerald Fenske, of Bemidji. "They would pick up golf balls as they farmed."

Many, many golf balls. Both sons said their father and uncle would hit balls by the pailful off into nearby woods for amusement.

The best modern-day reference point for the old golf course — all three Fenskes mentioned it — is the interchange of U.S. Highways 2 and 71, an interchange that was built on the golf course grounds. Gerald Fenske said the course ran as far south as the current Pete's Place South convenience store and that the northeast corner of the golf course corresponds to a fenced-in, state-owned retention pond near property he owns. He used to operate a welding shop that was on the golf course property, and he said that as recently as about three years ago, there was a remnant of the course — a machine shed that stored mowers — still standing, though the roof had caved in.

Bemidji Municipal's opening date remains a mystery. Gerald Fenske said his father used to cut grass at the course, perhaps in 1930 or '31.

NORTH OF TOWN, BEMIDJI TOWN & COUNTRY CLUB, ON the shore of Lake Bemidji, has been a bellwether of outstate golf since 1916 and the host of the highly regarded Birchmont Tournament since 1926.

CHAPTER 42

Silos and Flagsticks

SOUTHWESTERN MINNESOTA IS KNOWN FOR FERTILE FARMLAND, CLOSE-KNIT SMALL TOWNS AND LAND AS LEVEL AS THE $13 FLAT-TOP AVAILABLE AT BERNIE'S BARBER SHOP IN WINDOM.

The region also can now be known for its lost golf courses.

Five (or six) of the state's southwesternmost counties — Cottonwood, Jackson, Lyon, Murray, Pipestone and Watonwan with an asterisk — are home to as many as 12 lost courses. Let's take a virtual visit, early 1900s style.

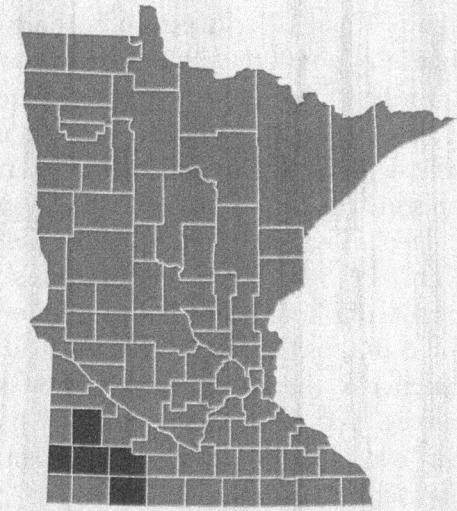

WINDOM

Considering the region's topography, our Southwestern Minnesota lost-golf course tour begins in an unlikely place.

On a hilltop.

The *Windom Recorder* of Sept. 5, 1924, reported on a road trip organized by President A.B. Fisch of the Windom Golf Club, in which the club officers and board of directors visited a site two miles east of the Cottonwood County seat. "Driving our car to the top of a small hill we stopped and found a beautiful view overlooking Summit and Wolf lakes," reported the writer, Paul Gillam. "… Our little city can be seen in the distance very prominently and a golfer would soon know that a mistake would not be made in selecting this spot for the home of the Windom Golf Club."

Fisch, Gillam et al. sketched out a nine-hole course covering approximately 2,760 yards. This apparently was not Windom's first golf course, however. Five days later, the Cottonwood County Citizen ran a story headlined "Golfers Vote to Change Course," detailing the club's settling on the aforementioned land east of town and including one direct reference to "the present course." Also, the 1926 *American Annual Golf Guide* listed Windom Golf Club's year of founding as 1922.

The new course's grounds would cover 65 acres, leased for $5 an acre per year. The land was rolling, the *Citizen* reported, and featured views of the city plus four lakes: Cottonwood, Summit, Wolf and Parsons. It seems likely the reference to the latter lake could have been "Parso," also known in the 1920s as Parso Slough. The western edge of Parso was, in fact, within probably 100 yards of the golf course, based on a 1938 aerial map that shows the routing of the course.

The course's southern border was County Road 17; its western border was what is now 500th Avenue. Just to the northeast of that intersection, up the hill referred to in the *Recorder* story, is the highest point within approximately five miles in any direction, 1,485 feet above sea level. That area is now a farm field.

The 1938 aerial photo indicates an unusual-looking shape for a clubhouse — a thin, upside-down "T." That lends credence to the notion, reported by two sources, that the clubhouse might have been two old railroad cars set perpendicular to each other.

The course had sand greens, played to a par of 34 and measured 3,167 yards in its almost-finished version, according to the 1926 *American Annual Golf Guide*. Almost-finished? Yes, apparently. The Jan. 30, 1928, issue of *The 10,000 Lakes Golfer* included this entry: "Windom GC to be reconstructed (only two holes unchanged) under direction of Prof. C.E. Carey, Mpls."

It isn't known when this site was abandoned, but the current Windom Country Club, northwest of the city, was established in 1947.

Jackson

Twenty miles south of Windom, down U.S. 71, is the city of Jackson, seat of Jackson County. Two miles south of downtown Jackson, on a rolling piece of land in Petersburg Township, Harold Swensrud began plying his boyhood craft in the early 1930s as a 9-year-old at the original Jackson Golf Club, just east of the Petersburg Road.

"I caddied there; then, when there wasn't anyone around, I played," said Swensrud, 90, a longtime Jackson resident who now lives in nearby Sherburn.

Swensrud and his caddieing buddies were more than just club-toters. They would set off on holes in advance of their clients, serving as caddie and forecaddie rolled into one.

"We started walking down the fairway, we'd be 50 to a hundred yards out there, and so we'd never lose any golf balls," Swensrud said. "The pay was terrible, but we didn't know any better — 10 to 15 cents. ... But they'd give you a ride home when you were done. I lived halfway between downtown and the golf course, so they'd drop you off. And sometimes you'd get more than a nickel, and I'd ride into town and get two bags of popcorn and bring one home for my mom and me."

Swensrud remembered the entire routing of the course, from No. 1, a 250-yard hole with a creek coming into play at about 200 yards, to No. 9, where he said he once saw a woman make a hole in one. The clubhouse was in a wooded area at the north edge of the grounds and was "just big enough to be an outhouse." The course had sand greens and no watering system, Swensrud said.

Jackson Golf Club dated to 1924, according to the 1930-31 *American Annual Golf Guide*, which listed its length as 3,152 yards and par as 33, with a membership of 58 and daily fee of $1. The Petersburg Township site was selected in May 1925, according to a story in the *Jackson Republic* newspaper. The site, the newspaper reported, was the "Fiddes land" and was selected on the advice of "Mr. Morton of Fairmont, an authority on proper golf grounds."

Bylaws were adopted on June 30, 1925. Local guests could play with members three times a year. Caddies couldn't charge more than 20 cents for nine holes or 30 cents for 18. Marked golf balls that were lost were returned to the club and could be repurchased for 10 cents. Golfers could not buy lost balls from caddies. Such terms perhaps contributed to Swensrud terminating his caddieing career upon graduating from high school in 1941. "I was done carrying these big bags for these cockroaches who paid me 10 cents," he said.

The *Jackson Republic* of July 17, 1925, noted the first birdie at the course, recorded by Frank Holecek while "displaying wonderful nerve and form." Holecek slayed the beast that was the 294-yard, par-4 third hole in three whacks, which, the newspaper reported, made him the first person entitled to play the course wearing knickers. Holecek played in a foursome that day, and his playing partners, the newspaper reported, "all have promised not to give out Frank's total score for nine holes."

The Petersburg Township site lasted into the early 1940s. The club began selling off equipment in February 1943, according to the Jackson Golf Club website, and "the remainder of 1943 and 1944 the Jackson Golf Club was almost closed as most golfers were serving in World War II. ... During this time, the course was turned into a pasture and never again used for golfing."

Jackson Golf Club re-emerged in 1947 north of town, its layout designed by Bim Lovekin, a golf professional in Worthington, for $100. The club is still in operation at that site. Swensrud, a six-state traveling menswear salesman, became adept at the game and won the 1970 men's championship at Jackson. He was nicknamed "Medicare," he said, for his smooth, untroubled swing.

LAKEFIELD

Now, things get flatter.

Farther west, 8½ miles from Jackson and four miles south of the city of Lakefield, lies what is now a squarish, moribund-looking plot of land that once served as Lakefield Golf Club, established in 1926. The club was immediately northeast of what was known as 4-Mile Corner: the intersection of Minnesota Highway 86 and Jackson County 34, which formerly was U.S. 16.

Wait a minute — moribund-looking?

Yes. I realize what they say happens when you assume, but judging by current aerial and elevation maps, and a tour through the countryside via Google's Street View feature, the old Lakefield Golf Club grounds, except for a creek's bed that's at most 10 feet wide, appears to have had all the character of a Manila envelope.

A *Lakefield Standard* reporter called the land "rolling" in an August 1926 story (perhaps he grew up in Kansas), and a story earlier in the month in the same newspaper had reported: "L.F. Adair, secretary-treasurer of the club, predicts tht (sic) Lakefield's course will be one of the best in the vicinity."

Well, then, we'll just agree to disagree.

It's unclear when the site was abandoned. A 1938 aerial map, the earliest readily available, shows no signs of a golf course still existing at the site. Lakefield's current course, Emerald Valley, was established in 1977 at the northern edge of the city. The Lakefield Golf Club site later became a county landfill, also now abandoned.

Heron Lake

Eleven miles northwest of Lakefield is Heron Lake, population 698. At the northern edge of the city, just across Minnesota Highway 60, is Laker Field, home of the Heron Lake Lakers amateur baseball team.

But before there were ground-rule doubles at the site, there were double bogeys.

Heron Lake Golf Club was organized in July 1925, with the *Heron Lake News* reporting, "It was decided to lease the race track property from the City and go ahead with the work. ... The present plot will allow about 1800 yard (sic) divided in nine holes." H.B. Triem was named club president. "Mr. Triem is well versed in the game and will have charge of laying out the course," the newspaper reported. Triem would lay out the Lakefield course the next year.

"Golf is described as a health game that everyone can play. ... It is a long time coming but when it comes it usually stays," the *News* had reported the week before, in a story headlined "Golf Club May Be Perfected."

The newspaper also reported that the Heron Lake course had sand greens and "stately built bunkers."

Don Steen of Heron Lake recalled a "bunker or barrier" around two of the nine holes. "The bunkers were about two-foot high dirt and grass and several feet wide," he wrote. "A rake and a carpet with a handle on each was used to smooth and level after playing the hole. The course was originally mowed with a three reel mower pulled by horses; later with a tractor. Men and women usually played after store closings."

The course, which had a racetrack used for high school sports and horse training within its confines, lasted at least into the mid-1930s. A Southwestern Minnesota Women's Golf Association event was to be held there in June 1930, according to the *News*, featuring eight clubs from the region, and in July 1934, 10 Fulda golfers won a match with the Heron Lake "mashie wielders" at the Heron Lake course, the newspaper reported.

Fulda

In the same Heron Lake newspaper story, it was reported a return match would be played at Fulda. That city's lost course was less than a mile east of town, on 40 acres near Minnesota Highway 62, said longtime Fulda resident and avid golfer Del Koopman. That would place it not far south of Fulda's current course, Town & Country, established in the early 1990s (and we have a good notion that Town & Country was not, as noted on one website, "built by Nick Faldo").

Koopman said Fulda's lost course had sand greens, and he thought there were only five or six holes. "When the second world war came along, it kind of went on its merry way," he said.

Chandler

A golf course without greens?

"Yes, indeed, Chandler did at one time have a golf course," Dean Peterson of Mankato wrote in a history book produced for the 100th anniversary of the city of Chandler, in Murray County. "It wasn't as extravagant as the golf courses we see now. There is doubt whether there were any greens on the course, but it was a golf course."

Little else is known about the course, except that it was built in a pasture just north of the former John Veld farm in Chanarambie Township, just over a mile northwest of Chandler. The course is said to have dated to the 1920s. There are no signs of the course still existing in a 1938 aerial photo.

Pipestone

Pipestone Golf Club, in the city of 4,300 just seven miles from the South Dakota border, apparently had three lost-course sites, judging by a 1982 *Pipestone County Star* story, before moving to its present site south of town.

The first site was the Even farm; the newspaper story did not describe that location in detail. Next was the Jerry Hines farm, north of the city and near U.S. Highway 75. The third site, the newspaper reported, was "the Johnson Quarry on the DN Kilby dairy farms, just below Indian Lakes, where the dam is." The sand-greens course featured a par-6 ninth hole with a slough on it. "An eight foot long bull snake resided in the slough," the newspaper reported. "Avid golfer Jack Dressen said the snake was a good addition as it kept the rodents out."

Tracy

Our southwestern tour ends in a farm field four miles north of Tracy, a city of 2,166 in Lyon County. The field gives rise to corn and soybeans on a rotating basis, but before that, it was a pasture. And before that, a golf course.

"We found one cup and one golf ball" on the grounds, Brian Ludeman said in a fall 2012 telephone interview while operating his combine on the SAN-MARBO Farms property he owns and farms with brothers Sandy and Cal, the latter a 1986 Minnesota gubernatorial candidate. "And we think there's maybe a green down in there; it's a wetland now. We've always had the inclination to take a metal detector and go down there to see if we can find another cup, but we've never done that."

The course's history was addressed in the book *The First 100 Years in Tracy*, by Merrill Starr:

"Tracy's first golf club was organized in October 1924. A field four miles north of town containing 65 acres of virgin prairie sod was leased, and an effort was made to prepare sand greens before the ground froze that autumn. It was hoped that at least 100 members would sign up.

"The next spring, the prairie grass was closely mowed, and the nine sand greens were given the final touches. The course was said to be one of the best in all of southwestern Minnesota, and players for miles around were attracted to a tournament in the summer of 1925."

Brian Ludeman said he thought the course lasted only five or six years. The main part of the 25-acre farm field is flat, he said, "but then there's a big ravine that cuts across it, and I think that was part of (the golf course). There's a river or creek that goes through there, and I think that was part of it, too. I mean, you've gotta use your imagination; we're not quite sure how it was set up."

Ludeman said he heard the course was mowed using Model-T Fords, raising the possibility that a Tracy auto dealer might have played a role in the course's operation. Ludeman's father, Sander, said an 18 by 30 clubhouse used to be on the land, but "I don't know what happened to the darn thing. It was long gone when we bought the farm" about 20 years ago.

Tracy's current golf course, Tracy Country Club, opened in 1948 two miles east of the city.

Special thanks to Michael Kirchmeier, director of the Jackson County Historical Society, for providing material for this chapter.

CHAPTER 43

Rebirthed

U. S. G. A. RULES APPLY EXCEPT AS
MODIFIED BY THE FOLLOWING
LOCAL RULES

1. Out of Bounds is defined by white stakes on right side of fairways No. 1, 2, 3, 8, 9.
2. Unplayable ball. Lift and drop not nearer hole. penalty two strokes.
3. Cultivated areas — drinking fountains — man holes — buildings are not hazards — ball may be lifted and dropped not nearer hole without penalty.

REPLACE DIVOTS
REPAIR BALL MARKS ON GREENS
LET FASTER PLAYERS THROUGH

The State Bank of Faribault
Faribault, Minnesota

FARIBAULT'S ONLY LOCALLY OWNED BANK
DEPOSITS INSURED BY
Federal Deposit Insurance Corporation

Faribault Golf and Country Club
Faribault, Minnesota

Golf — Swim — Relax

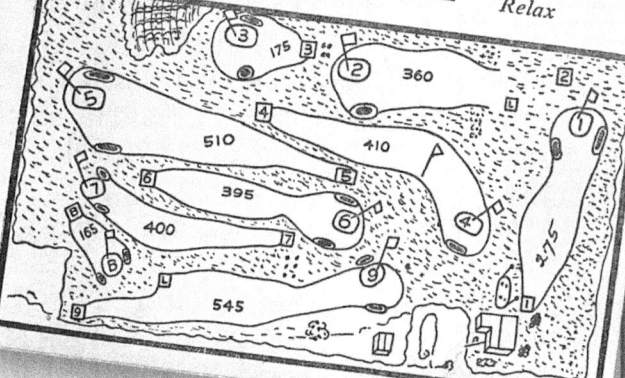

SCORECARD COURTESY OF JON VEE

207

FORE! GONE.

Not all lost golf courses were like the old soldiers in Douglas MacArthur's farewell address. They didn't all just fade away. Some soldiered on, either as the same club at a new site or as an altogether new course at the same site.

Two of these "rebirthed" golf courses are in the southern Minnesota city of Faribault. One was practically in Dick Carlander's yard.

Carlander grew up in the 1940s and '50s in a house on the corner of 6th Avenue Southwest and 8th Street Southwest in Faribault, about a mile from downtown. Across 8th Street was the first green at the nine-hole Faribault Golf and Country Club.

"The first hole was a par 4, probably 250, 260 yards," Carlander said. "The way they hit balls now, we would have had a number of balls in our yard."

The clubhouse, too, was not far from Carlander's childhood home. Within earshot of his second-floor bedroom, in fact.

"They used to have some real wingdings in the clubhouse ... bands playing, people hooting and hollering," Carlander said.

At age 14 or 15, Carlander was hired to clean the clubhouse bar and locker room area. He remembered sweeping up beer bottles and cigarettes, and "I can remember vaguely when they had slot machines."

Occasional reprobate activity notwithstanding, Faribault Golf Club carries significant stature in Minnesota golf history. The club's website says the club was founded in 1910, though there is ample evidence that it dates back earlier than that, usually referred to as Tatepaha Golf Club.

The book *History of Rice and Steele Counties, Minnesota*, published in 1910, includes this entry: "Tatepaha Golf Club. This club was organized in the spring of 1900. ... Grounds were leased in the southern part of the city and a club house erected. The grounds are pretty and picturesque, and form an ideal place for golf and other recreation. The club is the only one of its size outside the Twin Cities in this part of the country. It is represented every year at the state golf tournament, and the local grounds have developed some excellent golf players."

The 1901 *Harper's Official Golf Guide* listed the course, then dispatched an arrow toward its backside: "Faribault Golf Club. ... Organized, 1900. Annual dues, $10. Membership, 62. A nine-hole course, with poor putting-greens."

In 1901, at a meeting in Winona, the Minnesota Golf Association was formed, with Tatepaha as one of seven founding clubs. Tatepaha, which means "windy hill" in the Dakota Indian language, garnered frequent references before 1910 in Twin Cities newspapers as a club that competed against Twin Cities-area clubs.

The club still was named Tatepaha in 1916, according to an entry in *Spalding's Official Golf Guide*. By 1925, it was going by the name Faribault Golf

Ray Budenske, on the practice green at Faribault Golf and Country Club, 1947
COURTESY OF JON VEE AND LISA EVERT

and Country Club, according to a scorecard from that year.

Carlander, now 75 and chairman of the State Bank of Faribault, said the layout "was a typical old-time old-style golf course. Small greens, small tee boxes, small bunkers. It wasn't a very long course." Total yardage was 3,085. The seventh green, Carlander said, lay across the south side of 8th Avenue, on a block separate from the rest of the course.

Carlander won six varsity golf letters at Faribault High School. As a senior in 1955, he played in the final Big Nine Conference golf tournament on the "Tatepaha" grounds. The next year, the course was abandoned in favor of a new site, two miles to the north and 1½ miles northwest of downtown. Interlachen Country Club professional Willie Kidd designed a nine-hole course at that location, and in 1957, Carlander won the second club championship on the new course. In 1966, Bob Carlson of Austin designed a back nine. Now known as Faribault Golf Club, play continues at that site today. Part of the old clubhouse was moved to the current location and is still in use.

The old-course plot was sold to Bosford Lumber Company, which subdivided it. The area is residential now, with Tatepaha Boulevard arcing through it, a block north of Carlander's boyhood home.

Other "Rebirthings"

Faribault, Part II

On the northeast side of Faribault, the 14th tee at Legacy Golf lies within shanking distance of the parking lot at

Shattuck-St. Mary's School. The two entities (the golf course and the school, not the golf course and the parking lot) are inextricably linked.

Legacy is an 18-hole course designed by noted architect Garrett Gill. It opened in 1998 and occupies land formerly owned by Shattuck-St. Mary's, a boarding school that dates to 1858. For decades, 42 acres of Shattuck-St. Mary's property served as the site of the nine-hole Shattuck Golf Course.

Shattuck Golf Course, according to a 1985 Minnesota Golf Course Superintendents Association newsletter entry written by former Shattuck superintendent Randy Nelson, opened in 1928. It was designed by C.W. Newhall Jr., Shattuck Class of 1923 and son of the school's headmaster. Newhall was assisted in layout and construction of the course by Charles Erickson, greenskeeper at the Minikahda Club in Minneapolis, and White Bear Yacht Club pro Tom Vardon. The course measured 3,110 yards and also was known as Shattuck Golf Club.

The course was private in its early years, with Shattuck cadets and others with Shattuck connections paying a yearly fee of $20. The course went public around 1936, Nelson wrote.

Mike Frankenfield, who came to the Shattuck school in 1986 as a teacher and coach, managed Shattuck Golf Course in its later years. "The course I came to see in the '80s had been decimated by Dutch Elm Disease," Frankenfield said. He suspected the course had a parkland look in its early years but said it was mostly wide open by the time he first saw it.

Shattuck Golf Course was popular among the area's residents, Frankenfield said, hosting upwards of 25,000 to 30,000 rounds annually at its peak. The course was closed in the mid-1990s — Frankenfield thought it was in 1995 — and by 1997, the entire Shattuck GC grounds was part of either the new Legacy course or residential development. None of the Shattuck routing was retained in construction of the Legacy course. Frankenfield said the old eighth green at Shattuck was close to the current 14th tee at Legacy and that there are remnants of the old course in the woods near the tee box. Homes along the southeast edge of the Legacy course have Newhall Drive as their addresses, and a cul-de-sac next to Legacy's southernmost hole is situated on Vardon Court.

Cannon Falls/Wanamingo

Cannon Golf Club, another course laid out by Vardon in the late 1920s, was originally known as Cannon Glen Golf Club. Vardon's creation, even though it featured sand greens, likely was a step up for the gentlemen of Cannon Glen Golf Club, who, according to a *Cannon Falls Beacon* story, "had been introduced to golf when they played on a course cut through the pasture of Adolph Nesseth near Wanamingo in 1926."

Northfield

Northfield Golf Club has a history similar to that of Tatepaha/Faribault, with the club originally based on one site and then moved to another. Entries from the Northfield Golf Club website provide details:

"The first movement was formed to organize a Northfield golf club in the mid 1920's. ... The committee leased the

70 acre Hollis tract along the Cannon River, south of town (NW of current Hwy. 3, Co. Rd. 1 intersection). ... A nine hole course of 3,000 yards was laid out with the assistance of C. B. Anderson, a golf professional of Minneapolis. The course was laid out in March and ready to play June 1, with greens of part sand and part grass.

"In March, 1925, President Dr. H. C. Remele appointed a committee to investigate a proposal to move the course to a new site near the city. ... In May, 37½ acres of land were leased from O. F. Pruett on the east edge of town (our current location). Seeding and work on permanent greens was started, with the new course expected to be ready for use in 1926."

Ortonville

Though the Great Depression killed off many Minnesota golf courses, it was more of an accessory to the crime in the demise of the original Ortonville Golf Club layout.

The course was designed in 1921 by Vardon and opened in 1922 on a 61-acre plot northeast of Ortonville, on what was known as "the diagonal road," or Big Stone County Highway 12. The site was less than optimal. "It was way out in the middle of nothing," said Barbara Johnson of Ortonville, who recalled being taken to the golf course often as a young girl by her parents. She would play with her dolls, she said, while her parents played the course.

The course had "pasture-land fairways and sand greens," Magdalene R. Sparrow wrote in her book *Big Stone County, Minnesota 1881–1991*. League play was popular, Sparrow wrote, among towns in Minnesota and nearby South Dakota, whose members comprised the Minnkota Golf League.

Par was 33, the course measured 2,200 yards, and it cost 75 cents per day to play in 1926.

Like Johnson, Vince Parker of Stillwater remembered the old Ortonville course. "When I was just a young kid, I used to go out to that golf course, and we'd wait around in sloughs and collect balls," Parker said. "We'd sell them back to golfers for 50 cents a ball. If they had a smile on them, of course, you wouldn't get that much."

The course survived almost the entire Great Depression, then sought a greener pasture, figuratively at least. Ortonville Golf Club's move to its current site, a mile north of downtown, perhaps could not have been made without the help of the Works Progress Administration, a Depression-era labor program.

"In September 1939," Sparrow wrote, "the city purchased 86 acres of land from Martin Schoen for $3,500. On this site, overlooking Big Stone Lake, the golf clubhouse and nine holes were constructed by W.P.A. labor from 1940 to 1942. By 1942, W.P.A. had 65 men on the project, with $54,987 approved for construction of a clubhouse, greens, tees, fairways, grading, landscape and watering system."

A second nine was added in 1974. Ortonville Municipal Golf Course, as it is now known, is something of an anomaly in small-town, outstate Minnesota — a city of 2,000 with an 18-hole golf course.

Part of the course's northern border is County Highway 12, which two miles east turns diagonally, near the original golf course layout. The lost course served as a trapshooting range long after the original course closed; the gun range no longer exists there.

Roseau

Golf in this northwestern Minnesota town, 10 miles from the Canadian border, originated on a layout that most certainly wasn't an inspiration on the sketchpad of a Donald Ross disciple. Britt Dahl of the Roseau County Historical Society passed along details:

"The Roseau Golf Course (Oakcrest) was previously located on the Roseau County Fairgrounds in Roseau, but was moved. The *Roseau Times Region* reported in 1936, 'The local golf association rented the fair grounds. They complained of having to share the grounds with a herd of sheep and purchased other land in 1936. One of the holes was a blind shot over the grandstand.'"

No word on whether the sheep approved of the arrangement. And, hey, if you're going out to watch the tractor pull, a word of warning: Fore!

CHAPTER 44

Let's Not Forget

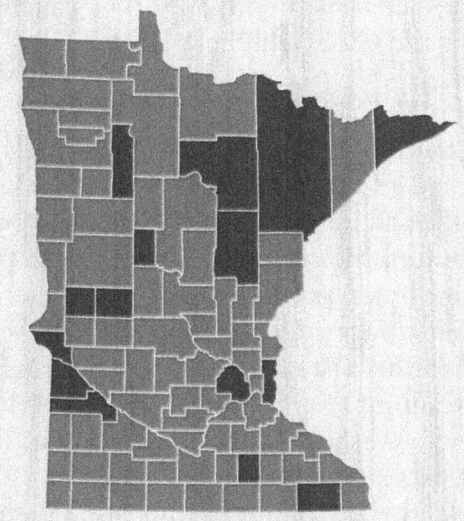

Arcadia Lodge

A nine-hole course and driving range used to be part of this resort, 30 miles northwest of Grand Rapids on the western shore of Turtle Lake. The lodge's Nikki Jones passed along this nugget from an original lodge brochure:

"Work on our nine hole golf course is being rushed to early completion and in all probability will be in readiness by July 1, 1926. The Golf Professional who has the work in charge pronounces it one of the best natural courses of which he has knowledge."

Jones said the course was defunct by the 1940s or '50s but that golf tees still are occasionally found on the grounds.

Beardsley

The 1930-31 *American Annual Golf Guide* lists a Lakeside Golf Club, established in 1924, five miles from the city of Beardsley, near the North and South Dakota borders. That location doesn't appear to coincide with any current golf course. The course was nine holes, 2,227 yards, par 33, with sand greens. E.G. Blackmun was the club president.

Blooming Prairie

A nine-hole course was said to have been built east of this southeastern Minnesota town, along Highway 30. It was said to have closed in the 1940s.

Boyd/Clarkfield

The same 1930-31 guide lists Boyd Country Club, also established in 1924, nine holes, 2,500 yards, par 33, sand greens, 27 members and "within city limits."

Six miles southeast of Boyd, in western Minnesota, lies the town of Clarkfield. The 1930-31 *American Annual Golf Guide* lists Orwoll Golf Club, established 1928, nine holes, 2,600 yards, sand greens, three miles from city, 40 members. The 1929 *Amateur Golfer & Outdoor Magazine* reported that five holes were in use at the new Clarkfield course, with four more being finished.

Though there is no established connection between him and the golf course, C.S. Orwoll was a president and/or director at more than a half-dozen outstate banks in the early 1900s, including the Clarkfield State Bank.

Camden Park, Minneapolis

The 1901 *Harper's Official Golf Guide* listed a Camden Park Golf Club, "Post-office address, Camden Place, and substation, Minneapolis." The course was nine holes, yardage 1,586, with only two holes longer than 200 yards. A 1905 city directory listed the course's address as "Camden Park Place Athletic Club, 4157 Washn Ave N." Beyond that, few details are known.

David C. Smith, Minneapolis parks historian, noted a *Minneapolis Tribune* entry from July 21, 1899, on his blog: "The Camden Park golf club has been organized among the young men in the employ of the C.A. Smith Lumber company," the newspaper reported. "It plays over a beautiful course of nine holes laid out in the Camden park region and crosses the creek three times." Smith presumed that the reference was to Shingle Creek.

The site might have been within a few hundred yards of the Mississippi River, near the current sites of I-94 and the Camden Bridge. A 2009 Camden Community News website entry written by Ron Manger reported that the original Camden Park was at this location, a few blocks east of the current Webber/Camden Park site.

An inquiry with a group with north Minneapolis connections was not answered.

Crestwood, Alexandria

Also known as Miller's Crestwood, for the family that was the second of three owners of the course. One website lists its opening date as 1972. It was a nine-hole, par-36 course on the east side of Lake Le Homme Dieu, a hilly layout that overlooked the lake. Neither the Millers nor Mark Klatte, the course's final owner, offered many other details on the course.

Klatte, a Plymouth native whose family owned Elm Creek Golf Course in Plymouth, bought Crestwood in the mid-1990s and sold it in, he believed, 1997. The course is now a housing development. Klatte also owns and operates Clarks Grove Golf Course in southeastern Minnesota.

Eko Backen

The "Eko Backen" name is best known as an outdoor recreational area, six miles east of Forest Lake on Manning Trail. It once had a par-34 golf course, too.

A 1977 directory described the course this way: "A rolling and hilly terrain (used for inner tubing in snow), two water hazards, sand traps on three holes, a few natural hazards, and small, watered greens."

Henry Houle of Forest Lake owned Eko Backen for one year in the mid-1970s and said the golf course likely was built in the early 1970s and likely closed by 1978 or '79.

Elbow Lake

Expansion, contraction ... Elbow Lake, 30 miles west of Alexandria, had a course that was built in 1930 just north of town, wrote Patty Benson, director of the Grant County Historical Society. The course began as a par-3, 1,335-yard layout, then was doubled in length to 2,790 yards. Benson speculated that the course lasted only into the 1940s.

Homewood, Minneapolis

Does this count as a lost golf course? No, but a May 22, 1921, *Minneapolis Tribune* story told the tale of two layouts crafted by boys of the Homewood neighborhood in northwest Minneapolis. One "course" was "in the street at Eighth and Russell avenues, where the dirt street made it possible to sink in cans for the holes."

Others laid out a course in Farwell Park, "keeping a sharp lookout for the majesty of the law." The boys made clubs out of furnace pokers, tree branches or umbrella handles, except for Nathan Bermau of 1125 Washburn, who, the *Tribune* said, was "the aristocrat of the bunch. Owns the only real club."

Itasca State Park

A five-hole layout, termed a "practice course," existed on the grounds of the Douglas Lodge, about 20 miles north of Park Rapids, reported Connie Cox, lead park naturalist at Itasca State Park. The course likely lasted into the 1940s.

A survey of annual favorite park activities and events was published in the Aug. 19, 1937, *Park Rapids Enterprise*. Golf ranked last among the 15 listed pastimes, with 40 participants, trailing, for instance, the Indian Pageant, top-rated with 8,600.

McGregor/Big Sandy

A 1908 golf course guide includes this entry: "Kare-Phree Resort ... Big Sandy. Oakes GC."

In fact, there was golf at the site, in one form or another, for almost a century. Whether it could be considered a golf course, and for how long, is open to debate.

A Hanson family bought and developed a lot on Davis Bay, at the south end of Big Sandy Lake, nine miles north of McGregor, in 1902 and opened Kare Phree Pines Resort. Presumably, they opened a nine-hole golf course on the site shortly afterward.

The resort was bought in 1948 by Newell and Marion Stringham. Newell Stringham died in 1984, but Marion Stringham apparently continued to make the golf course grounds available — strictly for lodge guests — after that.

Carol Beauchem of Palisade, who worked for Stringham for more than 20 years beginning in the early 1970s, considered the grounds more of a practice grounds than anything.

"I don't think it was really a golf course. She (Stringham) didn't have it mowed around the edges or anything," Beauchem said. "I never saw anybody out on the golf course. I never saw anybody who stayed there use it. She didn't have the greens mowed short or anything like most courses do."

Stringham sold the resort property in 2001 to Arlyce and Dennis Richardson of Blaine. At that time, Arlyce Richardson said, "The grounds were there, the flags were there, but it wasn't like it was a golf course."

Richardson said guests would check out clubs — wood-shafted — at Stringham's place. "It was just a little nine-hole course" with grass greens, Richardson said.

The Richardsons updated and expanded Kare Phree Pines and reopened it as Big Sandy Lodge & Resort. They no longer own it.

Menahga

An early plot of the north-central Minnesota city shows a golf course near Spirit Lake on the south end of town.

Midiron Country Club, Mountain Iron

This course, owned by stockholders, was built in 1927 in the Iron Range city just west of Virginia. One entry in the June 1928 issue of *10,000 Lakes Golfer* listed the course as being in Mountain Iron; another entry in the same issue listed it as being in Virginia. A story in the July 10, 1937, *Winnipeg Free Press* that listed "Arrowhead Golf Clubs" included Midiron Country Club of Mountain Iron. A 1938 Iron Range phone directory also lists the club as being in Mountain Iron. By 1942, the club was no longer listed in the phone book.

Naniboujou Lodge, Grand Marais

It never was a golf course, but the details are too rich to not pass along. Founders of the lodge, 14 miles east of Grand Marais on Lake Superior's North Shore, had grand plans in the late 1920s to build a lodge with a golf course, tennis courts and bath house on a 3,000-acre plot. Signed-and-sealed lodge members included baseball player Babe Ruth, boxer Jack Dempsey and sportswriter Ring Lardner. But construction of the golf course never began, and the 1929 stock market crash scuttled the grand plans. Naniboujou Lodge remains open today, albeit on a much smaller scale.

Sand Lake

The *Duluth News-Tribune* of July 30, 1914, published a story headlined "First Range golf course to be laid out at Sand Lake." The course was to be laid out at Birch Point, a peninsula along the western shore of the lake. The newspaper reported the site as seven miles north of Virginia, though the actual distance is 10 miles. The closest town is Britt, 5½ miles east.

"A nine-hole course will be laid," the *News-Tribune* reported, "with an expert Michigan golfer supervising the work. The links will be installed next month. At Octora lodge, a tennis court is being laid out."

Scot-Tees

This par-3 course and driving range was on Lakeland Avenue in the north metro. Though a 1977 course directory listed its mailing address as Osseo, the course was in Brooklyn Park. It measured 705 yards, with a greens fee of $1.50 in 1977. "Water hazards on five holes, out-of-bounds on three holes, and small, rolling greens," the directory reported. Charles Mingo was the manager.

The course was almost adjacent to the former Brooklyn Park Golf Course, also known as Joyner's. The Scot-Tees property is now a Wal-Mart.

Spring Valley

This southeastern Minnesota city's first golf course opened in July 1929, part of a recreational area built around the former Lake George on the western edge of town. The club's specific name was not mentioned in an Aug. 2, 1929, story in the *Spring Valley Mercury* newspaper and forwarded by the Fillmore County History Center, but the newspaper said the club's first tournament would be played Aug. 4.

"Work is still in progress on the fairways where considerable leveling is being done," the newspaper reported. "The club now has 75 members. ... About $3,000 already has been spent on the course, and the committee in charge propose to spent (sic) a large sum next spring in building hazards and changing two or three greens."

A 2011 *Spring Valley Tribune* story reported that the golf course was on the western shore of Lake George and featured two grass and seven sand greens. The course lasted at least through 1940, judging by a photo of golfers on the course dated 1940.

The Spring Valley history book *Tales of Our Town* alluded to a possible factor in the demise of the golf course. "In the flood of 1942," the book reported, "the dam that had created Lake George was washed out and much of the recreational activities of the area ended."

The clubhouse still stands; it is now a private residence in Spring Valley. Golf in town re-emerged in 1960 at a site four miles south of town, where Root River Country Club still operates.

Tower

"Everett Point Golf Course. Located on the shore of Lake Vermilion," reported the 1927 guide *Golf Courses in the Minnesota Arrowhead Country*. "Reached by County Highway No. 77. Five miles from Tower by boat. Nine hole course. Green fees, $1.00."

A 1926 *Moorhead Daily News* story had reported more details: "A 60-acre tract on Lake Vermilion adjoining McKinley park and 200 acres nearby have been offered by the Oliver Iron Mining company for a summer hotel site and golf course."

In 2004, the *Ely Echo* reported that Ely-area resident Dave Brude had unearthed a leatherette photo album featuring photos of the course, which was owned by Arthur and Tom Brude of Virginia. Arthur Brude, an accountant, was said to have enjoyed using dynamite while sculpting the course.

The newspaper speculated the highly regarded Wilderness at Fortune Bay resort course might now be occupying some of the lost-course grounds. Another source says the course was "across" Everett Bay from the Wilderness site, and a 1940 aerial photograph lends credence to that notion, with a golf course-sized plot of land cleared north of Everett Bay and south of Lake Vermilion proper, on or near the site of Everett Bay Lodge. Brude has died, and his widow, Carol, said she doesn't know anything about the lost course.

Twin Valley

A *Northern Pacific Railway Golf Directory*, likely from 1925, included a listing from the small town near Mahnomen in northwestern Minnesota: "Twin Valley Golf Course. Nine hole course being laid out — to be ready by mid-summer 1926. Edge of town. Altitude 1,117 feet. Visitors will be welcome. Green fee to be moderate."

Warroad

An Internet entry of errata from the *Warroad Centennial Book* includes this passage: "Warroad had 3 golf courses; south side of the river, at Bloom school, and the Estates." Warroad's only current course is Warroad Estates, an 18-hole layout north of town.

A 1940 aerial photo appears to show a golf course site at the southwestern edge of the city, south of the Warroad River, at the point where the river makes a 90-degree turn into the city. At least six bright dots, classic indications of sand greens, are seen on the photo.

The Bloom school was in Moranville Township, about two miles south of downtown.

Bucket List

Are there any lost courses in Minnesota you wish you could have played? How about any current Minnesota courses you'd like to play but haven't?

_____

_____

_____

_____

_____

_____

_____

_____

_____

_____

_____

_____

_____

_____

_____

_____

Be sure to visit ForeGoneGolf.com to post your favorites!

"In order to win, you must play your best golf when you need it most, and play your sloppy stuff when you can afford it. I shall not attempt to explain how you achieve this happy timing."

– BOBBY JONES

Fore! Gone. Gallery

All photos by Peter Wong except Westwood Hills, taken by Joe Bissen.

Whitewater Valley Golf Course

Mike Rak, Hilltop Public Golf Links

Thor Nordwall, Matoska Country Club

"Golf is deceptively simple and endlessly complicated. ... It satisfies the soul and frustrates the intellect. It is at the same time rewarding and maddening — and it is without a doubt the greatest game mankind has ever invented."
– ARNOLD PALMER
(PHOTO OF WHITEWATER VALLEY GOLF COURSE)

"Don't play too much golf. Two rounds a day are plenty."
– HARRY VARDON

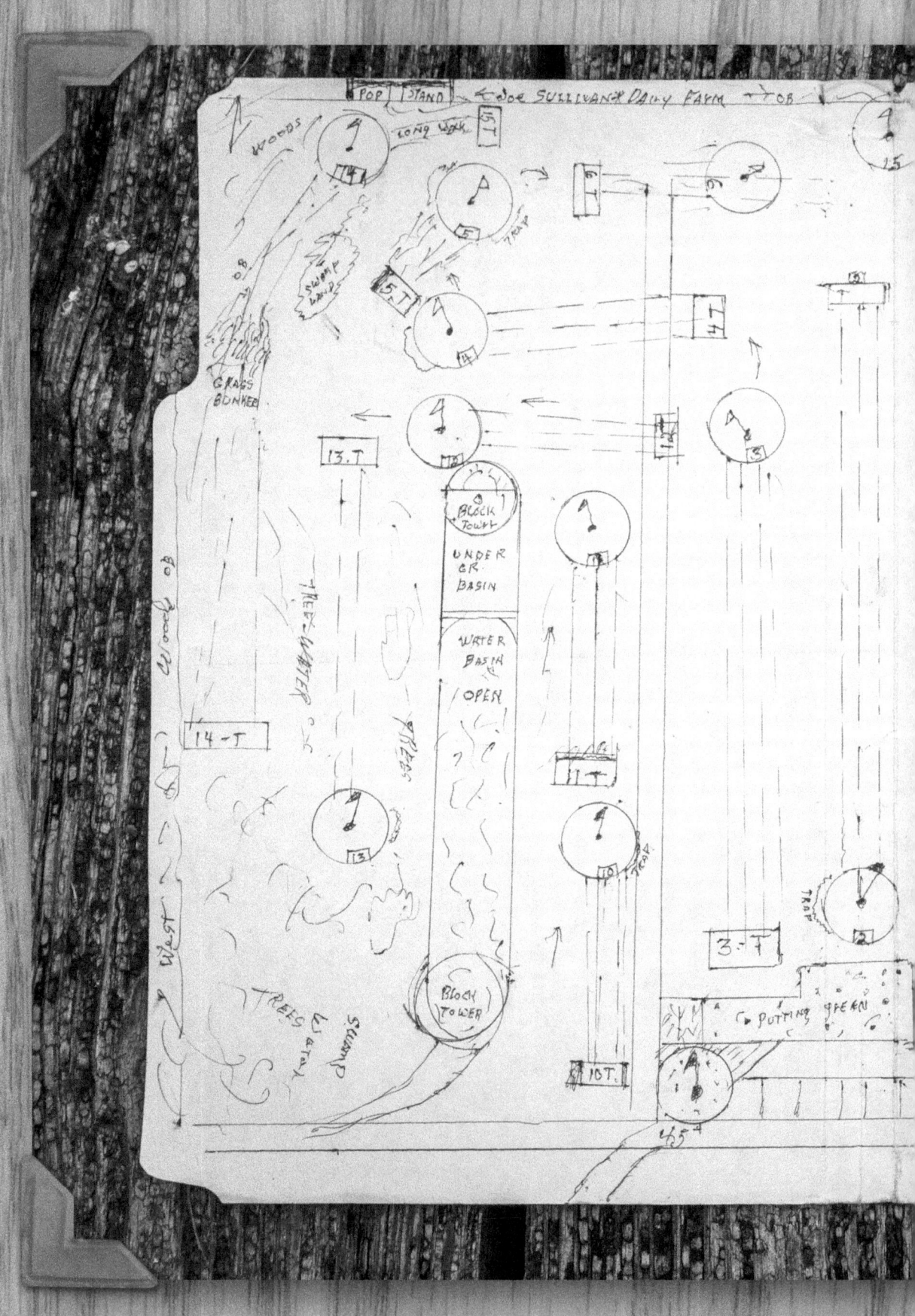

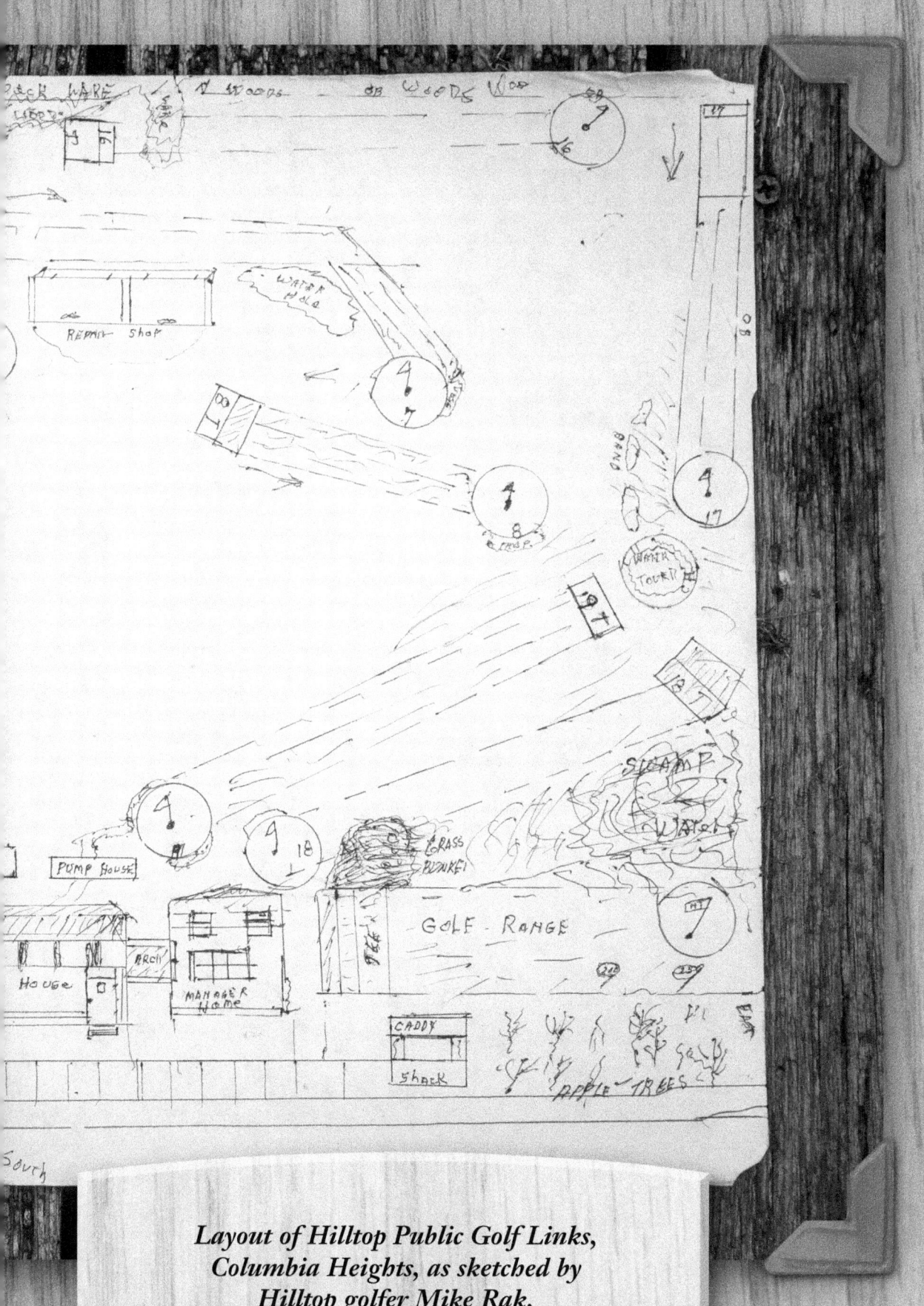

Layout of Hilltop Public Golf Links, Columbia Heights, as sketched by Hilltop golfer Mike Rak.

PHOTO: Jim Bjork, son of Clifford and Maybeth, pictured.

LEFT: *Clifford and Maybeth Bjork enjoying a beverage on the grounds of Hilltop Public Golf Links in Columbia Heights, circa 1940/1941.*

BOTTOM: *Cartoon from the Minneapolis Tribune of June 2, 1940 — a look at Westwood Hills Golf Course in St. Louis Park.*

John Burton, The Minnetonka Club

Peanuts Bell, Bayport Golf Club

Westwood Hills Golf Course

www.ingramcontent.com/pod-product-compliance
Lightning Source LLC
Chambersburg PA
CBHW060420010526
44118CB00017B/2287